TRADIVOX

VOLUME XX

TRADIVOX

CATHOLIC CATECHISM INDEX

VOLUME XX

INDEX

Edited by
Aaron Seng

SOPHIA INSTITUTE PRESS
MANCHESTER, NEW HAMPSHIRE

South Bend, Indiana
www.Tradivox.com

Printed in the United States of America.

Cover and interior design by Perceptions Design Studio.

Sophia Institute Press
Box 5284, Manchester, NH 03108
1-800-888-9344

www.SophiaInstitute.com

Sophia Institute Press® is a registered trademark of Sophia Institute.

ISBN 978-1-64413-388-0
LCCN 2025933887

Dedicated with love and deepest respect
to all the English Martyrs and Confessors.
Orate pro nobis.

CONTENTS

Acknowledgments xi

Systematic Index 3

I. Divine Revelation 3

Revelation Is Possible and Necessary (I a) 3

Revelation in Itself (I b) 3

Revelation Is Accepted by Faith (I c) 5

Reason Has Powers, Duties, and Limits (I d–e) 6

Revelation Is Contained in Scripture and Tradition (I f) 8

II–III. The Catholic Church 11

The Church in Itself (II a–b) 11

The Church's Power of Teaching (Infallibility) (II c–d) 14

The Church's Power of Governing (Jurisdiction) (II e–f) 16

The Church in the World (II g–i) 17

The Roman Pontiff (III a–i) 18

IV–V. God in Himself 23

God's Essence and Attributes (IV a–c) 23

The Blessed Trinity (V a–e) 25

VI–VII. Creation 30

The Natural Order (VI a–g) 30

The Supernatural Order (VII a) 34

Original Man (VII b) 34

Original Sin (VII c) 35

Fallen Man (VII d) 37

VIII. Incarnation (a–f) 39

Jesus Christ Is True God (VIII a) 39

Jesus Christ Is True Man (VIII b) 40

The Hypostatic Union (VIII c–f) 41

VIII. Redemption (g–k) 44

Jesus Christ Is Redeemer (VIII g) 44

The Life of the Redeemer (VIII h) 46

The Mother of the Redeemer (VIII i–k) 49

IX. Justification 52

X. Grace 56

Actual Grace (X a–e) 56

Sanctifying Grace (X f) 58

The Distribution of Graces (X g–i) 59

XI–XIII. Virtues and Precepts 62

The Virtues and Laws in General (XI a) 62

The Theological Virtues (XI b–d) 63

The Ten Commandments (XI e–t) 67

The First Commandment (XI e–f), 67; The Second Commandment (XI g), 70; The Third Commandment (XI h), 71; The Fourth Commandment (XI i–p), 71; The Fifth Commandment (XI q), 75; The Sixth and Ninth Commandments (XI r), 76; The Seventh and Tenth Commandments (XI s), 77; The Eighth Commandment (XI t), 78

The Sacraments (XII a–p) 78

The Sacraments in General (XII a–b), 78; Baptism (XII c–d), 81; Confirmation (XII e), 84; The Eucharist (XII f–h), 86; Penance (XII i–l), 93; Extreme Unction (XII m), 99; Holy Orders (XII n), 101; Matrimony (XII o), 103; The Sacramentals (XII p), 105

Christian Perfection (XIII a–e) 106

XIV. The Last Things 111
XV. Catholic Memory Lists 117
  Select Prayers 117
  On the Church 127
  Commandments and Precepts 130
  Sin 131
  Virtues 134
  Gifts, Fruits, Beatitudes, and Counsels 135
  Works of Mercy 138
  Four Last Things 139

Alphabetic Index **141**

About This Series 207

ACKNOWLEDGMENTS

THE publication of this series is due primarily to the generosity of countless volunteers and donors from several countries. Special thanks are owed to Mr. and Mrs. Phil Seng, Mr. and Mrs. Michael Fitzmaurice, Mr. and Mrs. Michael Over, Mr. and Mrs. Jim McElwee, Mr. and Mrs. John Brouillette, Mr. and Mrs. Thomas Scheibelhut, Mr. and Mrs. Kyle Barriger, as well the visionary priests and faithful of St. Stanislaus Bishop and Martyr parish in South Bend, Indiana, and St. Patrick's Oratory in Green Bay, Wisconsin.

Of the many editorial volunteers who have contributed to this twenty-volume series, particular mention must here be made of Mrs. Charlie Baxter, Mrs. Jeff Burns, Mrs. John Dettmer, Mr. Nathan Dibley, Mr. Jonas Dlugi, Miss Michele Ensign, Mrs. Ame Enwright, Mr. Seth Galemore, Miss Sharon Kabel, Mr. Griffin McHaffie, Miss Patricia Rupchock, Mrs. Charles Scheibelhut, Dr. Nancy Schmeing, Mr. Nathan Seymour, Mr. Shany in honor of the Immaculata, Mr. Trey J. Sorg, Mr. Travis Walker, and Miss Claire Wingfield. May your names, recorded here, appear also in the Book of Life at the last day.

May God richly reward these and all men and women endeavoring to hold and pass on the Catholic faith today.

TRADIVOX

VOLUME XX

TRADIVOX

Systematic Index

Divine Revelation

Revelation Is Possible and Necessary

I a

In the proper sense, *revelation* is the speaking of God to man, 9:249, 10:185, 11:95, 14:100, 16:101–102, 17:10, 18:104

it is both possible and useful, 10:185, 11:95, 14:100

truly supernatural, 10:185, 11:95, 14:100

morally necessary for knowledge of natural religious truths, 10:185, 12:89, 14:100, 14:168

absolutely necessary for knowledge of supernatural truths, 7:35, 8:6–8, 10:18–20, 11:90, 12:89, 14:168, 16:101–102, 18:253.

Revelation in Itself

I b

God has made a revelation to man, 2:113, 3:41, 3:147, 6:22, 6:40, 7:36, 9:249, 10:61, 10:185–186, 10:334, 11:95, 11:105, 14:100, 14:136, 14:167, 14:180–181, 15:41, 15:57–58, 16:172, 17:9, 17:117, 18:252–253, 18:440–441, 19:12–13, 19:136

through the patriarchs and prophets, 3:147, 6:40, 7:36, 10:19–22, 10:61–63, 10:186–188, 11:96, 13:106, 14:100, 14:136, 14:167, 14:181, 17:9, 17:117, 18:253, 18:262, 19:12–13

and ultimately Jesus Christ, 3:147, 6:22, 6:40, 7:36, 10:27, 10:63, 10:186–188, 11:19, 11:107, 13:106, 14:100, 14:136, 14:167, 14:181, 17:9, 17:117, 18:253, 19:12–13.

Revelation is not a work of man or some philosophical discovery, 6:22, 8:337, 10:185, 13:325–328, 18:259, 18:439–440

nor a mere evolution of man's understanding about God, 8:337, 10:186–188

nor an ongoing process of personal or communal discernment, 8:337

nor is it to be changed in any way into another meaning, 5:193–194, 8:337, 10:183–184, 10:186–188, 13:328–329, 14:326, 18:251, 18:259

but rather, revelation is a propositionally determined body of doctrine, 4:9–10, 4:16, 5:184, 5:192–194, 6:191, 6:199–200, 7:47, 10:27, 10:334–336, 11:95–101, 11:157, 14:5–6, 14:100–101, 14:251, 15:6–7, 16:190, 16:194–195, 17:154, 18:103–106

immutable, 5:192–194, 8:337, 10:39, 10:183–184, 10:186–188, 11:154–155, 14:168, 14:251, 14:326, 16:190, 16:194–195, 17:154, 18:251

externally verifiable, 5:190, 10:334–336, 14:251, 15:6, 17:154

applicable to all times and all men, 6:69, 8:337, 10:183–184, 10:194–197, 11:154, 14:251, 15:147, 16:126, 16:193, 17:21

understandable by the human mind and the senses, 6:191, 6:199–200, 10:27–28, 11:90, 11:154, 11:225, 13:8, 14:100, 16:172, 17:121

it concluded in history with the death of the last apostle, 17:28

and is now also called the *deposit of faith*, 2:139, 11:151, 18:106, 18:259–260, 18:337.

Besides truths accessible to human reason, Christian revelation also contains true mysteries, 2:113, 3:102, 4:16, 4:105, 5:184–186, 5:195, 6:40, 7:35, 8:325, 10:64, 11:11, 11:90, 11:94–99, 13:261, 14:169–170, 15:57–58, 15:130, 16:11, 16:101–102, 16:112–114, 16:218, 17:83, 17:121, 17:126, 18:102, 18:252, 18:339–440

naturally inaccessible to human and even angelic reason, 2:113, 3:102, 4:16, 4:105, 7:35, 7:52, 9:10–11, 10:64, 10:151, 11:90, 11:95, 12:89, 13:261,

14:168, 15:57, 15:130, 16:101–102, 16:112–114, 16:218, 17:121, 17:126, 18:102, 18:252–253, 18:439–440, 19:16

nevertheless, mysteries do not contradict reason (*irrational*), 3:102, 5:185–186, 8:326, 10:28, 11:95, 14:102, 14:170, 17:124, 17:126

but they do exceed it (*suprarational*), 2:113, 3:102, 5:195, 7:35, 8:325, 9:10–11, 11:94–95, 12:89, 14:169–170, 16:101–102, 16:112–114, 16:218, 17:121, 17:126, 18:252–253

remaining always somewhat obscure in this life, 3:102, 4:16, 4:105, 5:195, 11:95, 14:170, 15:57, 15:130, 16:112–114, 18:252.

Revelation Is Accepted by Faith

I c

Divine revelation requires man's internal assent, 1:19, 3:122, 5:183–186, 7:45, 7:48–50, 8:338, 9:10, 11:75, 12:117–118, 14:5–6, 14:165, 16:112–114, 16:172, 17:11, 17:121, 18:108, 18:437, 19:136

which is properly called *divine faith* or *supernatural faith*, 5:8, 6:21, 9:11, 9:249, 11:89, 14:5–6, 14:165, 14:345, 16:172, 17:11, 17:121, 18:232, 18:319.

Divine faith is not an assent based on mere probability, 1:19, 6:23–24, 11:75, 11:89, 14:5, 14:165, 14:345, 16:112–114, 16:172, 17:14, 17:84, 17:121, 18:232

nor is it to be confused with the merely natural act of belief, 5:183, 6:23–24, 8:108–109, 11:89–91, 11:95, 17:121, 18:175

nor is it merely a subjective experience, interior sense, or private inspiration, 8:337–338.

All men are summoned to respond to God's revelation by embracing the true faith, 1:18–19, 1:25, 1:34, 2:114, 2:316, 3:5, 5:184–186, 7:45, 9:11, 10:17–18, 11:25–26, 11:145, 11:149, 12:6, 13:324, 14:5–6, 14:165–169, 16:126, 17:20, 17:90–92, 17:121–122, 17:179–180, 17:268, 18:106, 18:138, 18:437, 19:127–128

which is retained whole and entire in the Catholic Church alone, 1:18, 1:22, 2:133, 2:315, 5:10, 5:149, 5:208, 6:4–5, 9:12, 10:47, 11:79, 11:89,

11:145, 11:149, 13:324, 14:5–6, 14:168, 14:251, 15:6, 15:32, 15:51, 15:73, 15:128, 16:9, 16:105–106, 16:126, 16:194–198, 17:20–22, 17:90–92, 17:107, 17:122, 17:179–180, 17:268, 18:106, 18:232, 19:136

although none should be forced to embrace this faith against their will, since coercion excludes real assent, 11:75, 18:138.

The invitation to true faith is properly called *evangelization*, a work of charity, 18:83–84, 19:106–108

it is not a violation of the intelligence, freedom, or dignity of man, 6:36, 12:350–353, 12:370–372, 18:138.

Once accepted on the teaching authority of the Church, revelation cannot be called into doubt by suspending assent, 3:5, 3:31, 3:41, 4:129, 5:10, 5:186–187, 6:4–5, 7:45, 7:48–49, 8:108, 11:89, 11:92–93, 11:153, 14:5–6, 14:165, 15:32, 15:41, 15:183, 16:84, 16:172, 17:84, 17:90–92, 17:107, 17:194–195, 18:138

the study of God and divine things, properly called *theology*, is therefore "faith seeking understanding" rather than investigation motivated by positive doubt, 8:107–109, 17:195, 19:139

all religious indifferentism and latitudinarianism is likewise a grave error, 1:18, 5:190–192, 11:144, 13:224, 14:166–167, 14:280, 15:67, 15:145, 16:126, 16:324–325, 17:42, 18:314.

Reason Has Powers, Duties, and Limits

I d

Not all certitude is founded on faith, 11:89

rather, many natural truths can be known with varying degrees of certitude by reason alone, 5:290, 6:22, 11:89–91, 14:102, 16:101–102, 17:7, 17:117, 18:104.

Apart from revelation and even without grace, unaided reason can know certain religious truths, 3:196, 7:35, 7:51–52, 14:100, 14:168, 16:172, 17:7, 17:117, 18:104, 18:233, 18:442

e.g., the existence of God, 7:50, 8:5, 8:337, 10:61, 10:68–72, 10:133–134, 11:102, 14:100, 14:180–181, 14:268, 17:7, 17:117, 18:103, 18:253–254, 18:442.

Before coming to divine faith, reason can know the motives for credibility, 6:24, 10:186, 11:90–91, 12:89, 14:136–139, 18:441

among the most outstanding of which are the prophecies and miracles of Christ, 3:5, 3:86–87, 3:96, 3:100, 5:17, 6:24, 10:186, 10:275–303, 11:79, 11:90–91, 11:106, 13:148–149, 13:176, 14:16, 14:136, 14:210–212, 14:223–224, 16:155–156, 17:14, 17:129, 18:104, 18:255–256, 18:441

and the Catholic Church itself, 3:377, 6:24, 11:35–36, 11:79, 11:90–91, 12:8, 12:89, 13:328–331, 14:117, 14:137–139, 16:168, 17:14, 18:441.

After coming to divine faith, reason can attain a degree of understanding of supernatural truths, 5:9, 7:50, 10:334, 11:91, 11:110, 14:100, 16:172, 17:129, 18:233.

Human reason is not immune from error, 3:99–100, 4:22–23, 4:111, 6:24, 11:90, 11:92, 12:19–20, 12:89, 13:325–328, 13:341, 14:100, 14:168, 18:233

and it is not to be exclusively or entirely relied upon, 5:187, 5:290–291, 6:24, 10:81, 11:89–90, 11:92, 12:19–20, 12:89, 12:314–315, 13:325–328, 14:132–134, 14:168, 16:101–102

nor is it autonomous, but subject to uncreated truth, 12:323–326, 13:329, 14:102, 14:132–134, 18:439.

Man does not have an unmodified freedom of feeling, speaking, writing, or otherwise acting, 12:314–315, 12:323–326, 14:102, 14:118–119, 14:132–134, 17:144, 17:211, 18:421.

I e

Revelation and reason cannot contradict one another, 4:16, 11:92, 14:102, 14:170, 17:126, 18:232–233, 18:272, 18:439–442

nor is faith opposed to human reason, 4:16, 6:23–24, 11:89–92, 14:170, 17:124, 18:232–233.

Reason explains, guards, and defends revealed truth, 3:101, 3:196, 11:91, 11:110, 16:322–323, 17:129, 18:440–442
while revelation frees reason from error, enlightening and strengthening it, 5:290–291, 6:24, 7:52–53, 10:81, 11:90, 11:92, 12:19–20, 12:89, 13:156, 14:100, 14:168, 18:233, 18:440–442
philosophy is ancillary to and under the authority of faith, 3:101, 6:22, 8:33, 12:314–315, 18:439
hence errors of reason are rightly and beneficially proscribed by the Church, 8:31, 12:19–20, 12:89, 12:205, 12:329, 13:325–328, 13:341, 18:233, 18:272, 18:320, 18:328, 18:439–442.

Theology is to be treated differently than other scientific disciplines, 18:233, 18:442
all theological speculation must be founded on the teaching of the Church and the fathers, 4:129, 8:12, 14:101
and theology must retain the commonly received terminology and utilize a reasonable form of words, 5:193–194, 7:56, 12:173, 17:25.

Revelation Is Contained in Scripture and Tradition

I f

There are two sources, fonts, or loci of divine revelation: scripture and tradition, 1:18, 2:115, 2:313, 3:332, 4:76, 5:189–190, 7:42, 8:326, 9:54, 10:63, 14:6, 14:100, 14:170, 14:172, 16:333, 17:10, 17:28, 17:91, 17:154, 18:105, 18:256–257, 18:319, 19:103–106.

The written source of revelation is sacred scripture, 2:115, 4:76–80, 8:12, 9:54, 9:58, 10:64, 14:6, 14:100–101, 14:170, 17:91, 17:154, 18:105, 19:104
consisting of forty-six books of the old testament and twenty-seven of the new testament, 8:12, 10:61–64, 14:171–172, 18:257, 19:329
which are properly referred to as the *canon* ("rule") of sacred scripture, 17:10, 18:258
of which the authentic version is had in the Vulgate, 8:13, 12:194, 18:257–258.

The canonical books with all their parts are sacred and canonical, 9:54, 18:257

because they have been written under the divine *inspiration* of the Holy Spirit, 6:63–64, 8:12, 10:64, 12:35, 14:100, 14:170, 17:10, 18:105, 18:256, 19:104

i.e., they have God as their author, 4:76, 6:210, 8:12–13, 10:64, 10:337, 12:173, 14:101, 14:170, 18:105, 18:257–259, 19:104

who, in composing the sacred books, worked in and through certain chosen men, 10:64, 12:15, 12:35, 14:170, 18:105, 18:258, 19:104

so that with him acting in and through them, they, as true authors, consigned to writing everything and only those things which he wanted, 8:12, 10:64, 13:110, 14:101, 18:258–259, 19:104.

Everything asserted in sacred scripture is asserted by the Holy Spirit, 4:27, 6:63–64, 10:64, 14:100, 18:105, 18:258, 19:104

and so sacred scripture possesses the quality of divine *inerrancy*, 3:330, 10:64, 18:258

i.e., the canonical books in all their parts teach the truth solidly, faithfully, and without error, 8:12, 10:64, 18:258.

The proper interpretation of scripture belongs to the Church's teaching office, 2:135, 3:12, 3:316, 3:330–331, 4:80, 8:14, 8:174, 9:67, 10:336, 11:256, 12:323–324, 14:101, 14:172, 16:333, 17:10, 17:91, 18:259, 19:104

ever maintaining the unanimous consent of the fathers and the received sense, 3:316, 3:331, 5:214, 8:14, 12:171, 14:101, 17:91, 18:335.

The reading of sacred scripture is neither necessary nor fitting for all, 2:135, 4:78–80, 7:405, 8:14–15, 12:323–324, 14:173, 16:333

but can be a great source of spiritual nourishment in prayer, 2:135, 5:356, 7:405, 12:54, 12:129, 12:189, 13:44, 14:173, 16:340, 17:277, 19:104

so that private reading is by no means forbidden, 4:80, 7:405, 12:54, 12:196, 14:173, 16:340, 17:30, 17:277, 19:104

in versions that have been officially approved, 4:80, 14:173, 19:104.

The other source of revelation is sacred tradition, 2:115, 2:313, 3:331, 4:76, 4:79, 5:189, 7:42, 8:15–17, 9:54, 9:55, 10:64, 12:324, 14:6, 14:100, 14:174, 16:333, 17:10, 17:91, 17:154, 17:159, 18:106, 18:335, 19:103–106

consisting of all matters of faith and morals taught by Christ and his apostles, and handed down in the Church by continual succession, 1:23, 1:59, 2:116, 2:134, 2:313, 3:332, 4:77, 5:190, 5:214, 8:16, 9:55, 10:39, 10:64, 11:99–100, 11:120–121, 12:101, 13:279, 14:6, 14:100, 14:174–175, 14:251, 17:10, 17:91, 17:154, 17:159, 18:106, 19:104

this teaching is found in the writings of the fathers and doctors, the decrees of popes and Church councils, the universal teaching of her bishops, and her received and approved rites, customs, and monuments, 1:59, 1:85–87, 2:115, 2:313, 4:79, 9:55–56, 10:39, 11:120–121, 11:221, 12:171–172, 13:8–12, 13:279, 14:175, 14:244, 17:154.

No other source of public revelation exists outside of the canonical scriptures and apostolic tradition, 5:192, 9:54, 9:59, 14:6, 14:100, 14:172, 14:251, 17:10, 17:28

the teaching office of the Catholic Church is not another source of revelation, but its guardian and expositor, 4:79, 5:192–194, 5:208, 5:214, 6:65, 8:337, 10:39, 10:336, 11:28, 11:89, 11:99–100, 11:152–157, 14:5–6, 14:101, 14:175, 14:251, 15:6, 16:190, 16:194–195, 16:333, 17:10, 17:28, 17:91, 17:122, 17:154, 18:106, 18:138, 18:316, 18:340

facilitating a secure progress in its understanding and dissemination through the ages, 3:93–94, 4:79, 5:192–194, 10:35, 11:154–157, 12:171, 13:152, 13:279, 14:5–6, 14:23–24, 14:175, 14:251, 15:147, 16:190, 16:194–195, 17:21, 17:154, 18:106, 18:138, 18:316, 18:340

always officially retaining the same teaching, the same sense, and the same meaning, 3:93–94, 4:79, 5:193–194, 5:214, 8:337, 10:39, 11:89, 11:154–157, 13:152, 14:23–24, 14:168, 14:251, 14:326, 15:147, 16:190, 16:194–195, 17:91, 17:154, 18:259.

The Catholic Church

The Church in Itself

II a

The Church is a society instituted by Jesus Christ, God, 1:22, 1:23, 1:118, 2:131, 2:313, 3:5, 3:35, 4:27, 4:31, 4:122, 6:66, 7:140, 8:184, 8:207, 8:337, 9:20, 9:59, 9:251, 10:250, 10:283, 11:144–146, 11:150, 11:432, 13:330–331, 14:22, 14:111, 14:203–204, 14:234–235, 15:66, 16:22, 16:177–178, 17:18, 17:28, 17:147–148, 18:49, 18:132, 18:136, 18:302, 18:311, 18:324, 19:91

it is united in one divine faith, end, and means of sanctification, 1:22, 1:118, 2:21, 2:131, 2:315, 3:13, 3:221–222, 4:29, 4:31, 4:119, 4:120–121, 5:20–21, 5:208, 6:66–67, 7:132, 7:142, 8:17, 9:21, 9:251, 10:336–339, 11:144, 11:146, 11:155, 13:10, 14:22–23, 14:234, 14:243, 15:14, 15:66, 15:145, 16:23, 16:25, 16:178–181, 16:190–192, 17:18, 17:23, 17:148, 17:156, 18:135, 18:302

constituting one mystical body under Christ the head, 1:22, 1:23, 1:118, 2:22, 2:131, 2:315, 3:12, 3:14, 3:106, 3:222, 3:239, 4:30, 4:120, 5:20, 5:208, 5:272, 6:66, 6:71, 7:131, 7:137, 9:59, 9:251, 11:135, 11:146, 11:161, 13:252, 14:22–23, 14:203–204, 14:236, 14:255, 15:13, 15:66, 15:145, 16:23, 16:178–181, 16:191, 17:19, 17:148, 18:134, 18:301, 18:359–360, 18:396, 19:96

formed from the side of Jesus Christ on the cross, 1:23, 2:131, 3:105, 13:56, 19:93

publicly manifested to the world at Pentecost, 2:297, 3:12, 3:259, 3:271, 4:27, 4:117, 4:177, 9:62, 12:7, 13:255–257, 13:264, 14:233, 18:48, 18:132.

The end of the Church is to communicate the divine life of grace to the world, 2:131, 3:5, 3:13, 6:192, 6:199–200, 7:531, 9:251, 10:283, 10:338, 11:144, 12:5, 12:402, 13:31, 13:249, 14:114, 14:229, 14:245, 15:145, 16:22–23, 16:177–178, 16:182, 17:19, 17:21, 18:49, 18:133, 18:136, 18:302, 18:311

by a threefold function of teaching (divine truth), governing (divine order), and sanctifying (divine mysteries), 1:118, 2:135, 3:12, 3:13, 6:199–200, 9:20–21, 9:61, 10:38, 10:337–338, 11:155, 13:249, 14:115, 14:235, 14:245, 15:66, 15:146, 16:23, 16:182, 17:21, 17:28, 18:50–51, 18:137, 18:302, 19:94–95, 19:100.

The Church is a perfect and independent society in itself, 1:118, 2:142, 8:210, 9:20, 9:59, 11:146, 11:150, 11:432–434, 12:159, 13:330–331, 14:234, 16:188–189, 17:148, 18:311, 18:324, 18:337

publicly visible and knowable by certain marks that distinguish it from other religious organizations, 2:135, 2:315, 3:320–321, 3:328–329, 4:30–31, 4:120–122, 5:214, 8:20, 8:207, 9:20–22, 9:59, 9:254, 10:338, 11:152–153, 11:158–159, 12:101, 12:177, 12:235, 13:328–331, 14:23, 14:236, 14:241–242, 15:14, 15:147, 16:24, 16:25, 16:178, 16:190, 16:198, 17:21, 17:147–148, 17:155–156, 18:49, 18:132, 18:136

there are four principal marks of the Church: she is one, 1:22, 2:132, 2:315, 3:13, 3:19, 3:321–324, 4:30–31, 4:120–121, 5:208, 6:66–67, 7:134–137, 8:19, 8:173, 8:209, 9:20–21, 9:251–252, 10:336–339, 11:153–155, 12:101, 12:177, 13:224, 13:331, 14:23, 14:116, 14:242–243, 15:14, 15:67, 15:147, 16:24–25, 16:178, 16:190–192, 17:21, 17:156, 18:136, 18:313, 18:317, 18:331, 19:119

holy, 1:4, 1:19, 1:22, 1:23, 2:21, 2:132, 2:136, 2:315, 3:13, 3:324–326, 3:329, 4:30–31, 4:120, 4:121, 5:208, 6:66, 6:67–68, 7:137–138, 8:19, 8:173, 8:210, 9:21, 9:252, 11:154, 11:155–156, 12:235, 12:339, 13:331, 14:23–24, 14:243, 15:14, 15:147, 16:25, 16:178, 16:192–193, 17:21, 17:157, 18:49, 18:132–133, 18:136, 18:262, 18:313, 18:322, 19:119

catholic, 1:4, 1:19, 1:22, 1:23, 2:21, 2:132, 2:315, 3:13, 3:326–327, 3:329, 4:30–31, 4:120, 4:121, 5:214, 6:66, 6:68–69, 7:138–139, 8:19, 8:173, 8:210, 9:21, 9:252, 10:336, 11:154, 11:156–157, 12:101, 12:235, 13:331, 14:23–24, 14:116, 14:244, 15:14, 15:147, 16:25, 16:178, 16:193–194, 17:21, 17:157–158, 18:49, 18:132, 18:262, 18:313, 19:119

and apostolic, 1:22, 1:23, 2:132, 2:142, 2:315, 3:13, 3:19, 3:328, 4:30–31, 4:120, 4:121–122, 6:66, 6:69–70, 7:139–140, 8:19, 8:173, 8:210, 11:154, 11:157–158, 12:101, 12:235, 13:331, 14:23–24, 14:244, 15:14, 15:147,

16:25, 16:178, 16:194–195, 17:21, 17:159, 18:50, 18:136, 18:262, 18:313, 19:119
hierarchically ordered, 1:23, 2:131, 3:199, 3:202–212, 6:74, 6:210, 8:161–162, 9:62, 10:338, 11:146–147, 11:155, 11:326–327, 12:235, 14:22–23, 14:240–241, 14:422, 16:191, 16:284–286, 18:50, 18:141–142, 18:426, 19:98
perpetual (immutable, indestructible, indefectible), 2:132, 2:135, 2:138, 2:315, 3:13, 3:320–321, 4:31, 4:32, 4:79, 4:123, 5:21, 6:69–70, 8:20, 8:213, 9:248, 10:337–338, 11:35–36, 11:147, 11:152–153, 12:235, 12:248, 14:22, 14:117, 14:138–139, 14:208, 15:14, 15:147, 16:24, 16:189–190, 17:20, 17:149, 17:150, 18:133, 18:324
and necessary to all for salvation, 2:133, 2:315, 4:29–30, 4:61, 4:119, 4:156, 4:203, 5:20, 5:191, 6:4, 6:67, 6:192, 7:140, 8:20, 8:211, 9:22, 9:248, 10:35, 10:213, 11:149–152, 13:220, 13:341, 14:251–252, 15:67, 15:146, 16:23, 16:126, 16:182–184, 17:20, 17:147, 17:158, 18:136, 18:144, 18:309, 18:312–316, 18:323–324, 19:120.

II b

In order to be saved, one must be a member of the Church at least in desire, 2:133, 2:315, 3:84, 3:206, 5:20, 5:191, 6:67, 6:192, 7:139–140, 8:20, 8:211–212, 9:22, 9:248, 10:35, 10:213, 11:149–151, 13:220, 14:251–252, 15:146, 16:23, 16:126, 16:182–184, 17:20–21, 17:147, 17:158, 18:51, 18:136, 18:143–144, 18:324, 18:384
members of the Church are properly the baptized, 1:61, 2:311, 3:55, 3:176, 3:335–336, 4:28, 4:29, 4:60, 4:118–119, 4:156, 4:194–195, 4:202–203, 5:148, 7:140, 8:208, 11:146, 11:148, 11:232, 14:52, 14:252, 15:91, 16:183, 17:158, 17:160, 17:222, 18:40, 18:51, 18:68, 18:135, 18:142, 19:97
including both saints and sinners, 1:23, 3:5, 3:12, 3:63, 3:84, 3:136, 5:208, 7:132–133, 11:148–149, 13:311–312, 14:254, 16:87–88, 17:160
those on earth, in purgatory, and in heaven, 1:23–24, 3:14, 3:173, 3:197, 3:358–359, 4:37, 4:127, 4:197, 5:21, 5:274, 6:69, 7:131–132, 8:17, 8:208, 8:220, 9:21–22, 9:252, 11:145–146, 11:161, 13:34, 13:124, 13:311–312, 14:24–25, 14:254, 15:15, 15:67–68, 15:185–186, 16:57, 16:87–90, 16:330, 17:79, 17:160, 18:51–52, 18:146–147, 18:330, 19:123.

The Church is not divided into various branches on earth, 1:22, 2:133, 2:142, 2:315, 11:91, 11:144, 11:146, 12:177, 13:224, 15:67, 15:145, 17:147, 17:155–156, 18:314, 19:119–120

rather, there are certain causes that separate a man from the body of the Church, 1:25, 5:208, 6:67, 6:74, 7:133, 7:505, 9:22, 11:148, 14:118–119, 14:250, 14:252, 16:365, 17:158, 18:51, 18:142

including obstinate rejection or pertinacious doubt of any of her defined doctrines (heresy), 1:25, 2:116, 2:133, 2:137–138, 3:54, 3:380–381, 4:80, 5:30, 5:208, 5:297, 6:66, 7:128, 7:133, 7:505, 8:17, 8:104, 8:220–221, 9:22, 9:253, 11:93, 11:148, 11:151, 12:172, 12:177, 13:152, 14:118–119, 14:126–129, 14:169, 14:252, 15:183, 16:55, 16:183–184, 16:191, 16:323–324, 17:42, 17:158, 17:194–195, 18:51, 18:142–143, 18:322, 18:459

refusing submission to her hierarchy or communion with her members (schism), 1:25, 2:133, 2:232, 3:206–207, 3:378, 5:297, 7:133, 7:505, 8:17, 8:220–221, 9:22, 9:253, 10:338, 11:91, 11:148, 11:151, 12:302–303, 14:122, 14:128–129, 14:252, 14:422, 16:324, 18:51, 18:142–143, 18:322

repudiation of the Christian faith in its entirety (apostasy), 1:25, 4:41, 4:133, 5:297, 8:220, 11:93, 11:148, 12:95, 12:179–180, 14:252, 16:323, 18:51, 18:142–143

and penal removal from her communion, either automatically or by judicial act (excommunication), 1:25, 2:138, 3:119, 4:55, 4:87, 5:54–55, 5:208, 5:255–256, 5:273, 6:74, 7:133, 8:17, 8:220, 9:22, 9:253, 11:148, 11:161–162, 12:172, 12:227, 14:252, 16:365, 18:51, 18:142, 18:460, 19:115, 19:217

so that the non-baptized do not belong to the body of the Church, 5:208, 7:133, 8:17, 8:220, 9:22, 9:253, 11:148, 14:252, 16:323, 17:158, 18:51, 18:142

nor do Jews, Muslims, or members of any other false religion, 1:25, 2:133, 7:505, 8:220, 9:22, 9:253, 11:148, 16:323, 18:312.

The Church's Power of Teaching (Infallibility)

II c

God has given the Church the divine right, duty, and power to guard and expound his revelation on earth, 2:139, 3:13, 4:123, 4:129, 5:207–208,

8:183–184, 8:337, 9:53, 10:35, 10:336, 11:28, 11:89, 11:97, 11:152–157, 12:172, 12:186, 12:197, 12:205, 12:220–221, 13:152, 13:249, 14:5–6, 14:101, 14:168, 14:246, 14:251, 15:14, 16:190, 16:194–195, 16:333, 17:10, 17:28, 17:122, 17:154, 18:26–28, 18:50, 18:106, 18:138, 18:316, 18:340, 19:7, 19:101

in doing so, the Holy Spirit preserves the Church from all possibility of error, 2:136, 2:315, 3:13, 3:93–94, 3:195–196, 3:319, 3:324–326, 4:32, 4:78–79, 4:123, 5:213, 6:70, 8:20, 8:212, 9:248, 11:96, 11:152–153, 12:229, 14:24, 14:101, 14:168, 14:246–247, 15:14, 15:146, 16:24, 16:25, 16:89, 16:185–189, 16:199, 17:20, 17:28, 17:150, 17:159, 18:49, 18:132, 18:138, 18:337, 18:459

through a unique charism (gift of grace) properly called *infallibility*, 2:134, 2:140, 4:32, 4:123, 5:213, 8:13, 8:20, 8:184, 8:212, 8:325, 11:91, 11:152–153, 12:15, 12:229, 13:341, 14:101, 14:168, 14:246–247, 15:146, 16:24, 16:25, 16:185–189, 16:199, 17:20, 17:24–25, 17:153–155, 17:159, 18:50–51, 18:138–139, 18:459

so that the Church has never erred, nor ever could err, in its official teaching, 2:135, 2:139, 3:13, 3:319, 3:93–94, 3:195–196, 3:324–326, 4:32, 4:123, 5:213–217, 8:20, 11:152–153, 14:24, 14:168, 14:246–247, 15:14, 16:89, 16:185–189, 17:153–155, 17:159, 18:254

although it remains possible for individual members of the Church (including clergy) to err, 2:134, 2:142, 5:217, 8:22, 9:56, 9:65, 11:91, 12:304–305, 13:341, 14:247–248.

II d

Even without the consent of the Church, the pope can teach infallibly, 2:134, 4:123, 7:604, 11:147, 14:168, 14:248–250, 15:146, 16:24, 16:185–189, 17:24–25, 17:153–155, 18:51, 18:319

properly convened and approved ecumenical (general) councils can teach infallibly, 2:137, 5:213, 8:22, 8:27, 14:248, 16:24, 16:185–189, 18:51, 18:139

regional, national, and otherwise local (particular) councils cannot teach infallibly by themselves, 8:27

the ordinary and universal teaching of all the bishops is infallible, 8:22, 14:168, 14:246–248, 15:146, 18:50, 18:138
individual bishops do not teach infallibly, 9:65, 14:247–248.

Only things pertaining to faith and morals can be taught infallibly by the Church, 4:123, 8:20, 9:53, 14:246–248, 15:14, 15:146, 16:89, 16:185–189, 17:20, 17:24–25, 17:153–155, 17:159, 18:50, 18:139
either by extraordinary acts or in her ordinary and universal teaching, 9:53–59, 16:24, 16:185–189, 17:25, 17:154, 18:50, 18:138.

The Church's Power of Governing (Jurisdiction)

II e

The Church has the same perpetual jurisdiction given to the apostles and their successors, 2:139, 3:13, 3:319, 4:31–32, 4:122–123, 5:213, 6:74, 6:169, 11:148, 11:432, 12:101, 14:24, 14:116, 14:239, 14:421, 15:14, 15:146, 16:23, 16:24, 16:181–182, 16:184–185, 17:21, 17:244–248, 17:263, 18:49–50, 18:133, 19:98.

II f

The objects and functions of ecclesiastical jurisdiction are especially these:
the administration of the sacraments, 2:231–233, 3:328, 6:73–74, 7:147, 7:531, 8:214, 9:74, 11:433, 13:249, 14:115, 14:233, 14:323–324, 15:14, 16:191, 17:263, 18:141–142, 19:110–112
preaching the divine word, 2:231–232, 3:12, 3:155, 3:320, 4:78, 9:68, 11:433, 12:6–11, 13:110–111, 13:249, 14:120–121, 14:233, 14:235, 14:327–328, 15:14, 15:146, 17:263, 19:74
the reading and interpretation of sacred scripture, 3:20, 3:316, 3:330–331, 4:78–79, 5:214, 8:14, 9:67–68, 11:153, 11:433, 13:105–106, 13:108–111, 13:220–221, 14:101, 16:333
the election and ordination of bishops and other clergy, 2:232, 4:32, 4:123, 4:170, 4:209, 9:122, 11:434, 12:17, 14:116, 14:234, 17:263
the care of religious and nuns, 11:434, 12:296

the granting of indulgences, 3:369, 4:70, 4:167, 4:209, 5:118, 5:250, 5:273–274, 6:169, 11:303–304, 11:309, 13:172–173, 13:236, 14:126, 14:414, 15:104, 17:76, 17:258, 18:219

the institution of feasts, 2:199, 3:32, 3:262–273, 3:333, 4:53, 4:147, 6:193, 7:423, 11:433, 13:41, 13:242–243, 13:261, 14:42–43, 14:325–326, 15:198, 16:64, 16:358–359, 17:48, 18:156

the direction of theological study, 12:205, 13:341, 14:124

the general care of all sacred things, and in some way even temporal things, 8:25–26, 11:434, 12:10, 13:317, 14:115, 14:233–234, 17:263, 18:325.

The Church in the World

II g

The Church in its own affairs is independent of the civil power, 8:24–26, 11:432–434, 12:250–251, 16:188–189, 18:145–146, 18:324.

The jurisdiction of the Church extends even over princes, kings, and entire nations, 2:138, 9:64, 11:432–434, 12:250–251, 13:249, 13:327, 16:187, 18:146

over public life, the family, and education, 12:340–343, 12:366–367, 13:327–328

it can declare unjust civil laws to be null and void, 5:41, 16:364–365, 18:146

in any conflict of laws, the Church is to be obeyed over the state, 11:432–434, 16:364–365, 18:146, 18:160.

The Church is not to be separated from the state, 13:204, 18:145, 18:326–327

and Catholicism should be the established religion of the state, 13:204, 14:118, 18:325–326.

The Church recognizes properly constituted states and their laws, 14:303–304, 16:364–365, 18:146, 18:159

and recognizes the power of civil rulers, even sinners, 6:106, 12:15, 12:250–251, 14:37, 14:303–304, 15:23, 15:76, 16:60, 16:185, 16:343, 16:364–365, 18:159

the state cannot govern without concern for the true religion, i.e., Catholicism, 12:289, 14:118, 18:145–146, 18:325–326

freedom of conscience and worship is a grave error, rightly opposed by citizens, 17:40–41, 17:144, 17:211, 18:325–326, 19:227

the state is not the source of all law, 16:364–365.

II h

The Church has authority over philosophers and philosophy, 12:19–20, 12:205, 12:329, 18:320

as well as all other sciences, 12:329, 18:320.

II i

The Church is not hostile to the good of human culture and temporal society, 11:101, 12:53, 13:15, 13:328–331, 14:121, 16:339–340, 18:146, 18:327

nor does it impede the free progress of science, 11:101, 14:102

nor is it an obstacle to true freedom, 13:327.

The Roman Pontiff

III a

Christ promised and directly conferred upon Peter the primacy of jurisdiction over the universal Church, 2:131, 3:203, 3:370, 4:32, 5:211, 8:28, 9:248, 10:34–35, 11:35, 11:146–147, 11:462–463, 14:111, 14:236, 15:145, 16:23, 16:182, 17:23–24, 17:28, 17:91, 17:149–152, 18:133–134, 18:303, 18:305, 18:307, 19:91, 19:98

hence Peter is the prince of the apostles, 3:317, 4:32, 4:122, 5:211, 8:175, 9:59–60, 11:35, 11:305, 14:114, 14:237, 16:23, 16:181–182, 17:24, 17:91, 18:302

the vicar of Christ, 1:22, 1:118, 2:21, 2:131, 2:315, 3:317, 3:370, 4:31–32, 4:122, 5:20, 8:175, 9:251–252, 10:34, 11:91, 11:146, 11:462–463,

12:302–303, 14:236, 15:145, 16:23, 16:181, 17:23, 17:91, 18:134, 18:309, 18:420, 19:91

the foundation of the Church, 1:23, 2:131, 3:370, 4:32, 4:122, 8:337, 11:147, 11:158, 14:111, 14:236, 14:237, 18:302, 18:304

the earthly head of the Church, 1:23, 1:118, 2:21, 2:131, 2:315, 3:313, 3:370, 4:32, 4:122, 5:20, 5:208, 5:211, 7:136, 8:28, 9:247–248, 9:251–252, 11:35, 11:91, 11:146, 11:155, 12:15–16, 12:27, 14:22, 14:111, 14:236, 15:13, 15:67, 15:145, 16:23, 16:181–182, 17:23, 17:28, 17:148–151, 18:49, 18:134, 18:302–304, 19:98

and the visible principle of the Church's unity, 1:23, 2:139, 3:13, 3:205, 4:32, 4:122, 5:211, 7:136, 8:19, 8:209, 11:146–148, 11:155, 11:463, 12:235, 14:116, 14:236, 15:67, 15:145, 16:23, 16:181–182, 17:23, 17:148–149, 17:157, 18:134, 18:136–137.

Peter has successors in the primacy, 1:23, 2:131, 3:13, 3:205, 4:32, 4:123, 5:20, 5:211, 8:215, 9:59, 11:147, 12:235, 14:22, 14:116, 14:237–238, 15:13, 15:67, 15:145, 16:181–182, 17:23, 17:28, 17:91, 17:151–152, 18:49, 18:134, 18:261, 18:302, 18:305, 19:98

these successors are perpetual in the Church, 2:132, 3:204, 3:372, 4:32, 4:123, 9:59, 11:147, 12:235, 12:302–303, 12:398–399, 14:24, 14:139, 14:237–238, 15:147, 17:151–152, 18:302, 18:304–305, 19:98

their succession is found in the episcopacy of the city of Rome, 1:23, 3:13, 3:205–212, 3:371–372, 4:31–32, 4:122, 8:27, 8:175, 8:215, 9:59, 11:146, 14:22, 14:116, 14:238, 15:67, 15:145, 16:181–182, 17:22, 17:151, 18:49, 18:134, 19:98

the diocese personally founded by St. Peter, 2:139, 3:206, 3:372, 4:31–32, 4:122, 12:14, 12:27, 16:325, 18:261

not merely by political accident, but by the ordination of divine providence, 3:204, 4:32, 4:122, 8:215, 12:14

where he was martyred (along with St. Paul), 1:23, 3:210, 3:372, 8:215, 12:26–27, 14:116, 16:169, 17:151, 18:49, 18:134, 19:98

his successors being therefore called *Roman Pontiff*, 2:131, 3:317, 3:372, 4:31, 4:122, 8:27, 8:215, 11:146, 14:116, 14:238, 17:91, 18:49, 18:134, 18:306

and the true faith appropriately called *Roman Catholicism*, 4:31, 4:122, 8:210, 11:146, 12:235, 14:23, 14:243, 16:182, 16:325, 17:22, 17:151, 19:120.

III b

The Roman pontiff holds, and has always held, primacy in the Universal Church, 2:139, 3:203, 3:208–209, 3:370–372, 4:31–32, 4:122, 5:211, 8:28, 9:59–61, 11:146, 11:155, 11:463, 12:27, 14:238, 17:22, 17:150–152, 18:49, 18:134–135, 18:261, 18:306–307

this primacy is supreme, full, ordinary, and immediate over all and each member of the Church, 2:131, 3:371, 4:32, 4:122, 8:26, 8:28, 9:60–61, 10:34–35, 11:146, 11:463, 12:79–80, 14:237, 16:181, 17:150–152, 18:135, 18:307–308, 18:310, 19:98

provided that he is duly elected, 12:249, 12:302–303.

III c

The Roman pontiff has authority over councils, 3:205, 4:32, 4:122, 8:27, 8:29, 11:147, 12:174, 12:197, 14:118–119, 14:134–135, 14:238, 18:51, 18:139, 18:308

jurisdiction over bishops and their churches, 3:208–209, 4:32, 4:122, 8:28, 11:146, 11:148, 11:463, 12:34, 12:79–80, 14:237, 15:67, 16:181, 17:24, 17:152, 18:50, 18:135, 18:141, 18:306–307, 19:98

a certain power over princes and nations, 5:211, 11:432–434, 12:250–251, 14:125, 14:238, 16:187, 18:306

and in general, all the baptized are subject to him in sacred things, 4:32, 4:122, 9:60–61, 10:338, 11:146, 11:155, 11:463, 12:79–80, 14:237, 17:151–152, 18:135, 18:159, 18:306–308, 19:98.

III d

The Roman pontiff alone establishes canons, 14:235

dispenses of the treasury of the Church by establishing indulgences, 5:118, 5:250, 6:169, 11:303–304, 11:308, 13:172–173, 13:236, 14:126, 14:414, 18:219, 18:420

establishes, transfers, and judges bishops, 11:148, 12:15, 12:303

dispenses in the laws of the Church, 11:147, 11:343, 14:235

is the supreme judge on earth, 11:147–148, 12:250, 14:238, 16:192, 18:306, 18:308–310.

III e

The Roman pontiff is the father and teacher of all Christians, 3:372, 4:32, 4:122, 7:604, 8:216, 11:147, 11:463, 14:238, 14:249, 15:13, 16:24, 16:185–190, 17:151–155, 19:98

he is not subordinate to any civil power, 11:432–434, 12:249–251, 14:238, 16:188–189.

III f

The Roman pontiff can establish articles of faith and laws of morals, 4:123, 7:604, 8:62, 11:89, 13:152, 14:235, 14:248–250, 15:146, 16:24, 16:185–189, 17:24–25, 18:51, 18:134, 18:319

not subject to the approval of Church councils, 7:604, 14:248–250, 18:319

and when making solemn definition of these (teaching *ex cathedra*), he is infallible, 4:32, 4:123, 7:604, 8:29, 8:216, 11:147, 13:152, 14:168, 14:248–250, 15:146, 16:24, 16:185–189, 17:24–25, 17:28, 17:153–155, 18:51, 18:139, 18:319, 19:101

hence he is the supreme teacher in the Church, 4:123, 8:216, 11:147, 14:238, 14:249, 16:24, 16:185–190, 17:151–155, 19:101

he has never erred in the solemn teaching of faith or morals, 4:32, 4:123, 8:216, 10:35, 11:147, 14:168, 14:248–250, 16:185–189, 17:28, 17:153–155, 18:260, 18:319

his office is to define and defend the truths of faith, 11:89, 12:302, 13:152, 14:235, 14:248–250, 16:24, 16:185–190, 17:153–155

and assent and obedience are due to his decrees, 3:122, 3:317, 4:78–79, 7:603, 7:604, 8:216, 10:338, 11:148, 13:152, 14:168–169, 14:248, 17:25, 17:28, 18:138–140, 18:306.

III g

The Roman pontiff lawfully holds a measure of temporal civil rule, 12:250–251, 14:135, 14:238, 16:188–189

abrogation of his temporal rule is not of benefit to the Church, 12:250–251, 14:135, 14:238, 16:188–189.

III h

The Roman pontiff is elected by the cardinals according to due process of law, 12:249

when rightly elected, he is the true head and pastor of the Church, 3:13, 5:211, 8:208, 12:249, 12:302–303, 19:98

even if he is a wicked sinner, 7:133, 9:132, 16:187.

III i

The Roman See is supreme over all local churches, 2:139, 3:205–209, 3:317, 3:372, 4:32, 9:60–61, 11:146–147, 12:235.

God in Himself

GOD'S ESSENCE AND ATTRIBUTES

IV a

God exists, 1:3, 1:4, 1:19, 1:116, 2:20, 2:30, 2:117, 2:156, 2:313, 3:5, 3:6, 3:63, 3:102, 3:316, 4:6, 4:95, 4:184, 5:10, 6:25–26, 7:50, 8:5, 9:10, 9:247, 10:68–72, 10:334, 11:102, 12:153, 14:100, 14:181, 15:41, 15:57–58, 16:10, 16:110, 17:7, 17:26, 17:98, 17:117, 17:124, 18:42, 18:108, 18:261–263, 19:12–13

which can be known with certainty by the light of reason, 6:23, 6:29, 7:50, 8:187, 8:337, 10:61, 10:68–72, 10:133–134, 11:102, 14:100, 14:180–181, 14:268, 17:7, 17:117, 18:103, 18:253–254, 18:442, 19:16

and reasonably demonstrated, 6:25, 6:29, 7:50, 8:337, 10:61, 10:68–72, 14:180–181, 18:103

God has also revealed himself, 1:116, 2:156, 3:41, 3:147, 6:23–24, 7:36, 9:41, 10:61–64, 10:334, 11:19, 11:105, 14:100, 14:180–181, 15:41, 15:57–58, 16:172, 17:9, 17:117, 18:103, 19:12–13

hence his existence can and ought to be believed, 1:4, 1:19, 1:116, 2:117, 2:157, 2:313, 3:41, 6:25–26, 7:50–53, 9:28–33, 10:68–72, 10:334, 11:46, 11:95–97, 11:102, 11:105, 12:20, 14:100, 14:180–181, 15:130, 16:172, 17:120, 18:108

although the immediate vision of God is not natural to the soul, 3:283, 3:301, 16:375, 18:114–115

nor is God immediately manifest in creation, 3:302, 13:338.

IV b

God is only one, 1:32, 1:116–117, 2:5, 2:20, 2:172, 2:312, 3:7, 3:122, 3:183, 3:316, 4:9, 4:13, 4:98, 4:102, 4:187, 4:190, 5:10, 5:12, 5:196, 6:25, 6:191–192, 6:199, 7:53, 8:187, 9:10, 9:12–13, 9:247, 9:253, 10:72, 10:140, 10:334, 11:95, 12:153, 12:173, 13:259, 14:7, 14:101, 15:8, 15:59, 15:129–130, 16:10, 16:84, 16:110–111, 17:26, 17:98–99, 17:125–126, 18:22, 18:42, 18:109, 18:261–263, 18:317

distinct from the world and high above all created things, 1:26–27, 1:120, 2:30, 3:6, 3:302, 3:316, 5:10, 6:31, 10:68, 10:72, 10:334, 11:96, 11:101, 11:104–105, 12:20, 13:259, 14:190–191, 16:110, 17:98, 18:109, 18:262, 19:22.

In God, various attributes are distinguished: he is infinitely simple, 8:36, 9:12, 14:181, 16:107, 17:26, 18:108, 18:262

immutable, 3:265, 6:149, 7:390, 9:13, 10:67, 10:72, 14:182, 18:108, 18:261–263, 18:288, 19:14

uncreated, 3:6, 6:4, 7:54, 10:72, 17:124–125, 18:261

eternal, 1:25, 2:276, 3:6, 3:41, 3:114, 3:122, 3:349, 4:14, 4:103, 5:11, 5:196, 6:4, 7:54, 8:50, 9:13, 9:253, 10:72, 10:140, 10:334, 11:96, 11:103, 14:7, 14:101, 14:182, 15:7, 15:60, 15:129, 16:9–10, 16:107, 17:26, 17:98, 17:124–125, 18:21, 18:42, 18:108, 18:261–262, 19:14

immense, 3:102, 4:13, 4:102, 5:196, 6:149–150, 8:38, 9:253, 10:72, 14:7, 14:182, 14:225, 14:232, 15:7, 15:59, 15:129, 16:10, 16:107–108, 17:125, 17:134, 18:21, 18:24, 18:43, 18:108, 18:261–262

incomprehensible, 1:25, 3:102, 6:4, 7:50, 9:13, 9:253, 10:67–68, 10:72, 11:95, 13:261, 14:190, 18:261–263

ineffable, 6:152–153, 10:67–68, 18:261, 18:263

invisible, 3:316, 7:50, 8:46, 14:7, 14:180, 15:129, 16:10, 16:106–108, 17:118–119, 18:334

a spiritual substance, 3:7, 4:14, 4:103, 5:11, 5:207, 7:51, 7:526, 8:35, 10:73, 10:140, 11:126, 14:7, 14:180–181, 15:8, 15:59, 15:128–129, 16:9–10, 16:106–108, 17:7, 17:118–119, 17:124–125, 18:21, 18:42, 18:108, 18:262, 18:270

happy in and of himself, 10:67, 11:96, 14:191, 16:115, 17:131, 18:90, 18:108, 18:262

however, there is no real distinction between his nature and his attributes, nor among themselves, 3:281, 5:196, 8:36, 8:41, 8:51.

IV c

God is omniscient, 2:117, 3:6, 3:281, 4:14, 4:103, 5:11, 6:25, 6:86, 7:58, 10:73, 10:140, 11:103, 14:182–183, 15:8, 15:60, 15:129, 16:10, 16:108–109, 17:125, 18:21, 18:42, 18:108, 18:262–263, 19:20

and omnipotent, 1:116, 2:20, 2:117, 3:6, 3:28, 3:99, 3:102, 3:237, 3:344, 4:6, 4:14, 4:95, 4:103, 4:130, 4:184, 5:11, 5:196, 6:4, 6:25, 7:57–60, 8:36, 8:50, 8:187, 10:72, 10:334, 11:54, 11:96, 11:103, 12:173, 14:7, 14:101, 14:183, 15:7, 15:42, 15:60, 15:129, 16:10, 16:84, 16:109, 17:124, 17:181, 18:43, 18:108, 18:181, 18:261–263, 19:28.

There is no twofold cosmic principle of good and evil at work in creation, 6:29, 8:38, 12:281, 13:30–31

rather, God is the source of all truth and power, 3:41, 4:129, 6:25, 7:51, 8:8, 11:87, 16:111

one and the same in the old and new testaments, 3:325, 3:333, 10:24, 10:61–64.

The Blessed Trinity

V a

God is a Blessed Trinity of three Persons who are nevertheless only one God, 1:3, 1:25, 1:32, 1:116, 2:5, 2:112, 2:117, 2:130, 2:312, 2:314, 3:4, 3:7, 3:272, 3:302, 3:316, 4:17–18, 4:106, 4:190, 5:12, 5:20, 5:196, 5:200, 6:4–5, 6:25, 6:191–192, 6:199, 7:53–54, 8:49–53, 9:10, 9:12–13, 9:247, 10:27, 10:140, 10:217, 10:334, 11:96, 11:103, 12:153, 13:102, 13:259, 14:8, 14:188, 14:345, 15:8, 15:41, 15:60, 15:130, 16:11, 16:111–112, 17:15, 17:26, 17:91, 17:98–99, 17:126, 18:16, 18:22, 18:41, 18:109–110, 18:131, 18:261, 18:263, 18:267–268, 19:87

the three divine Persons are one in nature, one in essence, one in substance, 1:25, 1:117, 2:6, 2:112, 2:314, 3:7, 3:316, 4:17–18, 4:106, 4:190, 5:13, 5:196, 6:4–5, 6:191, 6:199, 7:55, 8:50, 9:12, 9:247, 9:253, 10:140, 10:334, 11:96, 11:136, 12:177, 13:260, 13:261, 14:188, 15:8, 15:60, 15:130, 16:11, 16:112, 17:99, 18:42, 18:109–110, 18:261–263, 18:267–268, 19:87

coequal in divinity and all attributes, 1:25, 2:113, 2:127, 3:7, 3:11–12, 3:302, 4:17, 4:106, 4:187, 4:190–191, 5:12–13, 5:196, 6:4–5, 7:55, 8:50, 8:53, 9:253, 11:96, 11:103, 11:136, 13:163, 14:8, 14:188, 15:60, 15:130, 16:11, 16:111–112, 17:26, 17:91, 17:128, 17:146, 18:42, 18:109–110, 18:261, 18:266–268, 18:289, 19:87–88

inseparable in being and acting, 2:113, 3:7, 3:302, 4:18, 4:106, 4:190, 5:200, 6:4–5, 7:55, 8:50, 11:100, 11:108–109, 11:137, 13:260, 14:189, 16:112, 18:110, 18:123.

V b

The Father is true God, 1:3, 1:20, 1:116, 2:5, 2:20, 2:117, 2:156, 2:314, 3:20, 3:302, 3:316, 4:17, 4:106, 4:190, 5:12, 5:196, 6:4, 6:192, 6:199, 7:56, 8:50, 9:12, 11:96, 13:171, 14:8, 14:188, 15:8, 15:60, 15:130, 16:11, 16:111, 17:98, 17:126, 18:131, 19:87–88

not made, not created, not born, not proceeding from another, 2:5, 2:20, 3:6, 5:196, 6:4, 6:192, 7:55, 8:52, 8:188, 9:13, 11:96, 11:103, 14:188, 17:124, 18:261

he has everything of himself, and is the principle without principle, 2:20, 3:6, 7:56, 8:52, 9:13, 9:253, 11:103, 14:189, 17:124

with the Son, he is the cause or principle of the Holy Spirit, 2:5, 2:130, 2:313, 3:12, 3:316, 5:196–197, 6:4, 6:63, 7:55, 8:53, 8:188, 11:96, 11:100, 11:103, 14:188, 14:230, 15:141, 16:20, 16:160, 17:26, 17:145–146, 18:109, 18:131, 19:80

he is the Creator of all things visible and invisible, 1:4, 1:20, 1:25, 2:20, 2:117, 2:313, 2:314, 3:6, 3:316, 4:9, 4:13, 4:98, 4:102, 4:187, 4:190, 5:197, 6:28–29, 6:192, 7:48, 7:60–63, 8:187, 9:13, 9:250, 11:96, 11:100, 11:102–103, 11:104–105, 12:91, 12:173, 14:8, 14:189, 15:127, 16:84–85, 17:98, 17:124, 18:43, 18:107, 18:261, 18:263, 18:268.

V c

The Son is true God, 1:4, 1:20, 1:117, 2:6, 2:20, 2:119, 2:313, 2:314, 3:7, 3:286, 3:302, 4:17, 4:108, 4:192, 5:13, 5:196, 6:4, 6:33–34, 6:199, 7:70, 8:50, 9:12, 10:224, 11:96, 11:100, 11:105, 11:106, 12:173, 13:139, 14:8, 14:188,

14:204, 15:8, 15:60, 15:130, 16:11, 16:111, 17:15, 17:98, 17:126, 18:120, 18:131, 18:290, 19:87–88

consubstantial with the Father—but not a kind of part, portion, or extension of the Father, 1:117, 2:20, 2:121, 2:314, 3:7, 3:316, 5:193–194, 5:196, 6:34, 7:71, 8:173, 9:14, 9:250, 11:96, 11:97, 11:106, 12:173, 13:129, 13:260, 14:204, 15:8, 15:61, 18:110, 18:261, 18:264, 18:289, 18:291

begotten of the nature or substance of the Father—but not created or made, 1:20, 2:20, 2:121, 3:5, 3:316, 5:193–194, 5:201, 6:4, 6:33–34, 6:192, 7:55, 7:70, 8:52, 8:173, 8:188, 8:195, 9:14, 9:250, 11:97–99, 11:103, 11:106, 12:173, 13:260, 14:13, 14:188, 14:204, 15:61, 15:137, 17:128, 18:109, 18:263–264, 18:268, 18:350

eternally proceeding from the Father, 2:20, 2:121, 2:314, 3:7, 3:267, 5:196, 7:55, 7:70, 8:52, 8:195, 8:205, 9:14, 11:96, 11:106, 14:189, 14:204, 15:61, 17:26, 17:128, 18:261, 18:289, 19:56

as the Father's natural Son, not as adopted, 1:4, 1:20, 2:20, 2:121, 2:313, 2:314, 3:5, 3:7, 3:267, 3:316, 4:6, 4:95, 4:184, 5:201, 6:33–34, 7:77, 8:77, 8:84, 8:195, 9:14, 9:250, 11:100, 11:106, 14:13, 14:204, 15:61, 16:85, 18:350.

Through the Son all things are made, 2:20, 3:316, 7:89, 8:173, 9:12, 10:80–81, 11:97–99, 11:103, 11:108, 12:136, 12:173, 13:139, 13:163, 13:228, 14:204, 14:213, 18:122, 18:268

he rules all things, 2:20, 3:6, 3:11, 3:316, 9:14, 11:58, 13:171, 13:177, 18:286

he alone became incarnate and suffered, 1:4, 1:20, 2:6, 2:122–123, 2:314, 3:8–9, 3:270, 3:316, 4:18, 4:107, 4:191, 5:15–17, 5:150, 5:200, 5:202, 6:34, 6:39, 6:199, 8:74–75, 9:15, 10:18, 11:96, 11:108–109, 11:112, 12:186, 13:163, 13:260, 14:13–14, 14:204, 14:214, 15:9–10, 15:137–138, 17:15, 17:27, 17:99, 17:128, 18:16, 18:22.

V d

The Holy Spirit is true God, 1:4, 1:19, 1:22, 1:118, 2:5, 2:21, 2:130, 2:313, 3:7, 3:302, 4:17, 4:190, 5:13, 5:196, 6:4, 6:62–63, 6:192, 6:199, 7:122–123, 8:50, 8:173, 8:205, 9:12, 11:96, 11:100, 11:136, 12:186, 13:254, 14:8, 14:21,

14:188, 14:230, 15:8, 15:66, 15:130, 16:11, 16:20, 16:112, 16:160, 17:98, 17:126, 17:146, 18:131, 19:80, 19:87–88

proceeding from the Father and the Son as from one principle, 1:22, 2:5, 2:21, 2:130, 3:12, 3:316, 5:196–197, 5:202, 6:4, 6:63, 6:192, 7:55, 7:125–126, 8:52, 8:173, 8:205, 9:20, 9:251, 11:96, 11:100, 11:103, 11:136, 14:188, 14:230, 15:13, 15:141, 16:20, 16:160, 17:26, 17:145–146, 18:48, 18:109, 18:131, 18:261, 18:263–265, 18:268, 19:80

he is to be adored as the Father and the Son, 1:118, 2:130, 3:316, 6:4–5, 6:62–63, 8:173, 9:20, 9:251, 11:97, 11:100, 11:136, 12:186, 13:102, 13:260, 14:8, 14:230, 15:142, 19:87

he is sent by the Father and the Son, 2:21, 2:130, 6:64, 7:125–126, 9:20, 9:251, 13:251, 15:142

he is not the Father of Christ, 4:18, 4:107, 8:51, 9:15, 11:108

he is the inspirer of the law and the prophets, 3:316, 6:63–64, 7:123, 8:173, 9:253, 11:96, 12:186, 16:206, 18:256

author of both testaments, 6:63–64, 18:256–257

cause of the incarnation, 1:4, 1:20, 1:31, 1:117, 2:20, 2:122, 3:5, 3:8, 3:316, 4:18, 4:107, 4:191, 5:14, 5:202, 6:36–39, 6:183, 6:192, 9:15, 11:11, 11:108–109, 12:186, 13:95, 14:13, 14:214–215, 15:9, 15:62, 15:138, 16:17, 16:85, 16:139, 17:15, 17:99, 17:134, 18:22, 18:46, 18:95, 18:122, 18:288, 18:290

and the vivifier, 2:273, 3:66, 3:68, 3:316, 6:63, 7:125, 8:207, 9:20, 11:96, 11:137, 11:161, 12:186, 13:251, 13:254, 14:230–231, 18:49, 18:132

he dwells in the Church, 1:22, 3:13, 3:93, 3:195, 6:66, 9:20, 9:253, 11:96, 11:137, 11:144, 13:154, 14:21, 14:232–233, 15:92, 15:142, 16:21, 16:25, 16:169, 16:199, 17:19–20, 18:49, 18:132, 18:136, 19:81

he is sent to the apostles and the faithful and works in them, 1:133, 3:12, 3:353–55, 3:336, 4:26–27, 4:116–117, 4:177, 4:194, 6:63, 6:72, 8:206, 9:253, 11:137, 12:6–7, 12:71, 13:81, 13:255–258, 14:114, 14:232, 15:13, 15:67, 15:142, 16:20–21, 16:160–161, 16:168–169, 17:18, 17:146–147, 17:226–227, 18:48–49, 18:132

he teaches in a universal (ecumenical) council, 1:22, 3:93–94, 6:65, 11:96, 11:137, 12:173, 15:14

he acts in the sacraments, 1:22, 3:27, 3:49, 4:61, 4:68, 4:156, 4:157, 4:203, 6:64, 6:134, 9:82, 9:86, 11:96, 11:137, 13:322, 14:231

he is received along with sanctifying grace in the soul, 1:25, 1:118, 3:68, 3:336, 7:127, 7:521, 11:96, 11:137, 14:22, 14:232, 14:359, 18:49, 18:132

he is sevenfold in his gifts, 1:10, 1:132, 2:242, 3:32, 3:70, 4:62, 4:157–158, 4:203–204, 7:127, 9:242, 11:139–142, 11:249, 13:44, 13:258, 14:231, 15:33, 15:153, 16:31, 16:217, 17:63, 17:269, 18:49, 18:132, 18:239, 18:445–446, 19:81

he is given in a special way in confirmation, 1:63–64, 2:215, 3:27, 3:66, 3:69, 4:62, 4:157, 4:203, 6:64,–45, 6:72, 6:136–137, 6:204, 6:215, 9:88, 11:247, 14:52, 14:374, 15:28, 15:91, 15:142, 15:152–153, 16:30, 16:214, 17:63, 17:105, 17:226–228, 18:23, 18:69, 18:195, 18:374–375, 19:164

and ordination, 3:199, 3:201, 9:126, 9:130, 11:331.

V e

The three divine Persons are among themselves really distinct, 1:25, 2:117, 2:130, 3:7, 3:102, 4:9, 4:17, 4:98, 4:106, 4:187, 4:190, 5:196, 6:4–5, 6:191, 8:51, 9:253, 11:103, 13:261, 14:188, 15:130, 16:11, 16:111, 17:91, 17:126, 18:16, 18:22, 18:42, 18:107, 18:263, 18:266

as are all their personal relations and properties, 1:25, 5:196, 11:103, 14:188, 18:262

but each is whole and entire in the others, in a wonderful manner (properly called *circumincession*), 2:130, 5:196, 18:263–264

the revealed truth of the Blessed Trinity is a mystery beyond the reach of human reason alone, 2:112–213, 5:13, 6:191, 8:49, 9:10–11, 10:217, 11:95, 13:261, 14:189–190, 15:58, 15:130, 16:11, 16:101–102, 16:112, 17:83, 17:126, 18:102, 19:87–88.

Creation

The Natural Order

VI a

The triune God created the world, 1:116, 2:20, 2:117, 3:6, 4:9, 4:13, 4:98, 4:102, 4:187, 4:190, 5:197, 6:192, 6:199, 7:64, 8:53, 8:187, 8:188, 9:253, 10:80–164, 10:136, 10:334, 11:96, 11:100, 11:104–105, 13:259, 14:8, 14:102, 14:190, 15:61, 15:131, 16:8, 16:12, 16:84–85, 16:100, 16:114, 17:26, 17:98, 17:124, 18:21, 18:43, 18:90, 18:111, 18:261–263, 18:268, 19:34

out of nothing (*ex nihilo*), 2:20, 2:117, 3:6, 3:237, 4:14, 4:103, 5:197, 6:30–31, 6:199, 7:48, 7:60, 8:53, 8:188, 9:10, 9:13, 9:250, 10:80–81, 10:150, 10:335, 11:104, 13:250, 13:291, 14:8, 14:101, 14:190, 15:7, 15:61, 15:131, 16:12, 16:84–85, 16:114, 17:124, 18:43, 18:90, 18:111, 18:261–262, 19:34

not from all eternity, but from the beginning of time, 3:237, 6:30, 6:199, 10:72, 10:80–81, 11:383, 13:259, 13:324, 17:26, 18:111, 18:261–262, 19:34

not out of necessity, but freely of his own divine goodness, 2:117, 4:9, 4:10, 4:98–99, 4:130, 4:187, 4:188, 5:197, 7:60, 10:72–73, 14:191, 16:115, 18:90, 18:111, 19:34.

VI b

Creatures of two kinds are distinct from God: corporeal (visible) and spiritual (invisible), 2:118, 4:20–21, 4:109–110, 6:192, 6:199, 7:61–63, 9:13, 9:250, 10:74, 10:150, 11:104, 12:91, 14:10–11, 14:194, 15:131, 17:98, 18:43, 18:90, 18:111, 18:261–262, 19:34–40

created nature, even material, is good of itself, 3:249, 3:308, 6:29, 7:543, 10:129–130, 10:163, 12:281, 13:29–30, 13:324, 14:191, 19:34

the created universe is not animate, 13:30–31

nor is it a single entity of itself, 10:67–68

nor does it immediately manifest divinity, 8:54.

VI c

Angels exist and are spiritual beings of intellect and will, 2:117, 4:13, 4:20–21, 4:103, 4:173, 4:212, 6:23, 6:179, 7:61, 8:55, 8:189, 10:150–153, 10:317, 11:104, 14:10, 14:194, 15:131, 16:12, 16:114–118, 17:27, 17:33, 17:118, 17:131, 18:44, 18:112, 18:261–262, 18:270–271, 19:36

they are immortal, 1:17, 4:20, 4:109, 17:118, 18:270, 19:36

and not propagated, 4:110

the devil is not a mere symbol or literary device, 3:37, 4:20, 4:109–110, 6:27, 7:61, 7:582, 10:150, 11:19–20, 11:104, 16:12, 16:118, 17:27, 17:34, 17:131, 17:161

but he and the other demons were created as good angels, 2:118, 3:283–284, 4:20, 4:109–110, 7:61, 8:57, 10:153, 13:291, 14:10, 14:194, 15:132, 16:12, 16:118, 17:27, 17:33–34, 17:131, 17:174, 18:44, 18:112, 18:261, 19:36

and became evil through their own free rejection of God in the beginning, 2:118, 3:283–284, 4:20, 4:21, 4:109–110, 4:173, 4:212, 7:62, 8:57, 8:190, 10:153, 13:291, 14:10, 14:195, 15:132, 16:12, 16:118, 17:27, 17:34, 17:131, 17:174, 18:44, 18:112, 18:261, 18:270–271, 19:36.

VI d

Man is not of the substance of God, 1:17, 4:15, 4:104, 10:147–148, 11:104, 14:197, 15:183, 16:118–119, 18:278

but is created, 1:17, 2:113, 2:118, 3:4, 4:15, 4:104, 5:7, 6:161, 7:62, 7:516, 8:60–61, 10:135–136, 10:182, 10:335, 11:100, 11:104, 13:29–30, 14:11, 14:102, 14:197, 15:5, 15:61, 15:127, 16:8, 16:13, 16:100, 16:118–119, 17:8, 17:27, 17:98, 17:117, 17:130, 18:20, 18:44, 18:90, 18:114, 18:261–262, 18:277–278, 19:38

consisting of two substances: a soul (rational spirit) united with a body (flesh), 1:17, 3:4, 4:15, 4:104, 5:7, 5:371, 6:39, 6:66, 7:62, 7:152, 8:59, 8:191, 10:136–138, 10:148, 10:335, 11:100, 11:130, 11:168, 12:245, 13:5, 13:9, 13:333, 14:11, 14:197, 15:5–6, 15:127, 16:8, 16:100, 17:7, 17:118, 18:111, 18:114, 18:261–262, 19:38–39.

The end of man is so that leading a life in society and ordered under God he may cultivate fully all his faculties for the praise of his Creator, and by fulfilling faithfully the office of his art or any other vocation he may obtain for himself both temporal and eternal happiness, 1:17, 1:114, 2:312, 3:4, 3:16, 3:194, 3:331, 3:353, 4:15, 4:104, 5:7, 5:175, 5:293, 6:31–32, 6:144, 6:159, 10:34, 10:146–147, 11:82, 11:87–88, 11:437–438, 11:461, 12:53–54, 12:279–280, 12:297–298, 13:260, 13:333, 14:5, 14:162–164, 15:5, 15:61, 15:127, 16:103–104, 16:126–127, 17:8–9, 17:117–118, 17:265, 18:44, 18:114, 19:6.

Adam was the first man, 2:119, 3:55, 4:20, 4:109, 4:196, 5:57, 6:49, 6:204, 8:60, 10:25, 10:148, 10:170, 11:84, 14:11, 14:102, 14:197, 15:132, 16:118–119, 17:27, 17:171, 18:44, 18:90, 18:115, 19:39
  not a myth, metaphor, or literary device, but a true and historical individual, 10:148, 14:102, 14:197, 15:132, 17:27
  from whom the whole human race is derived, 4:20, 4:109, 4:196, 5:57, 6:204, 10:25, 10:148, 10:335, 11:84, 12:20, 14:12, 14:199, 15:132, 16:118–119, 17:27, 17:171, 18:44, 18:90, 18:115, 19:39.

The human soul is created directly by God, 2:113, 2:118, 3:4, 3:179, 4:15, 4:104, 10:137, 10:163, 11:225, 13:326–327, 14:11, 14:282, 17:27, 17:118, 18:116, 19:38
  from nothing, 18:115–116, 19:38
  it does not pre-exist or evolve, 10:163
  it is not generated by human parents, 7:431, 18:116
  but infused before birth, 7:431, 14:11.

The soul is a spiritual substance, 2:113, 3:4, 4:15, 4:104, 5:7, 8:59, 8:191, 10:138–139, 10:335, 11:100, 13:9, 13:326–327, 14:101, 14:197, 15:127, 16:8, 16:100–101, 17:118–119, 18:114, 18:273, 19:39
  rational and intellectual, 1:17, 2:113, 3:4, 4:15, 4:104, 5:7, 7:62, 7:543, 8:191, 10:138–139, 14:197, 15:5–6, 15:127, 16:8, 16:100–102, 17:27, 17:127, 18:114–115, 18:273, 18:278, 19:39
  not one in all, but unique to every individual, 2:113, 10:137–138, 18:272

immortal, 1:17, 2:113, 2:118–119, 3:4, 4:15, 4:104, 5:7, 5:58, 5:210, 6:32, 6:79, 7:152, 8:59, 8:192, 10:139–140, 10:335, 11:7, 11:99, 11:168, 13:11, 13:326–327, 14:11, 14:101, 14:134, 14:197, 15:5, 15:127, 16:8, 16:100–101, 17:100, 17:118–119, 18:114, 18:272–273, 19:39

essentially united to the body as its form, 3:102, 11:170, 13:9, 18:272

created free, 3:4, 6:32, 7:62, 8:59, 8:192, 10:139, 10:335, 11:100, 13:326–327, 14:197, 15:5, 15:127, 16:8, 16:100–102, 17:27, 18:273, 18:278, 19:39

which may be known and proven by reason alone, 10:138, 17:7.

VI e

Man by his nature is a social being, 10:131, 19:255–257

and human society is comprised of various ranks, 10:47, 18:157

each ordered to mutual assistance for the common good, 10:142–143.

VI f

The end of all creation is the glory of God, 3:4, 3:38, 4:14, 4:104, 4:212, 6:32, 10:74, 10:129–130, 11:83, 11:87, 13:29–30, 13:66, 13:259–260, 14:191, 15:131, 17:26, 19:34–35

who is the beginning and end of all things, 1:33, 3:6, 5:293, 8:337, 9:13, 10:30, 10:67–68, 10:144, 11:83, 13:49, 13:66, 13:259, 14:100, 17:8, 18:152, 19:34–35.

VI g

By his providence God protects and governs all things, 3:283, 5:11, 6:25–26, 6:146, 6:199, 7:54, 7:63–64, 7:516–521, 8:38–40, 8:231, 9:13–14, 9:250, 10:15–16, 10:74–80, 10:133–134, 11:29–30, 11:96, 11:100, 11:202–205, 12:24, 12:198, 12:220, 12:263, 13:265, 14:9, 14:185, 14:191–194, 16:10, 16:76–77, 16:108, 16:236, 18:43, 18:111, 18:262, 18:269, 19:18

he truly acts upon the world and men, 6:25–26, 6:199, 8:38–40, 10:20, 10:74–80, 11:29–30, 11:202–205, 11:386, 12:13, 12:84, 12:102, 12:352–353, 13:265, 14:9, 14:185, 14:192–194, 16:108, 17:26

he does not will evil as he wills good, 4:130, 6:25–26, 6:171–172, 8:37, 8:38, 10:74, 13:277, 14:184–185, 14:192–194, 18:111–112, 18:270, 19:24

but only permits evil as the consequence of sin, 3:177, 4:111, 6:25–26, 6:174–175, 7:585, 8:37, 11:80, 11:208, 14:192–194, 18:111–112, 18:269–270, 19:24.

Man is not under the direction of the stars, 6:28, 6:84–85, 6:150
nor is he ruled by fate, hereditary traits, or any other deterministic force, 6:28, 6:150, 11:104.

The Supernatural Order

VII a

God elevated rational creatures (angels and men) to a state exceeding the needs of nature, 8:61, 10:147, 10:169–171, 10:182, 11:183, 14:197–198, 17:27, 17:35, 17:131, 18:44–45, 18:116, 18:276
to a supernatural end, unknown to reason without revelation, 10:147, 14:100, 14:261–262, 16:207, 17:27, 17:35, 17:131, 17:178–179, 18:44–45, 18:115–116
consisting in the vision and enjoyment of God, 2:313, 3:284, 4:109–110, 5:22, 5:199, 6:32, 6:79, 8:191, 10:147, 10:159, 10:182, 11:175–176, 13:251, 13:300, 14:195, 14:261, 15:17, 16:68, 16:375, 17:178–179, 18:44, 18:114–115, 18:250
to which man ought to tend through supernatural acts, 3:16–17, 11:180, 14:356–358, 15:17, 17:27, 17:178–179, 18:176–177
distinction can therefore be made in man's works: as merely naturally good, or as also meriting of supernatural reward, 7:544–545, 11:160, 11:457, 14:277, 14:357–358, 14:361, 16:128, 16:170, 17:57, 17:166–167, 17:181, 18:62, 18:176–177, 18:237, 18:243, 18:275, 18:353.

Original Man

VII b

The first man was formed without any sin, 2:119, 4:20, 4:109, 4:196, 6:204, 8:61, 8:192, 10:335, 14:11, 14:197, 15:132, 16:13, 16:119, 17:35, 18:278, 19:39

in sanctity and justice, 2:119, 4:20, 4:111, 6:161, 6:204, 7:62, 7:543, 8:61–62, 8:192, 10:17, 10:147, 13:324–325, 14:11, 14:102, 14:197, 15:132, 16:13, 16:119, 17:27, 17:35, 18:45, 18:116, 18:283, 19:39

he had free will, 4:20, 4:111, 6:32, 6:161, 7:62, 8:192, 10:146, 11:184, 14:197, 16:122, 17:27, 18:115–116, 18:278, 19:39

and supernatural gifts of bodily integrity and immortality, 4:20–21, 4:111, 6:161, 7:62, 8:61, 8:192, 10:17, 10:147, 13:324–325, 14:11, 14:102, 14:197, 16:91, 18:44, 18:116, 18:283–284, 19:39.

The grace (justice) of the first man was not due to him, nor the simple result of his creation, 8:61, 8:193, 10:146–147, 10:171, 10:182, 14:198, 16:123, 18:115, 18:275–277, 19:39, 19:43

but a gift freely bestowed upon him by God, 2:119, 4:20–21, 4:111, 6:204, 7:543–544, 8:61, 8:193, 10:147, 10:171, 10:182, 11:183, 14:198, 16:123, 18:44–45, 18:115–116, 18:277, 19:39, 19:43.

Original Sin

VII c

At the suggestion of the devil, man sinned, 2:119, 3:15, 4:20, 4:109, 6:27, 6:184–185, 7:581, 10:164–165, 11:100, 14:11, 14:102, 14:198, 16:120–121, 17:27, 17:35, 18:45, 18:117, 18:261, 19:41

this sin effected Adam and all his progeny, 2:119, 2:247, 3:15, 4:21–22, 4:111–112, 4:196, 5:57, 5:279–280, 6:44, 6:204, 7:65, 8:62, 8:193–194, 9:142, 10:170–171, 10:242, 10:335, 11:88, 13:152, 14:12, 14:101, 14:102, 14:199–200, 15:16, 15:62, 15:68, 15:133, 16:13–14, 16:121–125, 17:34–36, 17:138–139, 17:172, 18:45, 18:91, 18:117, 18:281, 19:42

excepting Christ and the Blessed Virgin Mary, 4:112, 4:219, 4:224, 6:181, 6:184, 7:603, 8:62, 8:194, 9:33, 10:201, 11:212, 12:272–273, 13:152–158, 13:284, 14:199, 15:179, 16:14, 16:124–125, 17:27, 17:36, 17:154, 17:172–173, 18:45, 18:118, 18:283–285, 19:42, 19:58.

Original sin is passed on not by imitation but by generation from Adam's seed, 1:130, 2:80, 2:119, 2:247, 3:15, 3:55, 4:22, 4:111, 4:196, 5:57,

5:279–280, 6:49, 6:204, 7:65, 8:193, 9:142, 10:171–173, 10:335, 11:88, 11:232, 12:68, 13:152, 14:12, 14:199, 15:16, 15:68, 15:133, 16:14, 16:121–125, 17:27, 17:171, 18:45, 18:117, 18:279, 18:281, 19:42–43

it is proper to every human person, 1:130, 2:80, 2:119, 2:247, 3:15, 3:55, 3:60, 4:22, 4:112, 4:196, 5:279–280, 6:204, 7:65, 8:62, 8:194, 8:329, 9:142, 10:171–173, 10:335, 11:88, 11:232, 12:67–68, 13:152, 14:12, 14:101, 14:102, 14:199, 15:16, 15:62, 15:68, 15:133, 16:121–125, 17:27, 17:34–36, 17:138–139, 17:172, 18:45, 18:91, 18:117, 18:281, 19:42–43

although not personal, 3:55, 5:279–280, 8:63, 8:193, 9:142, 10:171–173, 14:199, 15:16, 15:68, 16:122–123, 16:125, 18:281, 18:283–284

and it differs from actual sin by reason of personal consent, 3:15, 3:55, 5:279–280, 6:204, 10:170–173, 14:199–200, 15:16, 15:68, 16:14, 16:122–123, 16:125–127, 18:85, 18:283–284

and by reason of its penalty, which for original sin alone is the lack of the vision of God, 2:80, 2:248, 5:206, 6:44, 6:47, 8:63–64, 8:329, 10:170, 11:232, 13:251, 14:18, 14:200, 15:62, 16:85–86, 16:121–123, 16:153, 17:171–172, 17:218, 18:371, 19:41.

Original sin is remitted by the baptism of regeneration, 1:60, 1:130, 2:80, 2:211, 2:248, 3:26–27, 3:55, 4:60, 4:156, 4:202, 5:57, 5:222, 5:225, 6:71, 6:135, 6:204, 7:146, 7:212, 8:138, 8:329, 9:142, 9:269, 10:171, 11:166, 11:231, 13:221, 14:368, 15:27, 15:91, 15:133, 15:150, 16:26, 16:28, 16:201–202, 16:205–207, 17:60, 17:171–172, 17:222–223, 18:68, 18:191, 18:279, 18:282, 18:367, 19:133

which must be received (at least in desire) in order to be saved, 1:60, 2:80, 2:210, 3:56, 3:335, 4:61, 4:156, 4:203, 5:57, 5:205–206, 5:225, 6:71, 7:206–210, 8:135, 9:22–23, 9:81–82, 10:82, 11:84, 11:166–167, 11:228, 11:232–233, 14:367–368, 15:150–151, 16:28, 16:29, 16:153, 16:207–208, 16:210–212, 17:61–62, 17:158, 17:225–226, 18:69, 18:143–144, 18:188, 18:194, 18:367, 19:134–136.

FALLEN MAN

VII d

Man through the sin of Adam was changed for the worse, 2:248, 3:15, 4:21–22, 4:111–112, 6:44, 6:161, 6:204, 7:65, 7:543–545, 8:62, 8:193, 9:142, 10:146, 10:167, 10:170–171, 11:24, 11:39, 11:80, 13:325, 14:12, 14:102, 14:199–201, 15:133, 16:13–14, 16:121–125, 16:136, 17:27, 17:35–36, 18:45, 18:91, 18:117, 18:278, 18:280–281, 19:41

he lost original sanctity and justice, 2:119, 4:21, 4:111, 5:279, 6:44, 6:161, 6:204, 7:65, 7:543–544, 8:62, 10:170–171, 11:167, 13:325, 14:198–200, 15:133, 16:13, 16:121, 17:35, 18:45, 18:117, 18:280, 19:41

was made mortal, 2:119, 4:21, 4:111, 4:196, 5:57, 5:280, 6:44, 6:47, 6:161, 6:184, 8:62, 8:193, 10:25, 10:165, 10:170, 11:39, 11:83, 11:167, 13:150, 13:325, 14:12, 14:102, 14:200, 15:133, 16:13, 16:91, 16:121, 17:35, 18:45, 18:117, 18:279, 18:281, 18:367, 19:41

subjected to the power of the devil, 3:37, 3:60, 4:22, 4:111, 5:148, 6:44, 7:580–584, 10:170, 11:24, 13:87, 13:149, 13:251–252, 14:196, 16:125, 16:136, 17:136, 17:173, 18:91, 18:280–281, 18:296, 19:41

and prevented from entering heaven, 4:22, 4:111, 5:57, 5:205, 6:44–45, 7:110, 8:62, 8:193, 10:167, 10:170–173, 11:116, 11:127, 13:251, 14:18, 14:102, 14:200, 14:222, 15:62, 16:85–86, 16:121–123, 16:153, 17:27, 17:35, 17:132, 17:138–139, 18:91, 18:455, 19:41

his intellect was darkened and obscured, 2:248, 4:22–23, 4:111, 5:280, 6:44, 7:543–545, 8:7, 8:61–62, 10:25, 10:167, 10:170, 11:13, 11:25, 11:82, 13:149–150, 13:325, 14:200, 15:133, 16:14, 16:123–124, 17:36, 17:234–235, 18:283, 19:41

his will was weakened, 2:248, 4:22–23, 4:111, 5:57, 5:80, 5:280, 6:44, 6:161, 7:543–545, 8:61–62, 10:167, 10:170, 11:13, 11:82, 11:184, 13:149–150, 13:325, 14:198, 15:133, 16:14, 16:123–124, 17:36, 17:234–235, 18:279, 18:283, 19:41

and his passions became disordered, 3:37, 4:22–23, 4:111, 5:57, 5:280, 6:44, 6:161, 7:546–547, 8:61–62, 10:25, 10:167, 10:170, 11:13, 11:82, 13:325, 14:200.

Creation: VII d

Man's free will was not entirely destroyed, 3:4, 8:100, 11:184, 14:126, 16:122–124, 17:27, 18:269, 18:353

therefore he can do certain morally good things even without grace, 4:23, 4:112, 8:97, 11:160, 11:457, 11:461, 14:357–358, 14:361, 17:57, 17:166–167, 17:181, 18:176, 18:243, 18:353

although there remains in fallen man an inclination to sin, called *concupiscence*, 2:197, 4:23, 4:112, 5:57, 5:84, 5:280, 6:44, 6:161–163, 6:172–173, 7:213, 7:216, 7:485, 7:546, 9:83–84, 9:148, 10:25, 10:167, 10:170–172, 11:13, 11:86, 11:231, 11:452–453, 12:66–69, 13:159, 13:325, 14:200, 14:368, 15:37, 15:133, 16:14, 16:88, 16:123–124, 17:36, 17:274, 18:45, 18:117, 18:283–284, 19:41–43, 19:185

from which he can never completely free himself in this life, 2:160, 4:23, 4:112, 5:84, 5:367, 6:44, 6:161–163, 7:215–217, 7:485, 7:546, 9:83–84, 9:148, 10:37, 10:172, 11:86, 11:231, 11:244, 12:169, 13:159–161, 14:368, 15:37, 15:133, 16:14, 16:88, 16:124, 17:274, 18:283–284, 19:185

involuntary motions of concupiscence are not sins of themselves, 2:197, 2:248, 5:282–283, 5:368, 7:213, 7:487, 8:254, 9:83–84, 11:231, 11:409, 15:25, 16:124, 18:283, 18:407.

Incarnation

Jesus Christ Is True God

VIII a

Jesus Christ is true God, 1:4, 1:20, 1:114, 2:20, 2:114, 2:120, 2:313, 3:7, 4:17, 4:19, 4:108, 4:192, 5:14–15, 5:201, 6:5, 6:33–34, 6:43, 6:183, 7:70, 8:173, 8:194, 8:197, 9:14, 9:19, 9:247, 10:224, 10:262–263, 10:334, 11:47–48, 11:96, 11:105–106, 12:30, 12:46, 12:89, 12:109, 12:117, 12:173, 13:139, 13:177, 13:341, 14:13–14, 14:118–119, 14:204, 14:209–215, 15:8, 15:61–62, 15:137, 16:16, 16:85, 16:137, 17:15, 17:99, 17:128, 17:191, 18:16, 18:22, 18:41, 18:46, 18:66, 18:120, 18:287, 18:291, 19:54

rightly called Son of the Father, 1:4, 1:20, 1:117, 2:20, 2:121, 2:312, 2:313, 3:5, 3:7, 3:316, 5:14, 5:201, 6:5, 6:33, 7:70, 9:15, 9:250, 10:219, 11:11, 11:36, 11:96, 11:106, 12:82, 12:173, 14:13, 14:204, 15:8, 15:61–62, 15:137, 16:16, 16:85, 16:137, 17:99, 18:46, 18:120, 18:287, 18:350, 19:53

and Word of the Father, 3:291, 4:19, 4:108, 4:192, 6:35–36, 7:71, 9:15, 11:11, 11:106, 11:108, 11:136, 12:109, 13:139, 13:163, 14:189, 14:213, 15:61, 17:16, 18:110, 18:122, 18:268, 18:286, 18:290, 19:56

he is consubstantial with the Father, 1:20, 2:20, 2:121, 2:272, 3:7, 3:16, 5:193–194, 6:5, 6:34, 7:71, 8:173, 9:14, 9:250, 11:96, 11:97, 11:106, 12:173, 13:129, 13:260, 14:204, 15:8, 15:61, 18:286–287, 18:289, 18:291, 19:54

one of the Blessed Trinity, 1:20, 2:6, 2:20, 2:114, 2:120, 2:312, 3:7, 4:18, 4:107, 4:191, 5:14, 5:201–202, 6:5, 6:33–34, 7:70, 8:194, 9:14, 9:250, 11:96, 11:108, 13:163, 13:260, 14:13, 14:204, 15:8, 15:61–62, 15:137, 16:16, 16:85, 16:137, 17:15, 17:99, 17:128, 17:134, 18:22, 18:122, 18:291, 19:56

begotten, not made, 1:20, 2:20, 2:121, 2:272, 3:7, 3:16, 3:267, 5:193–194, 5:201, 6:5, 6:33–34, 7:70, 8:173, 9:15, 11:97, 11:106, 12:173, 14:204, 15:61, 17:128

through whom all things are made, 2:20, 2:272, 3:316, 6:36, 7:89, 8:173, 9:14, 10:80–81, 11:97, 11:103, 11:108, 12:136, 12:173, 13:139, 13:163, 13:228, 14:204, 14:213, 18:122, 18:268

his divinity is proven in the canonical gospels, 1:20, 2:120, 6:33–34, 11:11, 11:36, 11:47–48, 13:139, 14:210–213, 18:121.

Jesus Christ Is True Man

VIII b

The same Jesus Christ is true man, 1:20, 1:114, 2:20, 2:114, 2:120, 3:7, 3:8, 4:19, 4:108, 4:191–192, 5:14–15, 5:201, 6:5, 6:37, 6:192, 7:74–75, 8:80, 8:197, 9:19, 9:247, 10:25, 10:262–263, 11:11–12, 11:65, 11:96, 11:108, 12:30, 12:160, 12:173, 13:177, 13:341, 14:14, 14:215, 15:8, 15:61–62, 15:137, 16:16, 16:137, 17:15, 17:99, 17:128–129, 18:46, 18:66, 18:123, 18:287, 18:291, 19:56, 19:68

conceived of the Holy Spirit, 1:4, 1:20, 1:31, 1:117, 2:20, 2:122, 2:272, 2:313, 3:5, 3:8, 3:291, 4:18, 4:23, 4:95, 4:99, 4:184, 4:187, 5:14, 5:202, 6:36–39, 6:183, 6:192, 7:75–77, 8:77, 8:173, 9:12, 9:250, 11:11, 11:108, 12:186, 13:95, 14:13, 14:214–215, 15:9, 15:62, 15:138, 16:17, 16:85, 16:139, 17:15, 17:99, 17:134, 18:22, 18:46, 18:95, 18:122, 18:288–289, 18:291

not by a natural human father (hence Saint Joseph is rightly called his foster father), 1:20, 2:20, 3:288, 4:96, 4:185, 4:220–221, 7:74, 8:80, 9:14, 9:250, 10:216, 10:258, 11:108, 14:15, 14:110, 14:216, 15:9, 16:137, 17:15, 17:134–135, 18:125, 18:293

and truly born of a human mother, 1:4, 1:20, 2:20, 2:122, 2:313, 3:7, 3:8, 3:267, 3:291, 4:18, 4:101, 4:154, 4:184, 5:201, 5:203, 6:5, 6:39, 6:192, 6:199, 7:77–78, 8:76, 9:12, 9:15, 9:250, 10:282, 11:11–12, 11:108–110, 12:153, 12:160, 13:164, 14:14, 14:110, 14:214, 15:9, 15:62, 15:137, 16:17, 16:139, 17:15, 17:99, 17:134, 18:46, 18:66, 18:95, 18:122, 18:286, 18:290, 19:56

he has a true human soul, 2:293, 3:7, 3:10, 3:105, 3:345, 4:18, 4:107, 4:191, 5:14, 5:202, 6:5, 6:39, 8:77, 8:81, 9:14, 11:96, 11:109, 14:14, 14:215, 15:9, 15:62, 15:137, 16:16, 16:137–138, 17:15, 17:128, 17:134, 18:22, 18:46, 18:122, 18:286–287, 18:289, 18:291, 19:56

and a true human body, 1:20, 2:20, 2:293, 3:7, 3:105, 3:345, 4:18, 4:23, 4:107, 4:112–113, 4:187, 4:191–192, 5:14, 5:202, 6:5, 6:38, 6:192, 8:77, 9:12, 9:15, 11:65, 11:96, 11:109, 13:170, 13:251–252, 14:14, 14:215, 15:9,

15:62, 15:137, 16:16, 16:137–138, 17:15, 17:128, 17:134, 18:22, 18:46, 18:122, 18:287, 18:291, 19:56

so that Christ is like us in all things, yet without sin, 1:20, 6:39, 9:14, 11:19, 11:109, 14:215, 16:137–138, 17:128, 18:285, 18:287, 18:291.

The Hypostatic Union

VIII c

In Jesus Christ there are two natures: human and divine, 1:20, 1:114, 2:20, 3:7, 3:102, 4:18–19, 4:107–108, 4:191–192, 5:14–15, 5:195, 5:201–202, 6:5, 6:39, 6:41, 7:74–75, 8:76, 8:198, 9:14, 9:247, 10:336, 11:35, 11:83, 11:96, 11:108–109, 12:30, 12:160, 12:197, 12:220–221, 13:177, 13:341, 14:215, 15:9, 15:61, 15:137–138, 16:16, 16:138, 17:16, 17:27, 17:91, 17:129, 18:47, 18:123, 18:286–287, 18:291, 19:56

they are undivided, 2:120, 5:195, 7:74–75, 11:35, 11:83, 11:109, 14:215, 15:94, 15:166, 18:287, 18:291

inseparable, 5:195, 5:205, 8:75, 11:83, 11:109, 14:215, 15:94, 15:166, 18:286–287, 18:291

unconfused, 11:83, 11:109, 14:215, 18:287, 18:289

always in perfect accord, 8:83, 11:83, 14:215, 16:138, 18:288.

VIII d

Christ is only one Person (and that divine), 1:90, 2:120, 3:102, 5:14–15, 5:195, 5:201, 6:5, 7:74–75, 8:75, 8:76, 8:198, 9:14, 11:60–61, 11:83, 11:96, 11:108–109, 12:197, 13:271, 14:215, 15:9, 15:62, 15:137, 16:16, 16:138, 17:16, 17:27, 17:129–130, 18:47, 18:123, 18:287, 18:289

God and man in him are one and the same, 1:90, 1:114, 2:120, 3:7–8, 6:5, 6:34, 9:14, 10:25, 11:83, 11:108–109, 13:271, 17:129–130

united in a wondrous union of subsistence, properly called the *hypostatic union*, 3:122, 5:195, 5:202, 6:37–38, 11:126, 13:271, 13:317, 17:91, 18:286–287

which occurred from the first moment of the incarnation, 3:8, 4:19, 4:108, 4:191, 5:202, 6:192, 15:9, 15:137, 17:16, 17:129

and remains ineffable, incomprehensible, and a mystery beyond the reach of human reason alone, 2:112, 5:195, 9:10–11, 11:11, 11:96, 11:108–109, 15:58, 16:138, 17:83, 18:102.

VIII e

The humanity of Christ is to be adored directly, as united with divinity, 1:33, 3:122, 6:41, 6:219–220, 8:85, 11:13, 13:164–165, 13:252, 13:260, 13:271, 14:14, 15:94, 15:166, 17:33, 17:131

the worship of *latria* is fitting especially to the Eucharistic Christ, 1:71, 1:99, 2:277, 2:291–292, 2:324, 3:116–117, 3:121–123, 4:11, 4:100, 5:95, 5:98, 5:162–163, 5:381–382, 5:387, 6:206, 6:219–220, 7:259, 7:266, 8:109, 8:284, 8:287, 9:94, 9:266, 12:288, 12:364, 13:85, 13:127, 13:260, 13:271, 13:341, 14:54, 14:382, 14:393, 15:94, 15:96–97, 15:166, 16:265–266, 17:66, 17:229, 18:171, 18:207, 19:176–178

and the most Sacred Heart of Jesus, 13:271, 16:277.

The man Christ is the only Son of God, 1:117, 2:20, 3:5, 3:7, 3:316, 4:19, 5:201, 6:5, 6:33, 6:183, 6:199, 7:71, 8:195, 9:15, 9:250, 10:245, 10:262–263, 10:334, 11:60–61, 11:96, 11:106, 11:108, 12:46, 12:81, 12:89, 12:173, 13:165, 14:13–14, 14:110, 14:118–119, 14:204, 14:214, 15:41, 15:58, 15:62, 15:137, 16:16, 16:137, 17:27, 17:99, 17:127, 18:16, 18:46, 18:286, 18:396

a "servant" only allegorically through obedience, 13:139

not the Son of the Holy Spirit, 8:77, 9:15, 11:108

but truly a Son of man, 2:114, 3:5, 3:7, 3:286, 9:15, 10:262–263, 10:334, 11:26, 11:108, 13:165, 15:9, 15:137, 15:180, 18:396

he has two "nativities": eternal (as God in heaven), and temporal (as man in Bethlehem), 2:20, 2:121, 2:122, 3:8, 3:267, 3:316, 4:18, 4:24, 4:113, 4:192, 5:201–202, 6:5, 7:71, 9:15, 9:250, 13:168, 18:287, 18:289, 19:56.

VIII f

Christ was conceived, born, lived, and died all holy and without sin, 1:20, 6:39, 6:167, 8:83, 9:14, 10:234, 11:19, 17:128, 18:280, 18:284, 18:291

not subject to passions, nor improved by progress, 13:154, 16:137–138

he did not offer sacrifice for himself (as he needed no purification), 11:83

he performed true miracles, 2:7, 3:5, 3:82, 3:86, 3:96, 5:17, 6:24, 10:245, 11:21, 11:33, 11:46, 13:148–149, 13:176, 14:15–16, 14:110, 14:136, 14:210–211, 16:155–156, 17:15, 17:129, 18:95

and pronounced true prophecies, 11:23–24, 11:51, 11:55–56, 11:106, 14:110, 14:211–212, 17:15

his human soul knew all things from the beginning in the Word, 5:203–204, 8:82, 11:17, 13:154, 13:229.

Redemption

Jesus Christ Is Redeemer

VIII g

Fallen man could not be restored through the powers of nature nor the Mosaic law, 3:17, 3:126, 7:65, 10:174–175, 11:116, 12:89–90, 13:67, 14:201, 14:219, 16:136, 17:133, 18:124, 18:281, 18:289, 18:355–356

but only through the merits of Jesus Christ, 2:121, 3:56, 3:173, 3:361, 4:60, 4:112, 4:125, 6:45, 7:65, 8:78, 9:22, 9:253, 10:174–176, 11:116, 13:68, 13:104, 14:25, 14:201, 14:219, 15:138, 16:125, 16:136, 16:142, 17:17, 17:28, 17:133, 18:124, 18:280–281, 18:356

and therefore Christ became man for our salvation, 2:120, 3:103, 3:316, 4:26, 4:34, 4:116, 4:125, 5:16, 5:200, 5:201, 5:204, 6:39–40, 6:192, 7:65, 7:81, 8:77, 8:194, 8:201, 9:19, 9:250, 10:174–176, 11:13, 11:80, 11:96, 12:173, 13:67–68, 13:112, 13:163, 14:12, 14:84, 14:201, 14:217, 15:9, 15:62, 15:138, 16:125, 16:136, 17:17, 17:27, 17:99, 17:127, 17:130–133, 18:16, 18:22, 18:41, 18:46, 18:123, 18:349, 19:57

so that he might repair man's fallen nature, 3:9, 4:155, 4:168, 4:202, 6:44–45, 7:65, 10:174–176, 10:242–243, 11:13, 11:24–26, 11:82–83, 13:67–68, 13:259, 16:125, 16:136

and free us from captivity to the devil, 1:28, 2:162, 3:60, 4:19, 4:83, 4:108, 4:180, 5:148, 6:45, 7:92, 10:245, 10:253, 11:24–25, 11:97, 13:221, 13:251–252, 14:448, 15:9, 16:125, 16:136, 17:17, 17:133, 17:136, 18:43, 18:91, 18:280, 19:63

and original sin, 2:247, 3:55, 5:16, 6:44–45, 7:65, 7:92, 9:142, 10:174–176, 11:13, 13:221, 14:12, 14:219, 15:9, 15:62, 15:138, 16:86, 16:125, 17:132–133, 18:93, 18:123, 18:280

by his redeeming death on the cross, 1:31, 1:114, 2:20, 2:114, 2:121, 2:312, 3:9, 3:270, 3:316, 4:11, 4:65, 4:100, 4:160, 4:205, 5:17, 5:150, 5:204, 5:373–374, 6:44–45, 6:199, 7:92, 9:250, 10:174–176, 11:13, 11:96, 13:68–69,

14:16, 14:104, 14:218–219, 15:10, 15:140, 16:136, 17:17, 17:70, 17:99, 17:136, 18:22, 18:41, 18:47, 18:121, 18:123, 18:288, 19:63

which was a true sacrifice, 2:124, 2:223, 2:324, 3:126, 4:64–65, 4:100, 4:160, 4:204–205, 5:373–374, 6:44–45, 6:199, 7:93, 8:200, 9:98–99, 10:219, 10:239, 11:106, 13:68–69, 13:264, 14:54–55, 14:104, 14:383, 15:168–169, 16:45–46, 16:274–275, 17:70, 17:240–242, 18:71–72, 18:123, 18:127, 18:200–203, 18:297, 19:65.

Jesus Christ redeemed us from sin and reconciled us to the Father, 2:120, 3:8, 3:126, 4:24, 4:114, 5:204, 6:44–45, 6:199, 7:65, 7:93, 8:195, 9:19, 9:250, 10:174–176, 11:13, 11:80–84, 11:96, 13:68–69, 13:214, 13:252, 14:16, 14:218–219, 15:137, 15:140, 16:136, 17:17, 17:84, 17:130–133, 17:217, 18:121, 18:123, 18:296, 19:57

solely out of love for the human race, 3:270, 4:24, 4:114, 5:204, 6:40–41, 6:44–45, 7:89, 8:200, 10:300, 11:109, 13:148, 13:324, 14:17, 14:220, 15:139, 16:18, 16:151, 17:251, 18:126, 18:296

dying to satisfy for the sins of the whole world, 2:124, 3:131, 4:24, 4:114, 5:17, 5:114, 5:204, 6:44–45, 7:90, 7:93, 8:200, 9:19, 9:250, 10:174–176, 11:13, 11:25, 13:68–69, 13:252, 14:113, 14:218–219, 15:10, 15:41, 15:140, 16:18, 16:21, 16:148–150, 16:152, 16:170, 17:17, 17:136, 18:126, 18:296, 19:26, 19:63.

Christ is the Redeemer and Savior, 2:114, 2:120, 3:41, 4:23, 4:112, 4:178, 4:222, 5:16–18, 5:200, 7:67–68, 8:114, 8:195, 9:14, 9:250, 10:174–176, 10:230, 10:249, 11:11–12, 11:105, 12:46, 12:173, 13:104, 13:172, 13:324, 14:13, 14:109–110, 14:203, 15:41, 15:137, 16:16, 16:85, 16:137, 17:133, 17:136, 18:95, 18:119, 18:121–122, 18:349, 18:359, 18:378, 19:88

Lord, 1:4, 1:20, 2:62, 2:121, 3:5, 3:7, 4:29, 4:119, 4:195, 5:10, 5:26, 5:158, 6:4, 7:72, 7:537–538, 8:195, 9:14, 9:250, 10:224, 11:106–107, 12:173, 13:122, 13:251, 14:13, 14:204–205, 15:137, 16:85, 17:17, 17:99, 18:46, 18:120, 18:130, 18:280, 18:286–287, 18:386, 19:47, 19:74, 19:157

teacher, 2:121, 4:179, 6:143, 9:14, 10:24, 11:17, 11:27–30, 14:15, 14:113, 14:203, 18:123, 19:48–49, 19:75

priest, 2:121, 3:127, 3:133, 4:11, 4:101, 5:159, 5:373, 7:69, 7:93, 7:284, 8:85, 8:195, 9:14, 9:98, 10:206, 10:216, 10:279, 11:106, 11:443, 12:34, 13:68–70, 13:116, 14:203, 15:168, 16:45, 16:266–267, 16:274, 17:70, 17:241, 18:121, 18:297, 18:386, 19:75

King and lawgiver, 2:121, 3:287, 4:178–179, 5:158, 7:69, 7:537–538, 8:84–85, 8:195, 9:14, 9:20, 10:206, 10:246, 10:266–267, 10:298, 11:63, 11:67, 11:105, 11:443, 12:34, 12:92, 12:94, 12:145, 12:250, 13:122, 13:150, 13:177, 14:203–204, 17:133, 18:121–122, 18:130, 19:75

ruling over all individuals and nations, 4:178–179, 5:98, 9:14, 10:157, 11:69, 11:105, 13:171, 13:177, 14:225, 17:17

as head of the Church, his mystical body, 1:22, 1:63, 1:118, 2:21, 2:131, 2:315, 3:12, 3:14, 3:106, 3:239, 4:30, 4:120, 5:20, 5:208, 5:272, 6:56, 6:71, 7:134, 9:20–21, 10:157, 11:135, 11:146, 11:161, 13:252, 14:22, 14:203–204, 14:236, 14:255, 15:13, 15:66, 15:145, 16:23, 16:178–181, 16:191, 17:19, 17:148, 18:134, 18:301, 18:359–360, 19:96

and present in the mysteries of the Church, 9:21, 14:225.

The Life of the Redeemer

VIII h

The coming of Christ was foreshadowed by the sacred signs, symbols, sacrifices, and ceremonies of the Mosaic law, 3:125, 6:40, 7:79–80, 8:196, 10:204–205, 10:238–239, 10:301, 11:52–53, 11:70, 11:77, 11:254–255, 12:151, 13:67–68, 14:105, 16:166, 17:238–242, 18:280

and promised before the law, 3:126, 4:23, 4:112, 10:19, 10:176–177, 10:204–206, 11:10, 11:57, 13:163, 14:103–104, 14:209, 16:139–142, 16:177, 17:15

even to our first parents, 4:23, 4:112, 7:65–67, 8:196, 10:19, 10:166–167, 10:205–206, 11:145, 13:163, 14:12, 14:102, 14:137, 15:138, 16:17, 16:139–142, 16:177, 17:27, 18:91, 18:119, 19:44.

Jesus Christ is a true and historical individual (not a myth, metaphor, or pious fiction), 4:19, 4:108, 4:192, 5:16–17, 9:14, 9:15, 11:11–12, 11:113–114, 14:110

he was conceived of the Holy Spirit in the womb of the Virgin Mary, 1:4, 1:20, 1:117, 2:20, 2:122–123, 2:164, 2:272–273, 2:313, 3:5, 3:8, 3:268, 3:291, 3:316, 4:18, 4:23, 4:95, 4:99, 4:184, 4:187, 5:14, 5:202–203, 6:36–40, 6:183, 6:192, 6:199, 7:74–77, 8:173, 8:197, 9:15, 11:11, 11:108–110, 12:186, 13:95, 13:163, 13:229, 14:214–216, 15:9, 15:62, 15:138, 16:17, 16:85, 16:139, 17:15, 17:99, 17:134, 18:46, 18:66, 18:95, 18:122, 19:56

and truly born in Bethlehem, 2:122, 2:295, 3:8, 4:24, 4:113, 4:192, 5:16, 6:39, 7:77–78, 8:81, 9:15, 10:266, 10:285, 10:287, 11:11–12, 13:50, 13:163–164, 14:14, 14:110, 14:206, 15:9, 15:139, 16:17, 16:143–145, 17:16, 17:135, 18:95, 19:44

during his life he experienced hunger, thirst, weariness, sorrow, and pain, 2:123, 4:192, 5:203–204, 8:78, 9:15, 10:224, 10:266, 11:13, 11:20, 11:81, 11:112, 13:171, 14:16, 14:215, 15:10, 15:63, 16:137–138, 17:128, 18:289, 19:56

he truly ate, drank, and slept, 11:20, 11:77, 17:128, 18:286

he was poor but not absolutely, 4:192, 5:16–17, 10:224, 11:13, 11:81, 11:380, 11:442, 12:51, 12:160, 13:171, 14:16, 14:217, 14:322, 16:18, 16:145, 17:16

he always had a consciousness of his Messianic dignity, 11:44

he suffered freely and willingly, 2:313, 3:8–9, 3:270, 3:316, 3:349, 4:6, 4:95, 4:193, 5:201, 5:203–204, 6:5, 6:41–42, 6:52, 6:192, 6:199, 7:87, 8:78, 8:199, 9:15, 10:219, 10:282–283, 11:13, 11:58–59, 11:81–82, 11:112, 12:160, 13:171, 14:17, 14:112–113, 14:218–219, 16:85, 17:135–136, 17:241, 18:22, 18:47, 18:96, 18:125, 18:289, 18:295, 18:297, 19:61

he was crucified under Pontius Pilate, 1:4, 1:20, 1:117, 2:20, 2:123, 2:273, 2:313, 3:6, 3:8, 3:316, 4:6, 4:95, 4:193, 5:203, 6:192, 7:84, 8:173, 8:199, 9:15, 9:250, 10:283, 11:66–67, 11:113–115, 14:16, 14:112, 15:10, 15:63, 15:139, 16:85, 16:149–150, 17:135, 18:47, 18:96, 18:125

he died, 1:4, 1:21, 1:117, 2:20, 2:112, 2:124, 2:273, 2:313, 3:6, 3:8–9, 3:127, 3:270, 3:316, 3:350–351, 4:6, 4:95, 4:193, 5:17, 5:203, 5:373, 6:5, 6:41–42, 6:47, 6:52, 6:192, 6:199, 7:86, 8:173, 8:199, 9:17, 9:250, 10:219, 10:280, 11:13, 11:69, 11:96, 11:115, 12:160, 13:214–217, 14:17, 14:113, 14:218, 15:10, 15:63, 15:139, 16:18–19, 16:85, 16:150–153, 17:16, 17:135–136, 17:241, 18:16, 18:22, 18:47, 18:96, 18:125, 18:289, 19:61–62

from his pierced side flowed blood and water, 1:70, 3:105, 11:70, 11:256, 13:88–89, 13:201, 14:113
he was buried, 1:4, 1:21, 1:117, 2:20, 2:124, 2:273, 2:313, 3:6, 3:8, 3:316, 4:6, 4:95, 5:18, 6:41, 6:47, 6:192, 6:199, 7:88, 8:173, 8:199, 9:17, 9:250, 10:280, 11:71, 11:96, 11:115, 12:186, 13:222, 14:17, 14:113, 14:218, 15:63, 16:19, 16:85, 16:154, 17:140, 18:47, 18:96, 18:125, 18:289, 18:298, 19:67
his soul descended into hell, 1:4, 1:21, 1:117, 2:21, 2:125, 2:313, 3:6, 3:10, 3:198, 4:6, 4:95, 4:193, 5:18, 5:204–205, 6:5, 6:47–51, 6:192, 6:199, 7:95–97, 8:84, 8:173, 8:202, 9:17, 9:251, 10:280, 11:72, 11:115–116, 14:18, 14:222, 15:11, 15:64, 15:140, 16:19, 16:85–86, 16:153, 17:138–139, 18:47, 18:96, 18:127–128, 18:288, 18:298, 19:67
he rose again on the third day, 1:4, 1:21, 1:117, 2:21, 2:125, 2:273, 2:313, 3:6, 3:10, 3:316, 3:345, 4:6, 4:95, 4:193, 5:18, 5:206, 6:5, 6:51–54, 6:199, 7:99–101, 8:81, 8:173, 9:17, 9:251, 10:267, 10:275, 10:280, 11:72, 11:96, 11:116–117, 12:20, 12:160, 12:173, 13:171, 13:223, 14:18, 14:113, 14:222–223, 15:11, 15:64, 15:140, 16:19, 16:86, 16:155–158, 17:27, 17:129, 17:140, 18:16, 18:22, 18:47, 18:96, 18:128, 18:289, 18:297, 19:68
as foretold in the scriptures, 2:125, 2:273, 3:316, 4:78, 7:101–102, 8:173, 9:17, 10:302, 11:47–48, 11:116–117, 12:186, 14:108, 14:207
by his own power, 3:10, 5:206, 6:48, 6:52, 7:102, 8:202, 9:17, 9:251, 11:72, 11:96, 11:117, 13:249, 14:18, 14:113, 14:211, 14:222, 15:11, 15:140, 16:86, 16:155–156, 17:27, 17:129, 17:140, 18:47, 18:128, 19:68
with a true resurrection of the flesh (the soul reanimating the body), 1:4, 1:21, 2:125, 2:314, 3:271, 3:345, 4:7, 4:193, 5:206, 6:54, 6:77, 6:192, 6:199, 7:99, 8:81, 9:17, 9:251, 11:117, 14:18, 14:222–223, 15:64, 16:156, 17:178, 18:47, 18:128, 18:289, 19:68
he ascended into heaven, 1:4, 1:21, 1:117, 2:21, 2:126, 2:273, 2:313, 3:6, 3:10–11, 3:288, 3:316, 4:7, 4:26, 4:95, 4:116, 4:184, 4:193–194, 5:18, 5:206, 6:5, 6:55–57, 6:192, 6:199, 7:106, 8:173, 8:203, 9:18, 9:251, 10:35, 10:250, 11:96, 11:125–126, 11:464, 12:160, 12:173, 13:171, 13:248–253, 13:280, 14:19, 14:114, 14:224–225, 15:11, 15:64, 15:141, 16:19, 16:86, 16:159, 17:27, 17:140, 18:22, 18:47, 18:96, 18:128, 18:288–289, 18:298, 19:73
with his body and soul, 1:21, 4:193, 7:106, 9:18, 11:125–126, 13:251, 14:19, 14:224, 15:64, 17:140, 18:47, 18:128, 18:289

he is seated at the right hand of the Father, 1:4, 1:21, 1:117, 2:21, 2:126, 2:273, 2:313, 3:6, 3:10–11, 3:288, 3:316, 4:7, 4:95, 4:184, 4:193, 5:207, 6:5, 6:55–56, 7:107–108, 8:173, 8:204, 9:18, 11:61, 11:126, 11:464, 12:186, 14:19, 14:225, 15:11, 15:64, 15:141, 16:19–20, 16:86, 16:159, 17:134, 17:140, 18:47, 18:96, 18:129, 18:289, 18:298, 19:66

he sent the Holy Spirit, 2:144, 3:155, 3:265, 3:316, 4:27, 4:32, 4:117, 4:123, 4:194, 6:64–65, 6:199, 7:110, 9:20, 11:127, 13:251, 13:254, 14:114, 14:232, 15:65, 15:142, 15:189, 16:20, 16:168–169, 17:146, 18:289, 19:78

he rules unto eternity, 1:4, 1:21, 3:11, 3:184, 3:271, 3:316, 6:57, 7:109, 9:18, 9:251, 10:298, 11:126, 14:204, 14:225, 15:64, 19:77

he will return in his glorified state, 2:21, 3:6, 3:11, 4:7, 4:95, 4:184, 5:19, 5:207, 6:55–57, 6:200, 7:113, 8:173, 9:18, 9:251, 10:302, 11:96, 11:129, 11:131, 11:464, 12:186, 13:148, 13:268, 14:20, 14:226–227, 16:369–370, 16:374, 17:39, 17:141–142, 18:48, 18:97, 18:129, 18:280, 18:288–289, 18:299, 19:76–78

to judge the living and the dead, 1:4, 1:21–22, 1:117, 2:21, 2:127, 2:273, 2:313, 3:11, 3:316, 4:7, 4:95, 4:184, 5:19, 5:207, 6:5, 6:57–60, 6:192, 6:200, 7:113, 8:173, 8:204, 9:18, 9:251, 10:286, 11:96, 11:129, 11:131–135, 11:464, 12:20, 12:173, 13:268, 14:20, 14:204–205, 14:226–227, 15:12, 15:65, 15:202–204, 16:87, 16:369–370, 16:374, 17:29, 17:84, 17:142–145, 18:48, 18:97, 18:129, 18:288–289, 18:299, 18:331, 19:76–78.

The Mother of the Redeemer

VIII i

Mary is the Mother of Christ and hence truly and properly the Mother of God, 1:30, 1:121, 2:164, 2:317, 3:284, 3:286, 4:6, 4:59, 4:100, 4:154, 4:184, 4:189, 5:145, 5:369, 7:76, 7:78, 8:76, 8:77, 8:198, 9:10, 9:33, 9:257, 11:108–110, 11:214, 12:197, 13:231, 13:277, 14:14, 14:69, 14:216, 14:288, 14:440, 15:20, 15:86, 15:138, 15:180, 16:17, 16:81, 16:139, 17:27, 17:91, 17:189–191, 18:66, 18:95, 18:124, 18:290–294, 19:57–58

but she gave birth only to the Son, not the Trinity, 1:117, 3:5, 3:8, 3:268, 3:291, 3:316, 4:19, 4:99, 4:107–108, 4:187, 4:191, 5:202–203, 6:34, 6:184, 6:192, 9:36, 11:108–109, 11:214, 13:281, 14:440, 17:189.

VIII k

Mary was conceived immaculate, i.e., without any stain of original sin, 4:112, 4:219, 4:224, 6:181, 6:184, 7:603, 8:62, 8:194, 9:33, 10:201, 11:212, 12:272–273, 13:152–158, 13:284, 14:199, 15:179, 16:14, 16:124–125, 17:27, 17:36, 17:154, 17:172–173, 18:45, 18:118, 18:283–285, 19:42, 19:58

by a unique and special privilege of divine grace, 1:29, 1:121, 2:163, 2:317, 3:285, 4:112, 4:219, 6:181, 7:603, 8:90–91, 8:194, 9:34, 10:201, 11:212, 13:152, 13:284, 14:199, 14:440, 15:179, 16:14, 16:124–125, 17:36, 17:172–173, 18:45, 18:118, 18:284, 19:58

not because of an uncorrupted seed passed on to her, 13:152, 17:172.

Mary was an inviolate Virgin, 1:31, 1:117, 1:121, 2:123, 3:287–288, 4:18, 4:191, 5:145, 5:203, 6:183, 6:192, 7:78–79, 8:81, 8:198, 9:34, 10:282, 11:109–110, 13:164, 13:229, 13:286, 14:33, 14:216, 17:91, 18:95, 18:125, 18:293–294

and remained so perpetually (before birth, in birth, and after birth), 1:31, 1:117, 2:123, 3:287–288, 5:145, 5:203, 7:78–79, 8:81, 8:198, 9:34–36, 10:282, 11:110–111, 11:212, 13:164, 13:229, 14:216, 18:95, 18:125, 18:294–295, 19:58

she needed no purification, 3:285, 6:183, 13:181.

Mary was always free from all sin, even venial, 3:285, 5:145, 6:167, 6:181, 6:183, 8:90–91, 9:36, 10:201, 11:212, 13:153, 14:199, 16:81, 17:173, 18:285, 19:125

excels all creatures in sanctity, 1:4, 2:33, 2:163, 2:317, 3:285, 3:286–287, 4:59, 4:154, 4:184, 4:189, 5:145, 6:180–183, 7:506, 8:85, 9:34–35, 10:201, 11:212–214, 13:153, 13:228, 13:281, 13:284, 14:69–70, 14:288, 15:179, 16:105, 17:79, 17:189, 18:184, 18:294, 19:125, 19:236

intercedes before God for men, 1:31, 1:121, 2:33, 2:317, 3:144, 3:245, 4:59, 4:88, 4:100, 4:154, 4:184, 4:189, 5:146, 5:370, 6:182, 7:506, 8:86, 9:35–37, 11:214–215, 12:295–296, 12:347, 13:59, 13:153, 13:235–243, 13:278, 13:289–290, 14:74, 14:288, 14:441, 15:20, 15:85, 15:179–181, 16:125, 17:189–191, 18:67, 18:179, 18:184–185, 18:360–361, 19:125, 19:236

because of which she is worthy of love and praise, 1:4, 1:33, 1:121, 2:162, 2:331–332, 3:285, 4:59, 4:154, 4:184, 4:189, 5:167, 6:180, 7:506, 8:85–86, 9:36–37, 11:210–216, 13:155–158, 13:229–230, 13:235–243, 13:276–283, 13:284, 13:289, 14:33, 14:69–70, 14:288, 14:440, 15:20, 15:179–181, 16:105, 17:79, 17:190–191, 18:53, 18:153, 18:184, 18:334, 19:236–237.

She is mediatrix of all graces, 3:286, 6:182, 9:33–37, 10:201, 13:278–279, 13:281, 13:284–285, 13:289

and coredemptrix with Christ, 9:33–37, 13:184, 13:202–203, 13:281, 18:359, 19:125.

She was assumed, body and soul, into heaven, 1:135, 2:102, 2:300, 3:272, 3:291, 4:85, 4:86, 5:370, 6:184, 8:203, 11:213, 13:279–280, 14:81, 14:442, 15:107–108, 15:124–126, 15:200, 16:304, 17:28, 18:18, 18:45, 18:119, 19:125.

Justification

IX a

Justification does not consist in the fact that sins are only covered over or not imputed, 8:95, 18:282

nor only in the remission of sins, 3:128, 3:186, 4:11, 4:65, 4:96, 4:167, 4:205, 4:209, 9:22, 18:350, 18:434

nor in obedience to the commandments, 1:82, 3:65, 3:114, 7:383–384

nor in the external favor of God or imputing of the merits of Christ, 3:173, 4:60, 4:112, 4:125, 8:94–95, 18:350

but it is a condition in which man in himself is made just and a friend of God, 8:89, 8:269, 11:35, 11:84, 11:160, 11:184–186, 14:49, 14:359–361, 15:155, 16:175, 17:9, 17:57, 17:182, 18:61–62, 18:175

adopted as a child of God and heir to eternal life, 1:26–27, 2:30, 2:117, 2:147, 2:156, 2:209, 3:55, 4:60, 4:156, 4:202, 5:222, 6:159, 7:127, 7:520–521, 8:89, 8:231, 8:269, 9:265, 11:88, 11:103, 11:231–232, 13:221, 13:252, 14:51–52, 14:359–361, 14:369, 15:27, 15:91, 15:150, 16:28, 16:205, 17:17, 17:60, 17:222, 18:61–62, 18:175, 18:279, 18:282, 18:350, 19:39, 19:133–134

and made a sharer in the divine nature, 2:149, 2:209, 3:105, 5:222, 6:41, 7:127, 11:88, 11:184, 11:231, 17:182, 18:61–62, 18:175, 19:39

by a true sanctification and internal renewal through *sanctifying grace:* the habitual principle of supernatural life in the soul, 1:27, 2:209, 3:55, 3:120, 4:33–34, 4:124–125, 4:196, 5:79, 7:187–188, 8:89, 8:269, 11:86, 11:184, 14:49, 14:51–52, 14:335, 14:356, 14:359–361, 15:134, 15:143, 15:148, 16:15, 16:21, 16:128–129, 16:171, 17:57, 17:175, 17:182, 18:61–62, 18:175, 18:350, 19:39

together with the infusion of the theological virtues (faith, hope, and charity), 1:9, 1:26, 1:132, 2:63, 2:150, 2:313, 3:5, 3:27, 3:31, 4:8–10, 4:83, 4:98–100, 4:131, 4:187–188, 5:79, 7:218, 8:101, 8:324, 9:9, 11:88–89, 11:184, 11:231, 13:227, 14:345, 16:171, 17:120–121, 18:350, 18:434, 19:134.

IX b

All that leads to justification is done through grace, 1:80, 3:186, 5:79–80, 5:272, 7:127, 7:184, 7:187–188, 8:88, 10:28, 10:335, 11:84, 11:113, 11:183, 12:190, 14:164, 14:357, 15:144, 17:57, 17:181–182, 18:61–62, 18:175–176, 18:354, 19:82

founded upon the merits of Christ, 2:115, 2:150, 3:173, 4:60, 4:112, 4:125, 5:17, 5:78, 5:81, 5:272, 7:149, 8:88, 10:28, 10:175–176, 11:84, 11:88, 11:180, 11:183, 13:104, 14:25, 14:218–221, 14:357, 15:27, 15:138, 15:143, 15:148, 16:125, 16:142, 17:17, 17:28, 17:57, 17:181, 18:296, 19:82

however, adults can and ought to dispose themselves to the grace of justification, 1:80, 8:93, 8:97, 11:88, 11:113, 11:160, 13:323, 14:164, 14:221, 14:357–358, 17:11, 17:57, 18:176, 18:352

by freely assenting and cooperating with the promptings of grace, 1:80, 3:186, 5:78, 5:78–85, 5:191, 6:161, 7:541–542, 8:78–79, 8:92, 10:177, 11:88–89, 11:113, 11:183–184, 14:164, 14:221, 14:358–360, 17:11, 17:79, 18:49, 18:111, 18:132, 18:352, 19:84

which are given to those outside the Church, 5:185, 8:42, 8:93, 8:105, 11:113, 14:221, 14:264

and which may be freely rejected, 5:80, 8:78–79, 11:113, 11:149, 11:184, 14:221, 14:264, 14:358–359, 15:144, 16:22, 16:175, 17:79, 17:143–144, 17:251, 18:111, 19:84.

A worthy disposition is made by acts of faith, hope, charity, penance, 1:9, 1:82, 1:115, 2:63, 2:150, 2:313, 2:327, 3:5, 3:41, 4:57, 4:98–100, 4:152, 9:38, 10:335, 11:88–90, 11:113, 11:160, 11:192, 12:20, 14:164, 14:221, 15:6, 17:11, 17:57, 18:352

and by observing the commandments, 1:8–9, 2:44, 2:46–54, 2:147, 2:148, 2:313, 2:321, 3:65, 3:114, 8:93, 8:97, 9:40, 10:335, 11:93, 11:113, 11:160, 14:164, 14:221, 14:357–358, 15:32, 15:138, 15:181, 17:11, 17:57, 18:144, 18:352.

Faith is the beginning of human salvation, 1:19, 2:114, 3:56, 4:30, 4:119–120, 5:197, 6:21–22, 7:288, 8:95, 9:10–11, 10:176, 11:89–90, 17:179–180, 18:443

and the necessary foundation and root of justification, 4:30, 4:119–120, 5:188, 5:197, 6:21–24, 8:95, 9:10–11, 11:89–90, 11:179, 11:186, 14:403
but it is not the first grace, 4:30, 4:120, 5:79, 11:183.

Faith alone does not suffice for salvation, 1:125, 2:115, 2:326, 3:16, 4:30, 4:120, 5:7–8, 5:188, 5:197, 8:95, 9:38, 10:31, 11:89, 11:113, 11:179, 12:32, 14:28, 14:164, 15:17, 17:13, 17:28, 17:179–180, 18:150, 18:351, 18:434
nor only prayers, 3:63, 5:8, 10:31, 11:93, 17:179–180
nor a mere confidence that one is saved, 4:35, 4:42, 4:133, 5:83, 8:95
but rather, one must hold explicit faith in the existence and justice of God, 1:115, 2:114, 2:316, 3:5, 3:186, 4:19, 4:108, 5:184–185, 6:22, 8:107, 9:10–11, 11:89–90, 11:99, 11:180, 17:12, 17:30, 17:179–180, 17:269, 18:82, 18:232, 18:438
and in the Trinity and incarnation, 1:19, 1:115, 2:20–21, 3:47, 3:186, 5:13–14, 5:185, 6:4–5, 6:32–33, 6:37, 7:65, 9:10–11, 10:175–177, 10:243, 11:89–90, 11:95–97, 14:190, 14:360, 15:138, 17:12, 17:30, 17:179–180, 17:269, 18:15, 18:41, 18:82, 18:102, 18:232, 18:438.

Penance consists not only in an amendment of life, 3:159, 4:34, 4:69, 4:166, 4:168, 4:187, 4:208, 5:107, 7:288, 8:150, 9:106, 11:278–279, 14:59–60, 14:360, 14:405, 18:404
nor only in confidence that one is forgiven, 3:15, 4:57, 4:67, 4:152, 4:163, 4:201, 5:83, 9:107, 11:278–279, 18:403
but is a hatred and detestation for sin with desire for the sacrament, 3:159, 4:34, 4:68, 4:98, 4:126, 4:187, 4:207, 5:103–104, 5:236, 7:288, 7:303, 9:106, 9:246, 11:164–165, 11:278–280, 14:59–60, 14:360, 14:399, 15:158, 16:36, 16:210–211, 16:236–237, 17:58, 17:73–74, 17:102–103, 17:248–249, 18:188, 18:404
together with the firm purpose of living a new life and observing the commandments, 3:157, 4:9, 4:34, 4:98, 4:126, 4:187, 5:83, 5:103, 5:236, 7:288, 7:384, 9:107, 9:246, 11:278–279, 14:59–60, 14:360, 15:31, 16:34, 16:36, 16:230–231, 16:234, 16:237–238, 17:58, 17:73–74, 17:103, 17:248–249, 18:404.

Contrition is always necessary for justification, 8:139, 8:150–151, 9:109, 10:263, 11:113, 11:278–279, 13:323, 14:404, 15:156, 16:183, 16:230, 17:226, 17:248, 18:400, 19:192

it can be perfect (motivated by charity) or imperfect (attrition), 2:225, 3:29, 3:169, 4:34–35, 4:68, 4:166, 4:207, 5:104–105, 5:236–237, 8:117, 8:152, 8:299–300, 11:279–280, 11:302, 14:403–404, 15:30, 15:101–102, 15:157–158, 16:35–36, 16:183, 16:235, 16:236–237, 17:73, 17:251–252, 18:76–77, 18:212–213, 18:404, 18:408, 19:193.

Contrition with desire for the sacrament justifies even before the sacrament is received, 1:65, 4:34, 4:126, 5:105, 5:236–237, 6:168–169, 7:304–305, 8:117, 8:152, 8:299, 11:164–165, 11:279–280, 12:30, 14:399, 15:158, 16:210–211, 17:58, 17:73, 17:176, 17:226, 17:252, 18:76, 18:148, 18:188, 18:364, 18:404.

IX c

See effects of baptism, XII c.

No one can know with the perfect certitude of faith that he is justified, 2:144–145, 5:84, 5:209, 8:96, 11:180

concupiscence remains in the justified, 2:197, 3:36–38, 4:23, 4:112, 5:80, 6:44, 7:213, 7:216, 7:485, 7:546, 9:83–84, 10:37, 11:86, 11:231, 11:244, 12:66–69, 12:169, 13:159–161, 15:133, 16:14, 16:88, 16:124, 17:274, 18:282, 19:41–43, 19:185

even the innocent are afflicted by God and exposed to sufferings in this life, 3:36–67, 5:77–78, 5:142, 7:521–522, 7:597–598, 10:177–181, 10:332–333, 11:15, 11:39, 11:44, 11:444–445, 12:10, 12:17, 12:55–56, 13:272, 13:338, 14:116–117, 14:129–130, 14:192–194, 14:355, 15:203, 16:206, 19:26.

Grace

Actual Grace

X a

Grace (actual) is a supernatural help of God, by which a man is made fit to act as he should to obtain eternal life, 1:27, 1:119, 2:31, 2:209, 3:17, 4:34, 4:40, 4:125, 5:78, 5:222, 7:544–545, 8:88–89, 8:270, 10:28, 10:200, 11:182, 14:356–357, 15:17, 15:82, 15:144, 16:21, 16:128, 16:170, 17:11, 17:57–58, 17:120, 17:181–182, 18:61–62, 18:175–177, 18:276, 18:354, 19:82–84

it is not only an external help, 10:200, 11:182, 17:120, 17:182, 18:176–177

but God acting "in us without us," 2:4, 2:111, 4:8, 4:189, 11:182, 17:120, 17:182, 18:176–177

both to heal and elevate our fallen nature, 2:249, 3:62, 4:9, 4:34, 5:223, 8:88, 10:28, 10:183, 10:200–202, 11:184, 13:67–68, 13:259, 14:165–166, 14:357, 18:350.

X b

There is a grace of illumination (in the intellect) and of inspiration (in the will), 1:18, 5:79–80, 7:523, 10:28, 10:200–201, 11:185, 12:52, 13:81, 14:165–166, 14:357, 15:144, 16:22, 16:174–175, 17:58, 17:182, 18:62, 18:176, 18:354, 19:83

preceding, accompanying, and following our good actions, 4:10, 5:79–80, 7:326, 7:498, 8:89–90, 11:185, 14:357, 17:58, 17:182, 18:177, 18:351, 19:83.

X c

Grace is necessary to all for salvation, 1:119, 3:17, 4:34, 4:125, 5:79, 6:71, 8:89, 10:28, 10:335, 11:183, 11:186, 12:190, 14:49, 14:221, 14:357–358, 15:17, 15:143, 16:22, 16:175, 17:28, 17:175, 17:181–182, 18:62, 18:176–177, 19:82

and for man to make supernatural acts conducive to salvation, 1:27, 1:119, 4:34, 4:55, 5:78–79, 7:326, 7:523, 8:89–90, 10:28, 11:183, 11:281,

11:461, 12:190, 14:49, 14:345, 14:357–358, 14:361, 15:17, 15:82, 16:128, 16:175, 17:57, 17:181–182, 18:62, 18:175, 18:351, 19:82.

Grace is necessary to know truth, 1:80, 3:159, 5:79–80, 11:185, 12:89
to avoid sin, 1:80, 2:31, 2:249, 3:29, 4:9, 4:125, 5:25, 5:79–81, 6:44, 8:90, 11:183, 14:49, 14:356, 15:82, 15:176, 17:67, 17:79, 17:103, 17:181–182, 18:177
to act well, 1:80, 2:158, 2:249, 4:10, 4:125, 5:25, 5:62, 5:79–81, 7:326, 7:544–545, 11:183, 11:185, 14:49, 14:356–357, 15:52, 15:82, 15:144, 15:176, 17:57, 17:79, 17:181–182, 18:62, 18:177, 18:355–357
to pray for grace, 1:27, 1:119, 3:17, 4:58, 5:80, 11:183, 17:79, 18:354–355
to desire salvation, 1:27, 3:56, 5:80, 11:183, 14:357, 14:360, 18:354–355, 19:83
for the beginning of faith, 3:186, 4:10, 5:79, 11:183, 14:357, 17:11, 18:175, 18:355, 19:82
and for perseverance in grace, 2:31, 3:84, 5:85, 8:91, 11:183, 14:357, 14:441, 15:144, 16:22, 16:175, 16:256, 17:11, 17:58, 17:103.

X d

The grace of justification is not owing to our own prayer or other dispositions, 3:186, 5:80, 11:89, 11:160, 11:183, 14:221, 14:360, 16:170, 17:57, 17:181, 19:43
for a man is called with no preceding merit of his own, 5:148, 5:272, 11:89, 11:183, 14:221, 14:360, 16:170, 17:57
but after justification, he can merit further, 1:119, 5:85, 5:272, 11:159, 11:183, 14:47–48, 14:49–50, 14:192–194, 14:361–362, 16:255–256, 17:182, 18:176, 18:276, 18:351, 18:415.

X e

Grace is not the omnipotent will of God which nothing resists, 2:249, 5:80, 8:92, 8:270, 10:335, 11:184, 14:221, 14:358, 15:144, 16:22, 16:175, 17:58, 17:143–144, 19:84.

Sanctifying Grace

See qualities of justification, IX a.

X f

Sanctifying (or habitual) grace is distinct from actual grace, 4:33–34, 4:124–125, 5:79, 8:89, 11:184–185, 14:49, 14:356, 15:143, 16:21, 16:171, 17:57, 17:182, 18:61, 18:175

it is a quality infused and inherent in the soul, by which man is formally justified, 2:209, 4:34, 4:125, 5:79, 5:222, 7:187–188, 8:89, 8:269, 11:86, 11:184, 11:231, 14:49, 14:356, 14:359–361, 15:143, 15:148, 16:21, 16:171, 17:57, 17:182, 18:175

is reborn and remains in Christ, 3:49, 5:222, 11:86, 11:231–232, 14:51, 14:359–361, 14:369.

It is the permanent principle of the supernatural life, 4:33–34, 4:124–125, 4:196, 5:79, 7:187–188, 8:89, 10:170, 11:86, 11:184, 11:186, 14:335, 14:356, 14:359, 15:134, 15:143, 15:148, 16:15, 16:128–129, 17:175, 18:175

called the "state of grace," 2:147, 3:28, 4:66, 4:163, 4:205, 11:186, 14:49, 16:217, 17:182, 18:176

not naturally observable by the senses, 3:67, 7:187, 8:96

conferred in baptism, 1:17–18, 2:62, 2:211, 3:49, 3:55, 6:71, 7:217–218, 8:94, 8:271, 8:273, 11:84, 11:184, 11:231–232, 14:49, 14:52, 14:360–361, 14:369, 15:148, 16:26, 16:201–202, 17:58, 18:193, 18:230–231, 19:133–134.

It can be increased especially through the reception of the sacraments, 1:27, 1:59–60, 1:129–130, 2:224, 3:26, 3:28, 3:317, 4:60, 4:62, 4:155, 4:202, 5:85, 5:222, 5:262, 7:187–188, 8:123–124, 9:264, 10:28–30, 11:247, 11:260, 14:56, 14:365, 15:17, 15:148, 16:26, 16:201–202, 17:18, 17:58–59, 17:182, 18:206, 19:84

and by good works, 1:9, 1:10, 1:125, 4:99, 4:125, 4:188, 5:85, 5:262–263, 8:97, 8:98, 11:159, 14:361–362, 17:18, 18:176, 18:351, 19:149.

It is lost by any mortal sin, 1:65–66, 2:80, 2:249, 3:15, 3:353, 4:33, 4:124, 4:196, 5:58, 5:82, 5:281, 7:569, 8:94, 8:219, 9:143, 10:170, 11:448, 14:49, 14:335, 14:361, 15:16, 15:69, 15:134, 15:143, 16:15, 16:128–129, 17:37, 17:58, 17:175, 17:182, 18:62, 18:85, 18:176, 18:243, 18:416, 18:444, 19:196

and can be regained (through the grace of God), 2:62, 3:28, 5:82, 8:94, 14:49, 16:26, 16:201–202, 17:58, 17:67, 17:182, 18:176, 18:416, 19:196

by the sacrament of penance or its desire, 1:65–66, 2:62, 2:80, 2:251, 3:30, 4:34–35, 4:125–126, 5:222, 5:235, 7:150, 8:94, 8:271, 9:115, 9:119, 11:164–165, 11:184, 11:278–280, 14:49, 14:360–361, 14:399, 15:148, 15:158, 16:26, 16:201–202, 16:210–211, 17:58, 17:67, 17:73–74, 17:176, 17:243–244, 17:252, 18:176, 18:188, 18:416, 19:196.

The Distribution of Graces

X g

God from eternity knew with certainty and immutably foreordained all future things, 10:73–74

but man remains free to do good with grace or to choose evil having rejected grace, 2:81, 2:88, 2:148, 2:248–249, 5:80, 6:161–163, 8:78–79, 8:91–92, 10:74–75, 10:335, 11:88, 11:149, 14:221, 14:264, 14:358, 15:144, 16:22, 16:175, 17:58, 17:130–132, 17:251, 18:111, 19:84.

God positively wills "that all men be saved," 2:148, 5:197, 6:156, 8:42, 8:92, 8:201, 10:42, 10:75, 10:176, 11:149, 11:152, 11:182, 11:185, 12:170, 14:264, 14:358, 16:88, 16:177, 18:43, 18:177, 18:269, 18:408, 19:8–9, 19:29, 19:84

and "Christ died for all," 3:41, 3:56, 3:142, 5:17, 5:373, 6:44, 8:201, 10:174–175, 11:52, 11:113, 11:185, 13:215, 14:17, 14:221, 14:264, 14:358, 15:41, 16:177, 17:217, 18:126, 18:295–297, 19:65, 19:92, 19:158 (*see also* VIII g–h).

God positively predestines all good works, 14:184
he has predestined no one to evil, 2:148, 6:174–175, 10:75, 17:13
no one is saved unwillingly, 5:80, 6:161–163, 8:78–79, 8:91–93, 10:74–75, 11:184–186, 14:221, 14:264, 17:217, 18:111, 19:84
and whoever is to be lost will be condemned from his own free choice of evil, 2:148, 2:248–249, 3:15, 3:36, 5:83, 6:161–163, 8:44, 8:78–79, 10:74–75, 10:155, 10:170, 11:88, 11:149, 11:181–182, 11:185–186, 14:221, 14:264, 17:143–144, 17:176, 17:251, 18:111, 19:84.

X h

God "does not abandon the justified, unless he is first abandoned by them," 5:82, 6:174–175, 7:541–542, 7:584–585, 8:92, 11:181–182, 13:29, 14:106
and does not permit anyone to be tempted more than they can bear, 1:28, 2:160, 3:18, 5:81, 6:171–172, 7:584, 9:139, 10:155, 10:177–181, 11:185, 11:208, 12:347, 14:358, 16:79, 16:124, 17:131–132, 18:183, 19:186
hence the commandments of God are impossible to no one, 2:170–171, 2:185, 2:198, 5:25, 5:80–81, 7:382–383, 8:92, 11:183–184, 11:185, 11:361, 14:126, 14:266–267, 14:358, 16:124, 17:120, 17:192, 18:333, 18:357
the grace of conversion is offered to sinners, 2:148, 3:159, 5:81–82, 8:93, 11:181–182, 11:185, 12:16, 14:201–202, 14:221, 18:43
and sufficient grace is given to all men for salvation, 2:148, 3:32, 5:81, 5:185, 5:197, 8:43, 8:78–79, 8:91–93, 10:75, 10:155, 10:176, 11:182, 11:185, 11:361, 12:66, 14:221, 14:264, 14:358, 15:32, 15:144, 16:124, 17:28, 17:107, 17:120, 17:180–181, 18:16, 18:43, 18:177, 18:357, 19:84.

Without a special revelation no one can be certain that he himself will be saved, 2:144, 5:84, 5:209, 8:96, 11:180
or after sin that he will be converted back to God's friendship, 2:145, 5:82, 11:180, 16:81, 16:152, 16:327.

The Catholic doctrine concerning justification is the only true one, 3:317, 11:182–186.

X i

In the state of the law of nature sufficient grace was not lacking to men for salvation, 3:126, 6:49, 8:107, 10:28, 10:30, 10:175–177, 14:201–202, 15:138, 16:17, 16:142, 18:275–276.

"The law" or old testament was good and a work of the one God, 1:126, 4:117, 7:380–382, 10:24, 10:237–238, 10:332–333, 12:151, 16:317, 18:93
but of itself it did not justify, 2:286, 3:126, 7:188, 10:30, 10:244, 13:67–68, 13:170, 14:201
rather, men were justified under the law by the blood of Christ, 3:126, 4:65, 4:117, 4:160, 4:194, 7:147, 10:30, 10:175–176, 11:145, 13:170, 14:201, 15:138, 16:17, 16:142
and in the hope of his coming, 3:126, 4:23, 4:112, 5:221, 6:48–49, 8:107, 10:30, 10:175–176, 11:145, 13:163, 14:201, 15:138, 16:17, 16:142, 18:119.

After the promulgation of the gospel, the ceremonies and legal precepts of the old testament became sinful to observe, 3:126, 5:297, 10:208–209, 11:383, 16:317
but the observance of the ten commandments remains binding on all, even in the new testament, 1:126, 2:44, 2:171, 5:25, 5:301–302, 6:160, 7:381, 7:383–384, 7:417, 10:336, 11:93, 11:149, 11:360, 14:28, 14:164, 14:266, 14:279, 15:20, 15:181–182, 16:52, 16:313–314, 17:28, 17:179–180, 17:193, 18:144.

The new law of the gospel will not cease with the coming of another law, 3:130, 10:246.

Virtues and Precepts

The Virtues and Laws in General

XI a

With sanctifying grace there are also infused virtues, 2:211, 5:78–79, 7:218, 8:101, 8:324, 10:200, 11:86, 11:184, 13:227, 14:345, 14:369, 16:21, 16:171, 17:120–121, 18:230, 18:445, 18:463, 19:134

distributed as theological and moral virtues, 1:9, 1:132, 2:63–64, 2:327, 3:31–32, 3:37, 3:47, 5:73–76, 6:196, 6:200–201, 9:9, 10:200–202, 11:88, 11:184, 11:456–461, 13:308, 14:345–346, 15:32–33, 15:73, 15:143, 16:171, 17:269, 18:81, 18:230, 18:463–464.

The acts of the theological virtues are necessary by divine precept, 1:33, 2:63, 5:7–8, 5:73, 5:76, 5:291, 6:201, 8:324, 11:79, 11:88–89, 11:183, 13:322, 14:47, 15:6, 15:72–73, 15:128, 15:183–184, 16:9, 16:104–105, 17:179–180, 18:82, 18:231.

There exists a twofold divine law: natural and positive, 17:31–32

no man is dispensed from observing the divine law, 3:76, 3:265, 5:25, 6:160, 7:383–384, 7:385, 11:93, 11:145, 11:149, 11:360, 14:28, 14:164, 14:266, 14:279, 15:71, 15:181, 16:52, 16:313–314, 17:28, 17:31, 17:120, 17:193, 18:144, 18:150, 19:222–223

human laws should conform to divine law, 11:360, 11:443, 12:148–149, 16:364–365

unjust laws need not be followed, 2:189, 5:35, 5:41, 5:306, 6:103, 7:435, 11:394, 12:8–10, 12:58, 12:232, 14:304, 16:60, 16:342, 16:364–365, 17:202, 18:160.

The Theological Virtues

See faith as acceptance of revelation, I c–d; as the foundation of justification, IX b.

XI b

Faith is a theological virtue, 1:9, 1:34, 1:132, 2:63, 2:313, 3:5, 3:31, 3:47, 4:39, 4:83, 4:129, 5:8, 5:73, 5:183, 5:291, 6:196, 6:201, 8:101, 8:103, 8:324, 9:10, 9:242, 9:249, 11:89, 11:94, 11:346, 14:47, 14:345, 15:32, 15:73, 15:143, 16:21, 16:172, 17:107, 17:120–121, 18:82, 18:230, 18:232

the act of faith is produced by a creature, not merely infused by God, 1:19, 1:34, 2:111, 5:78, 11:75, 11:89–90, 14:165–166, 17:120–121

it is not a blind assent or contrary to reason, 3:374, 5:186, 8:108, 11:75, 11:89–91, 14:170, 16:172, 17:121, 18:232

but it is above reason, 1:35, 5:186, 8:33, 9:10–11, 11:89–91, 11:94, 14:165, 14:170, 16:172, 17:121, 18:232

it is at the same time an act of intellect and will, 1:34, 3:5, 11:90, 14:166, 18:437

founded on the authority and truthfulness of God the revealer, 1:19, 2:64, 2:112, 2:313, 3:5, 3:31, 3:41, 4:39, 4:129–130, 5:8, 5:10, 5:187, 6:23–24, 8:103, 8:324, 11:79, 11:89–91, 11:95, 14:5, 14:73, 14:165–166, 14:345, 15:6, 15:41, 15:51, 15:118, 16:113, 16:172, 17:14, 17:84, 17:107, 17:120–121, 18:16, 18:82, 18:108, 18:232, 18:437, 19:136.

The act of faith falls under a special precept, 2:111, 4:9–10, 11:89–92, 11:177–178, 14:5–6, 14:165–166, 15:72, 15:183, 17:120–122, 17:179–180, 18:437

and should be elicited several times in life, 2:111, 3:41, 4:30, 4:40, 5:9, 5:187–188, 8:103, 8:107, 10:177–181, 11:89–90, 11:177–178, 14:47, 14:178–179, 14:345, 15:41, 15:184, 16:30, 16:55, 16:215–216, 16:321–326, 18:83, 18:231, 18:233, 18:436–437

the hiding of faith can be sinful in certain circumstances, 2:111–112, 5:187–188, 8:110, 11:90, 11:99, 11:177–178, 15:184, 16:55, 16:215–216, 16:321–326, 17:42, 18:233.

By divine and Catholic faith those things are to be believed which are revealed by God (in scripture or tradition) and proposed by the Church defining or teaching ordinarily, 1:18, 1:34, 2:5, 2:64, 2:113, 2:114, 2:311, 2:313, 3:5, 3:31, 3:59, 3:322, 4:39, 4:78–79, 4:129–130, 5:8–10, 5:149, 5:183–184, 6:4–5, 8:325, 9:11, 9:66, 9:249, 11:79, 11:89, 11:92, 13:341, 14:5–6, 14:73, 14:165, 14:168–169, 14:345, 15:6, 15:32, 15:51, 15:118, 15:143, 16:9, 16:94, 16:105–106, 16:172, 17:11, 17:84, 17:90–92, 17:107, 17:122, 17:154, 17:179–180, 18:16, 18:82, 18:106, 18:139–140, 18:232, 18:438, 18:459.

The most grievous sins against faith are heresy and apostasy, 1:35, 2:116, 3:322, 3:379, 11:89, 11:92–93, 11:177–178, 12:95, 14:169, 14:280, 15:183, 16:55, 16:321–325, 17:42, 17:194–195, 18:233

and occasions posing dangers to faith are to be avoided, 1:35, 3:29, 3:157, 3:159–60, 3:318, 5:31, 11:93, 11:94, 14:179, 14:280, 15:158, 15:172, 17:195, 18:234.

Faith is not lost by any sort of sin, 5:82, 14:169, 18:444

but only grave sins against faith, 1:36, 2:116, 5:82, 8:102, 8:325, 11:89, 14:169, 18:233

hence it can exist (although dead) in the soul without charity and hope, 6:40, 11:90, 11:160, 11:192, 14:177, 18:236, 18:434, 18:444.

In the next life faith will be done away with, 3:359, 6:21–22, 8:48, 8:102, 10:47, 11:348, 18:274, 19:314.

XI c

Hope is a theological virtue, 1:9, 1:26, 1:132, 2:63, 2:150, 2:316, 3:31, 3:47, 4:39, 4:130, 5:73, 5:132, 5:291, 6:196, 6:201, 8:101, 8:112, 9:26, 9:242, 9:254, 11:179, 11:346, 14:47, 14:345, 15:32, 15:73, 15:143–144, 16:22, 16:172–173, 17:107, 17:180, 18:82, 18:230, 18:234

it can exist without charity, 11:160, 18:236

and in the next life it will be done away with, 3:359, 8:102, 10:47, 11:348, 18:274.

The act of hope should be elicited at times during life, 1:18, 2:150, 2:316, 3:41–42, 4:10, 4:40, 4:130, 5:133, 5:292, 8:103, 9:27–28, 9:254, 10:177–181, 11:180, 14:47, 14:345, 15:41–42, 18:83, 18:231, 18:436.

XI d

Charity is a theological virtue, 1:9, 1:32, 1:132, 2:63, 2:166, 2:319, 3:31, 3:47, 4:40, 4:83, 4:131, 5:73, 5:291, 6:196, 6:201, 8:101, 8:115, 9:39, 9:242, 9:257, 11:347, 14:47, 14:345, 15:32, 15:73, 15:143–144, 16:22, 16:173–174, 17:107, 17:192, 18:82, 18:230–231

never present in the soul without grace, 2:166, 8:116–117, 9:38, 11:164, 14:269, 17:175, 18:236

supernatural charity is to be distinguished from merely natural love of God or neighbor, 1:34, 2:166, 4:40, 4:83, 4:131, 9:39, 14:267–268, 17:192.

Perfect charity destroys sin of itself, 2:169, 8:117, 9:175–176, 11:261, 11:302, 14:269, 17:252, 18:406, 18:435–436.

God is to be loved more than one's neighbor, 1:34, 1:38, 1:124, 1:127, 2:64, 2:166, 2:319, 3:5, 3:32, 4:40, 4:83, 4:131, 5:12, 5:26, 5:292–293, 6:200, 7:391, 7:429–430, 8:115, 8:327, 9:39, 9:243, 9:258, 11:17, 11:348, 14:28, 14:268–269, 15:33, 15:36, 15:144, 16:173, 17:13, 17:85, 17:107, 17:120, 17:273, 18:83, 18:235, 19:143.

Imperfect charity is not dishonorable, 13:249, 14:268–269, 14:403–404, 16:36, 16:237.

The act of charity is produced by a creature not merely infused by God, 1:34, 2:64, 2:167, 4:10, 5:78, 9:39, 9:258, 14:266, 17:192

it should be elicited several times in a lifetime, 2:319, 3:42, 3:190, 4:40, 5:294, 8:120, 8:169, 9:40, 11:350, 14:47, 14:345, 15:41–42, 18:83, 18:231, 18:436.

Man is bound to fraternal charity, i.e., to love his neighbor, 1:9, 1:83, 1:125, 2:166, 2:169, 2:319, 3:32, 3:42, 3:190, 5:25, 5:34–35, 5:73, 5:293–294,

6:131, 6:147, 6:194–195, 6:200, 7:389–390, 7:429–430, 8:119, 8:327, 9:39, 9:258, 11:28–29, 11:38, 11:199, 11:351–357, 12:30, 12:62–65, 13:211, 13:262, 14:29, 14:270–272, 15:33, 15:36–37, 15:72, 15:144, 15:181–182, 16:22, 16:53, 16:173–174, 16:314–315, 17:13, 17:32, 17:107, 17:274, 18:83, 18:445, 19:145

by an internal and formal act as well as external acts, 1:9, 1:10, 1:83, 1:125, 2:168, 2:319, 3:42, 3:190, 5:73–74, 6:131, 8:120, 11:28–29, 11:351–359, 12:62–65, 14:270–275, 15:36–37, 17:274, 18:83, 18:445, 19:146.

The wealthy are obliged to give alms to the poor from their superfluity, 5:352–353, 7:466–467, 10:314, 11:355–356, 12:51, 12:297–298, 13:160, 18:84, 18:237.

The souls in purgatory are helped by almsgiving, 3:34, 3:166, 3:197, 3:351, 3:360, 5:21, 5:274, 6:51, 8:220, 8:312, 9:118, 11:119, 11:159–160, 12:65, 12:113, 13:314, 14:25, 14:255, 15:68, 15:203, 16:68, 16:90, 16:373, 17:166–167, 18:84, 18:147, 19:123.

Care should be taken to avoid setting any example that would lead another to sin (scandal), 1:46, 2:334, 3:23, 3:37, 3:133, 3:210, 4:48, 4:141, 5:187, 5:294–295, 6:109–110, 6:210, 6:213, 7:114, 7:438, 8:252–253, 9:156, 11:43–44, 11:177–178, 11:398, 11:405–407, 12:66–69, 12:246, 12:256–257, 13:262, 14:37, 14:298, 14:309–310, 15:23, 15:75, 15:77, 15:192, 16:147, 16:227, 16:372, 17:45, 17:203–204, 18:161, 18:247, 19:277

schism is among the gravest sins against charity, 6:195, 11:357, 12:309–310, 18:436

one cooperates in the sin of another by various ways, 1:45–46, 1:48, 1:51–52, 1:53–54, 2:196, 2:252–253, 2:331, 5:70, 5:285, 6:109–110, 7:442, 7:465–466, 7:476, 9:156–163, 9:271, 11:402, 11:406, 11:421, 14:82, 14:343–344, 15:35, 16:121, 16:350–351, 17:45, 17:272, 18:247, 19:277.

THE TEN COMMANDMENTS

The First Commandment

XI e

God ought to be worshiped interiorly and exteriorly, 1:8, 1:33, 1:34, 1:126, 2:44, 2:172, 3:5, 3:20, 3:132, 3:265, 3:327, 4:39, 4:129, 5:332–333, 6:86–88, 6:201, 8:242–243, 9:41, 9:259, 10:164, 10:336, 11:225, 11:362–363, 13:6–10, 13:260, 13:299, 14:31–32, 14:279–285, 15:169, 15:182–184, 16:104–105, 17:42, 18:152, 19:229

this being man's primary moral obligation, 1:32, 2:319, 3:5, 3:20, 3:121, 3:132, 3:265, 5:12, 5:26, 6:86–88, 7:391, 9:40, 9:262, 11:362–363, 13:5, 14:431, 16:104–105, 17:211

in particular adoration is due to the humanity of Christ, 1:33, 3:122, 6:219–220, 8:85, 11:13, 13:164–165, 13:252, 13:260, 13:271, 14:14, 15:94, 15:166, 17:33, 17:131

the most Sacred Heart of Jesus, 13:271, 16:277

and the most Holy Eucharist, 1:71, 1:99, 2:277, 2:291–292, 2:324, 3:116–117, 3:121–123, 4:11, 4:100, 5:95, 5:98, 5:162–163, 5:381–382, 5:387, 6:206, 6:219–220, 7:259, 7:266, 8:109, 8:284, 8:287, 9:94, 9:266, 12:288, 12:364, 13:85, 13:127, 13:260, 13:271, 13:341, 14:54, 14:382, 14:393, 15:94, 15:96–97, 15:166, 16:265–266, 17:66, 17:229, 18:171, 18:207, 19:176–178.

True and fitting worship is retained in the Catholic Church alone, 1:18, 1:22, 1:35, 2:173, 6:66, 6:86–88, 7:138, 10:336, 11:149, 11:366–367, 12:271, 13:10, 13:104, 13:133, 16:126, 16:317, 17:211, 17:238–242

the worship (and invocation) of the saints is laudable, 1:33, 1:122, 2:177, 2:317, 3:14, 3:21, 3:63, 3:360–365, 4:42, 4:43, 4:134, 5:26, 5:31, 5:137, 5:217–220, 5:335–336, 7:391–395, 7:507, 8:87, 8:174, 8:244, 9:42, 9:259, 11:189, 11:367–369, 12:72, 13:6, 13:297–311, 14:32–33, 14:285–288, 15:19, 15:21, 15:74, 15:179–181, 15:185–186, 16:56–57, 16:88–89, 16:105, 16:328–330, 17:29, 17:79, 17:91, 17:160–163, 17:186–187, 17:198, 18:53, 18:153, 18:329–330, 18:334, 18:453, 19:157, 19:234

the veneration of sacred images (icons) is licit, 1:33, 2:175, 2:318, 3:21, 3:317, 4:43, 4:134, 5:27–30, 5:31, 5:330–335, 7:395, 7:397–398, 8:87, 8:175, 8:245, 9:46, 9:259, 11:370–371, 12:46, 12:230, 13:6–7, 13:294–295, 14:33, 14:127, 14:284, 14:288–289, 15:21, 15:74, 15:186, 16:57–58, 16:297, 16:331–334, 17:80, 17:91, 17:196–198, 18:53, 18:154, 18:334–336, 18:453, 19:234

the veneration of relics is licit, 1:33, 1:122, 2:178, 2:318, 3:21, 3:355, 4:43, 4:134, 5:30, 5:31, 5:335–336, 7:393–395, 8:87, 8:174, 8:245, 9:46, 11:369–370, 12:72, 12:84, 12:209, 13:98, 13:292–294, 13:320, 14:289–290, 15:21, 15:74, 15:186, 16:57, 16:330–331, 17:80, 17:198–199, 18:53, 18:154, 18:329, 18:453, 19:234

the rites of the Church in the solemn administration of the sacraments should not be contemned, omitted, or changed, 1:91, 1:101, 3:68, 5:166, 7:181, 9:79–80, 9:265, 10:39, 10:52–53, 11:256, 11:364, 11:366–367, 13:14–16, 14:291, 14:450, 17:199–200

they contain many mystical meanings and significations, 1:87–101, 2:213–214, 2:282–295, 2:304–307, 5:371–372, 5:378–383, 7:181–182, 7:285, 9:43, 9:97, 9:265, 10:43–44, 11:220–221, 11:333, 13:7–8, 13:16, 14:371–372, 14:387–389, 14:446–448, 15:92, 15:152

the improper treatment of sacred persons, places, or things constitutes the sin of *sacrilege*, 1:36, 3:162, 3:378, 4:44, 4:136, 5:31, 5:296, 6:224, 8:244, 9:47, 10:261, 11:364, 12:86, 12:384–385, 13:271–272, 14:284, 15:90, 15:149, 16:27, 16:202, 17:197, 17:266, 19:240

simony is illicit, 9:50, 11:364, 12:11, 12:247–248, 14:285, 16:276, 17:197, 18:153

active participation in any non-Catholic worship is gravely evil, 2:44, 2:172–173, 3:20, 3:322, 6:201, 14:283, 15:21, 16:126, 16:317, 17:42, 17:195, 17:203.

XI f

Prayer is the raising of the mind and heart to God, 1:83, 1:120, 2:30, 2:151, 2:316, 2:326, 3:17, 3:39, 3:153, 3:166, 4:56, 4:151, 4:201, 5:133, 5:354, 6:36, 7:496, 8:226, 9:189, 11:187, 12:52, 14:65, 14:430, 15:17, 15:82, 15:176, 16:51, 16:306, 17:183, 18:63, 18:178, 19:151

it is either public or private, 1:32, 2:317, 3:166, 3:190, 5:138, 7:513, 8:226, 9:189, 11:196, 12:52–53, 13:43–44, 18:178

public prayer (also called *liturgy*) is offered in the name of the Church and by her ministers, 3:123, 3:146–149, 3:350, 8:226, 11:196, 13:8, 13:60, 13:260, 18:178–179

liturgical prayer properly makes use of a sacred language, 3:150–154, 3:350, 5:161, 5:374–377, 8:150, 13:62–63, 14:388, 16:194, 17:25, 17:242–243.

Prayer presupposes grace, 1:119, 2:156, 3:17, 4:56, 4:150, 4:202, 5:80, 5:82, 5:174, 6:144, 11:183

it is necessary, 1:119, 2:156, 3:17, 3:34, 3:190, 3:360, 4:56, 4:151, 4:201, 5:8, 5:134, 5:169–174, 5:363, 7:493–495, 8:227, 9:191, 10:29, 11:187, 11:194, 11:449, 13:8, 14:66, 14:411, 14:431, 15:17, 15:82, 15:176, 16:52, 16:307, 17:28, 17:78–79, 17:103, 17:120, 17:183, 18:63, 18:178, 19:152

it is made for four ends: praise, thanksgiving, adoration, and petition, 1:26–29, 1:83, 1:120, 2:316, 3:117, 4:56, 4:58–59, 4:129, 4:151, 4:201, 5:98–99, 5:133, 5:162, 5:354–355, 6:144, 7:499, 8:226, 9:189, 11:186–187, 12:53, 13:44, 14:430, 15:39, 15:176, 16:51, 16:306, 17:184, 18:63, 18:178, 19:151

petition made on behalf of others is also called *intercession*, 2:153, 2:318, 3:112, 3:274, 3:278, 3:358, 3:360–361, 4:59, 4:88, 4:127–128, 4:134, 4:197–198, 9:191, 13:6

prayer does not exclude reasoning, 5:354, 7:496–497, 11:195–196, 14:434–435, 15:82, 16:306–307, 17:183

it is suitably helped by images, 2:176, 2:317, 2:318, 3:21, 3:365–368, 4:43, 4:134–135, 5:28–29, 5:331–333, 7:398, 9:259, 11:189, 12:46, 13:5–8, 13:215–216, 13:297, 14:435, 15:74, 15:186, 16:297, 17:196, 18:154, 19:156

it is hindered by willful distractions, 3:17, 4:57, 4:152, 5:361–362, 5:364–366, 7:496–497, 7:508–510, 8:228, 11:190–191, 11:196, 11:210, 11:390, 14:43, 14:65, 14:327, 14:432, 15:18, 15:82, 16:52, 16:312, 17:184, 19:154.

The Second Commandment

XI g

To swear an oath is a good and holy act, 2:182, 4:44–45, 4:137–138, 4:199, 6:88–93, 7:406, 8:246, 10:248, 11:373–374, 14:292, 15:74, 16:58–59, 16:335–336, 17:200, 19:241

whereby God is called as witness to an assertion, 2:182, 4:45, 4:137–138, 4:199, 5:298, 6:88–93, 7:407–408, 8:246, 9:47, 10:248, 11:373–374, 14:292, 15:74, 15:187, 16:58, 16:335, 17:200, 19:241

licitly performed when undertaken with truth, discernment, and for a just cause, 2:181, 4:45, 4:137–138, 5:32, 5:298–299, 6:88–93, 7:406–409, 8:246, 11:374–375, 14:292, 15:75, 15:187, 16:58–59, 16:335–336, 17:200, 19:241

even to confirm human contracts or civil business, 4:45, 4:137–138, 6:88–93, 11:374, 16:58–59, 16:335–336, 19:241

whereas swearing falsely (perjury) is always a mortal sin, 1:40, 2:44, 2:181, 3:165, 3:173, 4:44–45, 4:136–137, 4:138, 4:199, 5:32, 5:299–300, 6:88–93, 6:201, 7:412, 7:473–474, 8:247, 9:47, 11:375, 14:40, 14:293, 14:317, 15:75, 15:187, 16:335, 17:43, 18:155, 19:241

even if done to protect someone or defend the faith, 1:41, 5:300, 6:88–93, 7:473–474, 14:40, 14:318.

Reverence is to be paid to the name of God, 1:8, 1:39, 1:126, 2:157, 2:165, 2:182, 2:319, 3:21, 4:44, 4:136, 5:15, 5:139, 5:300, 6:88–93, 6:151–154, 6:193, 6:201, 6:223–224, 7:403–406, 7:412–414, 7:531–532, 8:246, 9:47, 9:260, 11:12, 11:105, 11:200, 11:373–381, 12:127, 13:124, 13:171–173, 13:275, 14:13, 14:33–34, 14:67, 14:205, 14:291–295, 14:436, 15:22, 15:74–75, 15:83, 15:187–188, 16:58–59, 16:227, 16:335–338, 17:43, 17:133, 17:199–200, 18:54, 18:154–155, 19:238

and to His saints and angels, 1:122, 2:182, 3:303, 3:355, 3:361–363, 4:44, 4:136, 5:26, 5:219–220, 6:88–93, 7:414, 8:246, 11:373, 11:376, 13:297–311, 14:10, 14:34, 14:291–292, 15:21, 15:74–75, 15:179–181, 15:185–187, 16:56, 16:58, 16:328–329, 16:335, 17:43, 17:199–200, 18:54, 18:155, 18:329, 18:453.

The Third Commandment

XI h

The precept of observing Sundays (and holy days of obligation) is binding on pain of grave sin, 1:8, 1:42, 1:55, 1:127, 2:44, 2:183, 2:198, 2:320, 3:21, 4:45, 4:138, 5:33–34, 5:303, 5:338, 6:93–101, 6:201, 9:47, 11:385, 11:389, 13:65, 14:42–43, 14:297–298, 14:324–328, 15:82, 15:189, 15:197–198, 16:64, 16:227, 16:339–340, 16:356–359, 17:31–32, 17:48–49, 17:210–211, 18:54, 18:57, 18:155, 18:166, 18:168, 19:245

the weekly time for this observance was Saturday under the old law, 1:41, 2:183, 3:262–264, 5:301–302, 6:93–101, 6:193, 7:421–422, 8:248, 10:164, 11:383–384, 13:41–42, 14:295, 15:189, 16:59, 16:340–341, 17:43, 17:201, 18:156, 19:244

and transferred to Sunday in the new law, 1:42, 1:55, 2:183, 3:262–265, 5:301–302, 6:93–101, 7:422, 8:248, 11:383–384, 13:41–42, 14:295, 15:189, 16:59–60, 16:340–341, 17:43–44, 17:201, 18:156, 19:244

in which time is set aside for divine worship and rest from servile labor, 1:42, 2:44, 2:183–184, 3:22, 3:262–265, 4:46, 4:139, 5:33–34, 5:147, 5:303–305, 6:93–101, 6:193, 6:201, 7:421, 7:424, 8:249, 9:47, 9:260, 10:164, 11:381–392, 13:41–43, 13:204, 14:35, 14:42–43, 14:295–298, 14:325–328, 15:22, 15:76, 15:89, 15:189, 16:59–60, 16:64, 16:338–341, 16:356–359, 17:44, 17:201, 17:210–211, 18:54, 18:57, 18:155, 18:166, 19:247

although certain works are still permitted on holy days, 1:42, 2:184, 5:33, 5:305–306, 6:97, 7:424, 8:249, 11:40, 11:384, 11:387–388, 14:296–297, 15:190, 16:60, 16:339–341, 17:201, 18:57–58, 18:167.

Civic officials and employers sin by requiring servile work on holy days, 4:46, 4:139, 5:33, 6:93–101, 11:385–387, 11:391, 14:297, 16:357, 18:160, 18:168, 18:341.

The Fourth Commandment

XI i

Authority is not the mere sum of numbers, material powers, or historical accident, 6:101

but a right and binding force coming from God, 3:161, 5:306, 6:103, 6:106, 7:435, 8:251, 10:191, 10:231, 11:66, 12:113, 13:327, 14:298, 14:306, 15:190–191, 16:111, 16:185, 18:159

so that even human laws should be obeyed, 4:46, 4:139, 6:103, 6:106, 7:434–435, 8:251, 10:190–191, 12:65, 13:327, 14:306, 16:364–365, 18:159.

XI k

The family is a society created by God, 6:103, 7:370–371, 11:334, 18:336

as an institution of natural law, 6:103, 7:366–367, 18:336

imperfect in itself, 8:251, 18:336

to be served and protected by wider civil society, 8:251, 18:336.

Parents are bound to love and provide for their children, 2:238, 3:22, 4:46, 4:139, 5:35, 5:130–131, 6:102, 7:374–375, 7:437–438, 8:183, 8:250, 9:48, 10:339–342, 11:230, 11:337, 11:396–399, 11:444, 12:54, 12:57–58, 12:59–62, 13:288, 14:280, 14:304–305, 14:425, 15:23, 15:191, 16:61, 16:291, 16:343–344, 17:44, 17:202, 17:222, 18:55, 18:158, 19:262

the father as head and the wife as heart of the home, 2:237, 3:239–241, 5:36, 5:130–131, 6:102, 6:116, 7:369, 7:374–375, 10:191, 10:231, 11:190, 11:336–338, 11:345, 11:443–444, 12:54, 12:59, 12:297–298, 12:299, 13:21, 13:288, 13:331, 14:425, 18:125, 18:158

while children are to love and obey their parents, 1:9, 1:43, 2:45, 2:185, 2:320, 3:22, 4:46, 4:139, 5:35, 5:306, 6:103, 6:193, 6:201, 7:430–433, 8:250, 9:48, 9:260, 10:191, 10:314, 11:381, 11:393–396, 12:54, 12:58–59, 12:232, 13:331, 14:15, 14:36, 14:217, 14:298–301, 15:23, 15:76, 15:190, 16:60–61, 16:227, 16:291, 16:342–345, 17:44, 17:202, 18:25, 18:54, 18:157, 19:257

and remain free to choose marriage or virginity, 2:238, 5:126–127, 5:261, 11:381, 11:398, 12:363, 13:286–287, 14:305, 14:422, 16:127, 18:160, 18:224, 18:349, 19:262.

XI l

See effects of baptism, XII c.

Rights: Members of the Church have the right to receive spiritual goods from the clergy, 2:188, 18:208

e.g., sacraments and proper doctrinal instruction, 9:73, 18:26–28, 18:208.

XI m

Obligations: Members of the Church are obliged to love the Church above their fatherland, 9:64, 18:146

being subject to the jurisdiction of the Church and recognizing its authority in private and public life, 1:44, 3:111, 3:381, 4:46, 4:78–79, 4:139, 5:54, 6:106, 6:193, 6:201, 7:433–434, 8:261, 9:260, 11:232, 13:199, 14:240–241, 14:254, 14:302–303, 15:23, 15:77, 15:79, 15:146, 15:191–192, 16:198, 17:32, 17:202, 17:208–209, 18:138, 18:159, 19:98, 19:266

observing the universal law of Christ, 1:44, 6:84, 9:67, 11:79, 11:232, 14:28, 14:254, 16:127–128, 17:31–32, 17:208–209, 18:182

and the precepts of the Church, 1:44, 1:55–56, 2:46–51, 2:198–203, 2:320–321, 3:25, 4:52–55, 4:144, 4:146–150, 4:200, 5:46, 5:338–350, 8:261, 9:66, 9:243, 9:263, 11:79, 11:151, 11:232, 11:432, 13:197, 14:41, 14:254, 14:323–325, 15:26, 15:79, 15:197, 16:52, 16:127–128, 16:228–229, 16:313–314, 17:31–32, 17:48, 17:208–209, 18:57, 18:138, 18:166, 19:266

receiving religious instruction, 2:44, 2:185, 3:56, 3:241, 4:69, 4:79–80, 4:166, 4:207, 5:53–54, 6:99–100, 6:201, 7:425, 8:165, 9:68, 11:93, 11:388–389, 11:457, 12:45, 14:164, 14:280, 14:327–328, 16:31, 16:55, 16:103, 16:216, 16:321–323, 17:30, 17:195, 18:25, 18:35, 18:138, 18:234, 19:262

and the sacraments, 1:56, 1:127, 2:49, 2:202, 2:320, 3:25, 4:29, 4:31, 4:118, 4:119, 4:202, 5:53–54, 5:338–342, 6:72, 7:276–277, 7:311, 7:425, 8:146, 8:154, 8:265–267, 9:73, 11:249, 11:434–435, 12:45, 12:292, 14:44, 14:332–334, 15:26–27, 15:80, 15:199–200, 16:65–66, 16:228, 16:361–362, 17:31–32, 17:50–51, 17:195, 18:15, 18:59–60, 18:169–173, 19:266–267

while supporting the clergy according to the precept of the Lord, 1:45, 1:127, 2:50, 2:203, 2:320, 3:25, 4:52, 4:55, 4:147, 4:150, 4:200, 5:55, 5:349–350, 6:106, 6:212–213, 6:220–221, 7:434, 8:266–267, 9:243, 12:9, 14:45, 14:334, 15:26, 15:81, 15:202, 16:66, 16:228–229, 16:362–364, 17:32, 17:51–52, 17:202, 17:215–216, 18:15, 18:61, 18:173, 19:266

and fulfilling the apostolate as befitting to their state, 11:151, 11:161, 16:229, 18:165, 18:182.

XI n

The law of ecclesiastical fast binds under pain of grave sin, 1:56, 1:127, 3:334, 4:53–54, 4:86–87, 4:147–148, 4:200, 5:47, 5:342–349, 9:185, 12:309–310, 13:144, 13:197, 14:43–44, 14:324–325, 14:332, 15:82, 15:197, 16:228, 16:345, 17:48, 17:49–50, 18:58–59, 18:168–169, 19:253

although there are exemptions from the norms of fasting, 3:250, 5:52, 5:344–345, 8:264, 13:143, 13:162, 13:197, 14:330, 15:81, 15:202, 16:228, 16:359–360, 17:50, 18:58, 18:168–169, 19:253.

XI o

See relations between Church and state, II g.

The state is a perfect society, 18:336

its end is the common good of citizens in this earthly life, 11:399–400, 12:289, 13:327, 13:331, 14:306, 18:325, 19:263

it should promote the true religion, 11:399–400, 12:289, 13:204, 14:118, 18:327

and repress unregulated liberty of feeling, expression, and action, 11:399–400, 12:289, 14:128

although false religions and their worships may be tolerated for reasons of prudence, 14:128, 18:325–326.

Sedition and rebellion are illicit, 13:327, 14:303, 15:76, 15:192, 18:160, 18:339–342

for the authority of all legitimate government is given immediately by God, 2:189, 4:47, 4:140, 6:106, 7:435, 8:251, 10:191, 11:66, 11:399, 12:113, 13:327, 14:306, 15:191, 16:111, 16:185, 18:159, 18:325, 18:339–340.

The civil power of government should promote the rights of its citizens, 18:341

it cannot intrude unnecessarily into the intimate affairs of individuals, 19:263

nor abolish the right to private property, 16:350, 19:284–286.

The state is to be loved and guarded by its citizens, 4:47, 4:140, 13:327, 14:303, 18:159, 18:339

just taxes are to be paid, 2:194, 12:33, 12:65, 14:303, 14:315

just laws are to be followed, 2:189, 6:106, 8:251, 10:191, 12:15, 14:306, 16:364–365, 18:339

each citizen should work for the public good according to his capacity, 2:189, 8:252, 12:53, 14:306.

XI p

Education is ordered to man's final end and accordingly it should be Christian, 4:46, 4:62, 4:139, 4:157, 6:102, 11:397, 12:57–58, 12:59–62, 12:340–343, 14:280, 14:304–305, 14:429, 17:44, 17:195, 19:262.

The office of educating belonging to the Church, the family, and the state, 12:366–367, 18:158, 18:336

to the Church as supreme teacher and supernatural mother, 2:282, 12:340–343, 12:366–367, 14:254, 16:90, 18:26–28, 18:158, 18:337–338

to the family as the primary custodians of those children given by God, 2:186, 2:238, 3:22, 4:46, 4:139, 5:35, 5:130, 6:102, 8:183, 11:337, 11:397, 12:57–58, 12:59–62, 13:288, 14:280, 14:304–305, 14:427, 17:44, 17:195, 18:35, 18:55, 18:158, 18:172

to the state in a subsidiary way, 18:158

promoting sound education in its territories, 12:340–343, 12:366–367

purely secular or areligious education is reprobated, 6:102, 11:398, 12:58, 12:314–315, 12:317, 14:280, 14:304–305, 14:429, 17:42, 17:195, 19:262

and coeducation, 12:340–343.

The Fifth Commandment

XI q

Man is bound to preserve his own bodily life, 1:45, 2:190, 5:310, 6:107, 6:110, 9:49, 11:402–403, 14:37, 14:308, 14:310, 15:192, 16:61, 16:345–346, 17:45, 18:55, 18:161, 19:268

as also its integrity, so that he cannot destroy or mutilate his members unless he cannot otherwise provide for the good of the whole body, 1:45, 5:310, 14:37, 14:308, 15:192, 16:345–346, 17:45, 18:55, 18:161, 19:268.

The civil government has no direct power over the bodies of its citizens, 1:46, 11:401.

It is licit to kill or wound another person in certain situations, 1:45, 2:45, 2:190, 5:308, 6:108, 7:440–441, 8:252, 11:401–402, 14:307, 18:342, 19:275
as when individuals defend themselves against unjust aggressors, 2:45, 2:190, 5:308–309, 6:108, 7:442, 8:252, 11:402, 14:307, 18:342, 19:275
and when a nation engages in a just war, 2:45, 2:190, 5:308–309, 6:108, 7:441, 8:252, 11:401–402, 12:259–261, 13:289–290, 14:123–124, 14:307, 19:275
or the execution of criminals, 1:45, 2:45, 2:190, 5:308–309, 5:342, 6:108–109, 7:440–441, 8:252, 9:160–161, 11:401–402, 12:295, 12:305, 14:307, 19:275.

All direct killing of the innocent is intrinsically evil, 1:9, 1:45, 2:191, 2:320, 3:22, 4:48, 4:141, 5:37, 5:66, 5:69, 5:308, 6:107–108, 6:193, 6:201–202, 8:252, 9:261, 11:401–405, 14:37, 14:306–308, 15:23, 15:77, 15:192, 16:61, 16:346, 17:45, 17:203–204, 18:55, 18:161, 18:342, 19:275
including abortion, 1:45–46, 2:191, 5:310, 6:110, 6:217, 7:367, 7:441, 11:243, 11:386, 11:401, 12:42, 12:358, 14:307, 16:273.

The Sixth and Ninth Commandments

XI r

Sexual temptations are to be resisted, 1:9, 1:48, 1:53, 2:46, 2:191, 2:257, 2:320, 3:24, 4:48, 4:50–51, 4:141, 4:143–144, 5:39, 5:63, 5:311–312, 5:327–330, 5:368–369, 6:118, 6:128–130, 6:203, 9:49, 9:261, 11:208, 11:408–412, 11:446–447, 12:185, 12:202, 14:38, 14:311–312, 15:24, 15:38, 15:136, 15:193, 15:196, 16:63, 16:227, 16:346–349, 16:355, 17:46, 17:204–205, 18:55, 18:162, 19:282

consent is required before sexual thoughts become sinful, 1:48, 1:108, 2:197, 2:248, 4:51, 4:144, 5:39, 5:63, 5:142–143, 5:312, 5:327–330, 5:368–369, 6:128–130, 6:203, 7:487–488, 8:254, 11:408–412, 11:446–447, 12:153, 14:41, 14:311, 15:78, 15:196, 16:63, 16:355, 17:142–143, 17:207, 18:56, 18:165, 19:282

any use of the sexual faculties outside of marriage is gravely sinful, 1:9, 1:47, 1:53, 2:45, 2:191–192, 2:320, 3:23, 3:24, 4:48, 4:50, 4:141, 4:143, 5:38, 5:310–311, 6:114–118, 6:194, 6:202, 6:217, 7:450, 9:49, 11:408–412, 14:310–314, 15:24, 15:77, 15:193, 16:61, 16:227, 16:347, 18:162, 19:282

unnatural sex acts (masturbation, sodomy, bestiality) are especially grave sins, 1:47, 1:81, 2:45, 2:192, 2:264, 3:34, 4:36, 5:38, 5:69, 5:288, 5:311, 6:194, 6:203, 6:217–218, 7:450–451, 9:49, 9:170–171, 9:271, 11:452, 14:312–314, 14:342–343, 15:77, 15:193, 16:61, 16:227, 16:347, 17:272, 18:162, 19:282

deliberate frustration of fertility in the marital act (even among spouses) is intrinsically evil, 1:45–46, 5:38, 6:73, 6:194, 6:217, 9:171.

The Seventh and Tenth Commandments

XI s

The right of property is founded in natural law, 6:194, 6:202, 7:460, 9:51, 11:417–418, 14:279, 17:46, 19:285

taking a thing belonging to another against their will (theft) is sinful, 1:9, 1:49, 2:45, 2:193, 2:320, 3:23, 4:48, 4:49, 4:142, 5:39, 5:283, 6:118, 6:120, 6:194, 6:202, 7:459–460, 8:255, 9:50, 9:261, 11:420, 14:39, 14:314–317, 15:24, 15:194, 16:62, 16:349–353, 17:46–47, 17:205–206, 18:55, 18:163, 19:287

although taking in extreme need is not itself theft, 8:256.

Civil governments should justly regulate commerce for the common good, 11:420

covetousness is an internal sin even apart from external acts, 1:9, 1:54, 2:46, 2:82, 2:197, 2:255, 2:329, 3:24, 4:51, 4:144, 5:39, 5:287, 5:327–329, 6:126–128, 6:194, 6:202, 7:460, 7:487–488, 8:260, 9:150, 9:261–262, 11:417, 11:422, 11:450, 14:41, 14:322–323, 14:339, 15:25, 15:78–79,

15:197, 16:63–64, 16:132, 16:355–356, 17:46–47, 17:142, 17:208, 18:56, 18:165, 19:288.

The Eighth Commandment

XI t

It is never permissible to tell a lie, 1:51, 2:45, 2:194, 3:23, 4:49, 4:142, 5:44, 5:321–322, 6:124–125, 6:194, 6:202, 7:477, 7:479–482, 8:258, 9:50, 11:426–427, 12:9, 12:60, 14:40, 14:318, 15:25, 15:78, 15:195, 16:62–63, 16:228, 16:353–355, 17:47, 17:206, 18:56, 18:164, 19:289–290

although the truth may be prudently hidden for a just cause, 7:479, 8:259, 11:426, 14:318, 19:290

respect for the reputation of others obliges under this commandment, 1:51–52, 2:45, 2:195, 2:320, 3:24, 4:50, 4:143, 5:43–45, 5:318–327, 6:123, 6:202, 7:475–476, 9:50, 9:261, 11:427–431, 14:40, 14:318–322, 15:25, 15:78, 15:195, 16:62–63, 16:228, 16:353–355, 17:47, 17:207, 18:164, 19:292.

The Sacraments

The Sacraments in General

XII a

The sacraments are means of grace, 1:18, 1:59, 1:130–131, 2:22, 2:209, 2:321, 3:26, 3:317, 3:335, 4:55, 4:60, 4:155, 4:202, 5:220, 5:222, 5:262, 6:74, 6:132, 6:204, 7:147, 7:531, 9:73, 9:264, 10:28–30, 11:217–218, 14:50, 14:363–367, 15:17, 15:27, 15:90, 15:148, 16:26, 16:199–200, 17:18, 17:28, 17:58–59, 17:182–183, 17:219–220, 18:22, 18:67, 18:177, 18:186–187, 18:361–362

being symbols or signs of sacred things, the visible forms of invisible grace, 1:59, 2:208, 2:321, 3:26, 3:49, 3:67, 3:335, 4:60, 4:155, 4:202, 5:86, 5:220, 6:131–132, 6:204, 7:173, 8:121, 8:268, 9:74, 9:77, 9:248, 10:29, 11:217–218, 14:51, 14:364, 15:27, 15:90, 15:148, 16:26, 16:199–200, 17:58, 17:219, 18:67, 18:186, 18:388.

The sacraments of the new testament contain and confer the grace that they signify, 1:59, 1:130–131, 3:26, 3:49, 3:317, 3:335, 5:86, 5:220, 5:222–223, 6:132, 7:176, 9:74, 9:77, 9:264, 10:29, 11:218, 14:365, 14:443, 15:27, 15:90, 16:199–200, 17:59, 17:219–220, 18:67, 18:186, 18:361–362, 19:111

they are instituted by Christ, 1:59, 1:130, 2:62, 2:208, 2:321, 3:26, 3:49, 3:316, 3:335, 4:60, 4:155, 4:202, 5:86, 5:223, 5:262, 6:133, 6:204, 7:184, 8:121, 8:174, 8:185, 8:268, 9:74, 9:248, 9:264, 11:217–218, 11:221–224, 14:50, 14:364–365, 15:27, 15:90, 15:148, 15:174, 16:26, 16:50, 16:199–200, 16:297, 17:18, 17:28, 17:58, 17:219, 18:22, 18:67, 18:186, 18:361–362, 19:111

they are exactly seven in number, 1:11, 1:59, 1:130, 2:55–61, 2:206, 2:321, 3:26, 3:316, 3:335, 4:60, 4:155, 4:202, 5:86, 5:222, 5:262, 6:132, 6:196, 6:204, 7:182, 8:132, 8:174, 8:269, 9:76, 9:248, 9:264, 11:222, 11:227–228, 14:51, 14:365–366, 15:27, 15:90, 15:148, 16:26, 16:200–201, 17:28, 17:59, 17:91, 17:221–222, 18:187, 18:361–362, 18:373, 18:422, 19:111

they are accomplished with due matter and form, 1:59, 2:208, 3:51, 4:60, 4:155, 4:202, 5:221, 6:133, 7:180, 8:128, 8:269, 9:75, 11:219–220, 17:219, 18:186, 18:361, 18:368–369, 19:111

with the necessary ministerial intention of "doing what the Church does," 1:61, 4:29, 4:31, 4:118, 4:119, 4:202, 5:221, 6:133, 7:185, 8:129, 8:269, 9:78, 11:220, 17:218, 18:186, 18:361–363.

The sacraments of the new testament not only nourish faith, 1:28, 1:59, 5:222, 7:179, 9:77, 9:265

but always confer grace by their own operation (*ex opere operato*), 1:59–60, 2:209, 3:49, 3:56, 3:317, 4:55, 4:60, 4:155, 4:202, 5:221, 5:262, 6:133, 7:187, 7:606, 8:122, 8:271, 9:74–75, 9:264, 11:219, 14:365, 14:444, 15:27, 15:149, 15:174, 16:27, 16:50, 16:203, 16:297–298, 17:60, 17:220, 18:187, 18:363

by the power of the Holy Spirit, 1:59, 3:27, 3:49, 3:56, 6:192, 6:199, 7:176, 9:74, 18:363, 18:368

upon all those who receive them without placing an obstacle to their effect, 1:59, 3:68, 3:317, 5:221, 6:134, 7:185, 7:606, 8:271, 9:77, 11:219, 14:365, 14:444, 15:27, 15:149, 15:174, 16:27, 16:203, 17:60, 17:220, 18:187.

Three sacraments furthermore imprint an indelible character in the soul, 1:61, 2:209, 4:73, 4:171, 4:210, 5:222, 6:134, 7:188, 8:126–127, 8:272, 11:218–219, 14:367, 15:149, 16:27–28, 16:204–205, 17:60, 17:220–221, 18:68, 18:189, 19:111

and cannot be repeated, 1:61, 1:64, 2:212, 2:217, 3:55, 3:67, 3:317, 4:73, 4:171, 4:210, 5:222, 6:134, 6:207, 7:189, 8:127, 8:174, 8:272, 9:140, 9:268, 11:219, 14:367, 15:90, 15:149–150, 16:27, 16:203–204, 17:60, 17:221, 18:68, 18:189, 19:111.

XII b

Only the proper minister can validly administer any given sacrament, 2:209, 3:50, 3:67, 5:222–223, 8:128–129, 9:78, 11:219–220, 18:186

which are conferred validly (per requisite form, matter, and intention) even if the minister be a sinner, 3:17, 3:51, 5:221–222, 6:133–134, 6:135–136, 7:185, 7:279–280, 8:129, 9:78, 11:219–220, 18:188, 18:387

or a heretic, 1:60–61, 3:51, 5:222, 6:135, 7:203, 8:129–130, 9:78, 14:370

or a schismatic, 3:51, 9:78, 14:370.

The recipient of the sacraments is a member of the Church (excepting in the case of baptism), 3:26, 9:79, 10:236

who is properly disposed, 3:28, 3:67, 3:68, 4:29, 4:31, 5:7, 5:86, 5:221, 5:389–393, 6:134, 8:122–123, 9:79, 10:234, 11:219, 15:90, 15:149, 17:30–31, 17:97, 18:37, 18:68, 18:187–188.

The sacraments are generally necessary for salvation (received in fact or desire), 1:18, 1:60, 1:65, 1:130, 2:208, 2:210–211, 2:248, 3:84, 3:316–317, 3:335, 4:171, 4:210–211, 5:7, 6:192, 7:183, 8:174, 8:201, 9:73, 9:77, 10:29, 11:146, 11:224–225, 11:227–228, 11:316, 14:444, 17:91, 17:176, 17:252, 18:37, 18:187–188, 18:190

although not all for each person, 3:316–317, 5:86, 8:174, 18:189–190.

Baptism

XII c

Baptism is the first sacrament, 1:60, 2:55, 2:210, 2:322, 3:26, 3:49, 3:51–52, 3:55, 4:60, 4:156, 4:202, 5:223, 5:263, 6:71, 6:135, 6:204, 7:192, 9:81, 9:265, 11:228, 14:51, 14:367, 15:27, 15:91, 15:150, 16:203–204, 17:60, 17:222, 18:22, 18:189, 18:361–362, 18:367, 18:373, 19:134
it succeeded circumcision, 3:52, 6:49, 7:207, 9:81, 18:370.

The remote matter is natural water, 1:60, 2:210, 3:27, 3:50, 3:51, 3:335, 4:61, 4:156, 4:203, 5:87, 5:221, 5:223, 6:71, 6:135, 6:213–214, 7:194, 8:132, 8:273, 9:82, 11:228, 14:51, 14:370, 15:28, 15:42, 15:91, 15:109, 15:150, 16:28, 16:208–210, 16:211, 17:61, 17:224–225, 18:69, 18:191, 18:367–369
the proximate matter is the washing, 1:60, 2:210, 3:27, 3:49–50, 3:54–55, 3:335, 4:61, 4:156, 4:203, 5:87, 5:221, 5:223–224, 6:71, 6:132, 7:194, 8:134, 8:273, 9:82, 11:229, 14:51, 14:368, 15:28, 15:42, 15:91, 15:109, 15:150, 16:28, 16:208–210, 16:211, 17:61, 17:224–225, 18:191, 19:129.

The form is the words: "I baptize thee in the name of the Father, and of the Son, and of the Holy Spirit," 1:60, 2:210, 3:27, 3:50–51, 3:63–64, 4:61, 4:156, 4:203, 5:87, 5:223, 6:71, 6:135, 6:204, 6:213–214, 7:196, 8:133, 8:273, 9:82, 11:229, 14:51, 14:368, 15:28, 15:42, 15:91, 15:109, 15:150, 16:28, 16:208–210, 17:61, 17:224, 18:69, 18:191, 18:367–369, 19:129
or among the Greeks: "Let him be baptized...," 3:54, 3:55, 7:197, 18:367–368
it may be conferred conditionally, 3:56, 5:224, 7:219–220, 8:134, 8:274, 14:370, 16:204, 17:93, 17:225, 18:37.

The effects are: the application of the merits of Christ, 1:60, 2:208, 2:211, 3:56, 4:60, 4:155, 4:202, 5:148, 6:71, 9:82–83, 11:233, 14:25, 17:17
and hence a change into a new creature, 1:60, 2:62, 3:49, 9:83, 9:265, 11:239
the remission of all sin (original and personal), 1:60, 1:130, 2:62, 2:80, 2:144, 2:211, 2:248, 2:322, 3:55, 3:57, 3:316, 4:60, 4:156, 4:202, 5:87, 5:148,

5:225, 5:254, 6:44, 6:71, 6:135, 6:204, 7:146, 7:212, 8:138, 8:174, 8:273, 9:81–83, 9:265, 10:171, 11:166, 11:231, 12:8, 13:221, 14:25, 14:51–52, 14:360–361, 14:368, 15:16, 15:27, 15:68, 15:91, 15:133, 15:150, 16:26, 16:28, 16:201–202, 16:205–207, 17:60, 17:222–223, 18:68, 18:191, 18:282, 18:367–368, 18:434–435, 19:133

the remission of all temporal punishment due to sin, 1:60, 2:227, 3:55, 4:61, 4:156, 5:87, 5:225, 5:254, 6:71, 6:135, 7:146, 7:214, 8:139, 8:273, 9:83, 11:231, 14:360–361, 14:368, 15:150, 16:28, 16:206–207, 16:247, 17:223, 18:68, 18:191, 18:367–368

the conferring of grace, 1:17–18, 1:59, 2:211, 2:213, 2:322, 3:49, 3:55–56, 4:60, 4:155, 5:87, 5:222, 7:217–218, 8:139, 9:83, 11:84, 11:184, 11:231–232, 14:49, 14:52, 14:361, 14:369, 15:148, 16:26, 16:201–202, 17:58, 18:193, 18:435, 19:133

divine adoption into the sonship of God, 1:18, 1:60, 1:130, 2:62, 2:111, 2:207, 2:211, 2:322, 3:55, 3:64, 4:60, 4:156, 4:202, 5:87, 5:222, 6:65, 7:217, 7:520–521, 8:231, 8:273, 9:84, 9:265, 11:231, 13:221, 13:260, 14:52, 14:361, 14:369, 15:27, 15:91, 15:150, 16:28, 16:205, 17:17, 17:60, 17:222, 18:366, 18:370, 18:435, 19:133

regeneration (rebirth), 1:60, 2:207, 2:211, 3:49, 3:64, 5:148, 5:222, 6:43, 6:71, 7:217–218, 7:520–521, 8:132, 9:81–84, 9:265, 10:29, 10:82, 11:19, 11:84, 11:241, 14:51, 14:369, 18:282, 18:361, 18:364, 18:367, 18:382, 19:69, 19:134

union with Christ, whose member the baptized person is made, 1:61, 1:63, 2:141, 2:207, 2:211, 3:49, 3:61, 3:64, 3:320, 3:335, 7:218, 7:224–225, 9:83, 11:84, 11:231–232, 14:51–52, 14:369, 15:27, 15:57, 15:91, 15:150, 16:28, 16:205, 17:222, 18:189, 18:367, 19:134

liberation from the power of the devil, 1:17, 1:62, 2:213, 3:27, 3:59–62, 4:61, 4:156, 4:203, 5:148, 6:214, 7:223, 9:84, 10:156, 11:240, 13:221, 13:254, 14:371–372, 15:28, 16:210, 16:222, 17:17, 18:367, 18:370

the infusion of virtues, 2:62, 2:211, 2:322, 3:47, 3:60, 5:87, 7:218, 8:101, 8:139, 8:324, 11:184, 11:231, 13:227, 14:369, 17:120–121, 18:230–231, 18:435, 19:134

the conferring of the gifts of the Holy Spirit, 1:62, 2:211, 2:213, 2:322, 6:158, 9:82–83, 11:184, 11:231, 12:8, 18:238, 18:446

the beginning of the spiritual life, 1:63, 2:211, 2:311, 3:49, 9:83, 9:85, 11:184, 11:232, 13:221, 14:366, 15:148, 17:17, 18:367

reception into the Church as a living member, 1:17, 1:61, 1:63, 1:130, 2:141, 2:212, 2:322, 3:26, 3:54–55, 3:61, 4:60, 4:118–119, 4:156, 4:194, 4:202, 5:87, 7:142, 8:132, 8:139, 8:273, 9:83, 11:232, 14:52, 14:252, 14:369, 15:91, 16:210, 17:222, 17:224, 18:23, 18:40, 18:68, 18:142, 18:189, 18:191, 19:97

the opening of heaven (possibility of salvation), 1:63, 1:130, 2:62, 2:111, 2:211, 2:322, 3:11, 3:55, 3:355, 4:60–61, 4:156, 4:202–203, 5:87, 5:149, 5:206, 6:135, 7:220, 8:273, 9:84, 9:265, 10:82, 11:84, 14:51–52, 15:150, 16:28, 16:205, 16:222, 17:17, 18:367, 19:134–136

the imprinting of a character in the soul (thus it cannot be repeated), 1:61, 2:209, 2:212, 2:217, 3:55, 3:67, 3:317, 3:321, 4:73, 4:171, 4:210, 5:88, 5:222, 5:224, 6:71, 6:134, 6:207, 6:213–214, 7:219, 8:139, 8:272, 9:81, 9:140, 9:268, 11:218–219, 11:232, 14:367, 15:90, 15:149–150, 16:27–28, 16:203–205, 16:211, 17:60, 17:221, 18:68, 18:189, 18:365, 19:134

the obligation and ability to fulfill the law of Christ, 1:17, 1:114, 2:111, 3:49, 3:62, 5:89, 7:192, 9:83–84, 11:107, 11:232, 12:60, 14:360–361, 14:371, 18:69, 18:193, 18:371

although concupiscence remains after baptism, 2:197, 3:60, 3:62–3:63, 3:154, 4:23, 4:112, 5:80, 6:44, 7:213, 7:216, 7:485, 7:546, 9:83–84, 10:37, 11:86, 11:231, 11:244, 12:169, 14:368, 15:133, 16:14, 16:88, 16:124, 17:274, 18:282, 19:185.

XII d

The minister must be someone other than the baptized, 2:211, 3:50, 4:61, 4:156, 4:203, 6:17, 9:82, 11:229–230, 15:42, 16:210

and in solemn baptism, a priest or deacon, 1:60, 2:211, 3:51, 3:155, 3:200, 4:61, 4:156, 4:203, 6:71, 6:135, 7:202, 8:135, 8:273, 9:82, 11:229–230, 14:52, 14:370, 17:61, 17:223–224, 18:192, 18:368, 19:129

in private baptism, anyone with the right intention, 1:60–61, 2:211, 3:51, 4:61, 4:156, 4:203, 5:87, 6:71, 6:135, 6:204, 6:213–214, 7:202, 8:135, 8:273, 9:82, 11:230, 14:52, 14:370, 15:42, 15:91, 15:109, 15:150, 16:28, 16:208, 17:61, 17:223–224, 18:37, 18:69, 18:192, 18:368, 18:369–370, 19:129.

Baptism is necessary to all for salvation, 1:60, 2:141, 2:210, 3:49, 3:53–54, 4:61, 4:156, 4:203, 5:87, 5:190, 5:225, 6:71, 7:206–210, 8:135, 8:276, 9:81, 10:82, 11:84, 11:166–167, 11:228, 11:232–233, 14:367–368, 15:150, 16:28, 16:207–208, 17:61, 17:158, 17:223, 18:69, 18:190, 18:194, 18:367, 18:371–372, 19:134–136

at least in desire (baptism of desire), 1:60, 2:210, 3:56, 5:87, 5:225, 8:135, 8:276, 9:81, 11:146, 11:229, 14:373, 15:150–151, 16:29, 16:210–212, 17:61–62, 17:225–226, 18:143–144, 18:188, 18:194, 18:323, 19:135–136

infants should be baptized as soon as possible, 3:52, 3:332, 7:208, 8:275, 9:81, 11:230, 11:397, 14:368, 15:42, 15:109, 16:207–208, 17:171–172, 17:218, 17:222, 18:193, 18:279, 18:282, 18:370, 19:134, 19:267

adults should have the intention and suitable preparation prior to receiving baptism, 3:56, 5:88, 5:225, 5:264, 7:210, 8:139, 9:84, 10:60–61, 11:165, 11:219, 11:232, 17:223, 18:37, 18:193

baptism should not be put off until death approaches, 3:57, 7:208, 16:207–208.

Confirmation

XII e

Confirmation is a true and proper sacrament, 1:11, 1:63, 1:130, 2:56, 2:214, 2:322, 3:27, 3:66–67, 3:336, 4:61, 4:156, 4:203, 5:89, 5:226, 5:264–265, 6:71, 6:136–137, 6:204, 7:227, 8:139, 8:278, 9:85, 9:265, 11:244, 14:52, 14:373–374, 15:28, 15:91, 15:152, 16:30, 16:214, 17:63, 17:105, 17:226, 18:23, 18:69, 18:187, 18:195, 18:361–362, 18:373, 19:161.

The remote matter is chrism, 1:63, 2:214, 3:27, 3:66, 3:70–71, 3:336, 4:61, 4:157, 5:90, 5:227, 5:265, 6:136–137, 6:204, 7:231, 8:278, 9:86, 9:265, 11:244–245, 14:52, 14:375, 15:92, 15:152, 16:30, 16:215, 17:63, 17:227–228, 18:195, 18:373, 19:162

the proximate matter is the imposition of hands, with the anointing, 1:64, 2:214, 3:27, 3:66–67, 3:70, 3:336, 4:61, 4:157, 5:90, 5:227, 5:265, 6:136–137, 8:140, 8:278, 9:86, 11:244, 14:52, 14:375, 15:28, 15:92, 15:152, 16:30, 16:215, 17:63, 17:227–228, 18:195, 19:161–162.

The form is "I sign thee...," 2:214, 3:69–70, 6:136–137, 7:232, 8:140, 8:279, 9:86, 9:265, 11:245–246, 14:375, 15:152, 16:30, 16:215, 17:63, 17:227–228, 18:195–196, 18:373, 19:162.

The effects are: communication of the Holy Spirit, 1:63–64, 2:215, 3:27, 3:66, 3:68–70, 3:336, 4:61, 4:62, 4:157–158, 4:203–204, 6:72, 6:136–137, 6:204, 6:215, 7:237, 8:139, 8:141, 8:278, 9:88, 11:247, 11:249, 14:52, 14:374, 15:28, 15:91, 15:142, 15:152–153, 16:30, 16:214, 17:63, 17:105, 17:226–227, 18:23, 18:69, 18:195, 18:374–375, 19:164

the increase of spiritual strength, 1:64, 2:62, 2:207, 2:215, 2:322, 3:27, 3:66, 3:68–70, 3:336, 4:62, 4:156, 4:157–158, 4:203–204, 5:89, 5:222, 5:226–227, 6:72, 6:136–137, 6:163, 6:204, 7:236, 8:139, 8:141, 9:88, 9:265, 11:247, 14:52, 14:366, 14:375, 15:28, 15:91, 15:152–153, 16:31, 16:203, 16:217, 17:105, 17:226–227, 18:23, 18:69, 18:189, 18:195, 18:361, 18:374–375, 19:164

the imprinting of a character in the soul (thus it cannot be repeated), 1:64, 2:215–217, 3:67, 3:317, 4:73, 4:171, 4:210, 5:90, 5:222, 5:227, 6:134, 6:207, 7:238, 8:141, 8:278, 8:280, 9:88, 9:140, 9:268, 11:218–219, 11:247, 14:367, 14:374, 15:90, 15:93, 15:149–150, 16:27–28, 16:203–205, 17:60, 17:105, 17:221, 18:68, 18:189, 18:365, 19:164.

The ordinary minister is the bishop alone, 1:64, 2:216, 3:27, 3:67, 3:336, 4:61, 4:157, 5:90, 5:227, 5:264–265, 6:136–137, 6:204, 7:233, 8:140, 8:279, 9:87, 9:265, 11:246, 14:52, 14:375, 15:28, 15:92, 15:152, 16:30, 16:215, 17:63, 17:105, 17:227, 18:196, 18:373, 18:375, 19:161

the extraordinary minister is a priest having the requisite faculty, 8:140, 14:375, 15:152, 16:215, 17:227, 18:196, 18:374–375, 19:161.

The subject is anyone baptized, 1:63, 2:215, 2:322, 3:66, 4:62, 4:157, 5:90, 5:226, 6:71–72, 6:215, 7:235, 8:140, 9:87, 9:265, 11:232, 11:248, 14:52, 14:376, 16:224, 17:63, 17:222, 18:69, 18:196, 18:376, 19:164

he is not however bound to receive it by necessity for salvation, 2:216, 3:68, 7:235, 8:140, 11:248–249, 14:53, 14:376, 17:226, 18:69, 18:197, 19:164

but to contemn it is a mortal sin, 2:217, 3:68, 4:63, 4:158, 4:204, 5:90, 5:228, 6:215, 7:235, 8:141, 9:88, 11:249, 14:53, 14:376, 15:93, 15:152, 16:31, 16:216–217, 17:63, 17:226, 18:69, 18:197, 18:374–375, 19:164.

The Eucharist

XII f

The Eucharist is a true sacrament, 1:11, 1:69, 1:130, 2:57, 2:218, 2:323, 3:26, 3:27, 3:72, 4:60, 4:64, 4:155, 4:158, 4:204, 5:92, 5:228, 5:265, 6:72, 6:137, 6:206, 6:219, 7:243, 8:141, 8:281, 9:89, 9:264, 11:54, 11:256, 13:143, 14:378, 15:93, 15:164, 16:41, 16:259, 16:274, 17:64, 17:228, 18:24, 18:72, 18:187, 18:203, 18:361–362, 18:373, 18:389, 19:168

instituted by Christ at the last supper, 2:218, 3:59, 3:73, 4:64, 4:159, 5:94, 5:228, 6:138, 7:240–241, 8:284, 9:95, 11:54–55, 11:255, 12:366, 13:18, 13:143, 13:209, 14:53, 14:112, 14:378–379, 15:164, 16:41, 16:259, 17:64, 17:231–232, 18:70, 18:72, 18:197, 18:203–204, 18:377, 18:379, 18:396, 19:166

as a symbol of mystical union, 1:70, 2:132, 2:221, 3:106, 5:228, 6:138, 9:90, 9:103, 11:224, 11:256, 13:115, 18:204, 18:377, 19:165.

The presence of Christ in the Eucharist is true, real, identical, 1:70–71, 1:99, 1:131, 2:62, 2:218, 2:323, 3:27, 3:73, 4:63, 4:66, 4:159, 4:204, 5:92, 5:229, 5:265–270, 6:72, 6:137, 6:206, 6:219, 7:255–261, 8:174, 8:281, 9:11, 9:90–91, 9:266, 11:54–55, 11:255, 11:260, 12:256–257, 13:43, 13:341, 14:53, 14:112, 14:378, 15:28, 15:65, 15:93, 15:164, 16:41, 16:259, 17:66, 17:91, 17:100–101, 17:134, 17:228–234, 18:24, 18:71–72, 18:190, 18:199, 18:203, 18:376, 18:384–385

accomplished by transubstantiation, 1:70, 2:219–220, 3:27, 3:96, 3:342, 4:63, 4:158–159, 4:204, 5:92–93, 5:194, 5:229, 7:264–265, 8:174, 8:282, 9:93, 9:266, 11:258, 13:125, 14:381, 15:93, 15:164–165, 16:42, 16:263, 17:65, 17:234, 18:198, 18:373, 18:378, 18:384–386

by which the substances of bread and wine cease to exist, 1:70, 2:62, 2:219, 2:323, 3:27, 3:73, 4:63, 4:158–159, 4:204, 5:92, 5:194, 5:229–230, 5:267–270, 5:373, 6:137, 6:206, 7:261, 8:142, 8:283, 9:93, 9:266, 11:54–55,

11:257, 13:43, 13:127, 14:53–54, 14:379, 14:381, 15:28, 15:93–94, 15:164–165, 16:42, 16:260–261, 17:65, 17:101, 17:233–234, 18:70, 18:197–198, 18:378, 18:384–386, 19:166

while the appearances (accidents, species) of bread and wine remain without a subject, 1:70, 2:62, 2:220, 2:324, 3:27, 3:72, 4:63, 4:158–159, 4:204, 5:92, 5:230, 5:267–268, 6:137, 6:206, 6:219, 7:266, 8:142, 8:283, 11:54–55, 11:257, 13:127, 14:54, 14:112, 14:379, 14:381, 15:28, 15:93–94, 15:165, 16:42, 16:260–263, 17:65, 17:101, 17:233–234, 18:70, 18:72, 18:198–199, 18:203, 18:376, 18:386, 18:390, 19:166

achieved by the words of consecration, 1:70, 1:131, 2:219, 2:324, 3:28, 3:97, 3:98, 4:64, 5:92, 5:230, 5:267, 5:373, 6:137, 6:206, 7:255, 8:282, 9:95, 9:266, 11:54–55, 11:257, 13:85, 13:126–127, 14:53, 14:381, 15:29, 15:93, 15:166, 16:43, 16:264–268, 17:66, 17:101, 17:234, 18:70–71, 18:199, 18:378, 18:385, 18:388–390, 19:168

so that Christ is whole and entire under each species, 1:70, 1:131, 2:220, 3:73, 4:63, 4:158–159, 4:204, 5:93–94, 5:230–231, 5:272, 6:137, 6:219, 7:260–261, 8:142, 8:174, 8:283, 9:99, 9:101, 9:267, 11:257–258, 11:269, 14:56, 14:381, 14:390, 15:94, 15:165, 16:42, 16:261–262, 17:65–66, 17:235–236, 18:199, 18:388, 18:390, 19:175

which mode of existing is sacramental, not natural, 2:220, 3:73, 3:124, 4:64, 4:158–159, 4:204, 5:230, 5:268–270, 7:260, 9:93, 14:381, 16:259, 18:199, 18:376.

The matter is wheat bread, 1:70, 2:221, 3:97, 5:228, 6:137, 6:206, 7:246–247, 8:141, 8:281, 9:90, 10:239, 11:54, 11:256, 12:238, 13:115, 16:276, 18:71, 18:199, 18:389

unleavened (in the Latin Church), 3:104, 5:228, 6:137, 7:246–247, 8:142–143, 9:90, 11:54, 11:256, 18:373, 18:384, 18:389, 19:178

or leavened (among the Greeks), 5:228, 8:143, 18:389

and grape wine, 1:70, 2:221, 3:105, 5:228, 6:137, 6:206, 7:248, 8:141, 8:281, 9:90, 10:239, 11:55, 11:256, 13:115, 16:276, 18:71, 18:199, 18:389, 19:178

with which a little water ought to be mixed as a symbol, 1:70, 2:221, 3:105, 5:228, 6:137, 7:248, 8:150, 11:256, 13:115, 18:389–390.

The form is the words of Christ, 1:70, 2:221, 3:28, 3:74, 3:97, 4:64, 4:159, 4:161, 5:92, 5:229, 6:137, 7:250–251, 8:141, 8:281, 9:92–93, 11:54–55, 11:257, 14:379, 16:43, 16:264–268, 17:65–66, 17:100, 17:234, 18:71, 18:200, 18:390, 19:168.

The consecrating minister is exclusively a priest with the proper intention, 1:71, 2:222, 3:28, 3:108, 4:64–65, 4:159–160, 4:161, 4:205, 5:159, 5:234, 6:137, 6:206, 7:279, 8:144, 9:92, 9:96, 11:255, 11:258, 13:73, 13:126, 14:53, 14:380–381, 15:165–166, 16:43, 16:263–268, 17:66, 17:234, 18:70, 18:387, 18:390, 19:166–167.

XII g

Consuming the Eucharist is distinguished in three ways: sacramental, spiritual, and both together, 5:100, 6:134, 7:270–271, 9:103, 11:225, 11:265, 13:135, 14:389, 16:277, 18:72, 18:203, 18:394, 19:172–173

sacramental reception (*Communion*) can be received under either species, 2:222, 3:106, 5:94, 5:271–272, 8:142–143, 9:90, 9:267, 11:269, 13:84, 14:390–391, 16:261, 17:68, 17:235–236, 18:29–30, 19:175

receiving from the chalice is not of divine precept for those not sacrificing, 2:223, 3:110, 5:94, 5:272, 6:219, 7:278, 8:143, 9:99, 11:269, 14:56, 14:390–391, 17:235–236

so that Communion under only one species is licit and should be retained, 2:222, 3:110, 5:94, 5:271–272, 6:206, 6:219, 7:278, 8:142–143, 9:100–101, 9:267, 11:269, 14:56, 14:390–391, 16:261, 17:68, 17:235–236, 18:29–30

Communion is ordinarily distributed by a priest, 1:71, 3:112, 5:234, 7:279, 8:144, 9:99, 11:269, 18:70

extraordinarily by a deacon, 8:144.

Those who reach the age of discretion are bound to communicate at least annually at paschal time, 1:56, 1:71, 1:127, 2:49, 2:202, 2:320, 3:118–120, 4:55, 4:149–150, 4:200, 5:54–55, 5:233, 5:340–341, 6:72, 6:218, 7:276–277, 8:146, 8:288, 8:289, 9:66, 9:263, 11:265, 11:435, 12:292, 14:44, 14:332–334, 15:26–27, 15:80, 15:95, 15:168, 15:199–200, 16:65–66, 16:228, 16:362,

17:51, 17:68, 17:91, 17:214–215, 18:15, 18:29–36, 18:60, 18:170–173, 18:207, 18:343–345, 19:175.

Faith alone does not suffice for lawful reception of the Eucharist, 1:71, 2:221, 2:324, 3:84, 4:66, 4:163, 4:205, 6:72, 9:105, 11:263, 13:43, 18:379

rather, the state of grace is required for the soul, 1:71, 1:131, 2:207, 2:221, 2:324, 3:28, 3:84, 3:114, 4:66, 4:163, 4:205, 5:96, 5:231–232, 6:72, 6:207, 6:218–219, 7:273, 7:606–607, 8:145, 8:285, 9:105, 10:234, 11:54, 11:263, 13:43, 14:56, 14:366, 14:391–392, 15:29, 15:95, 15:149, 15:167, 16:44, 16:203, 16:269–270, 17:67, 17:101, 17:221, 17:236–238, 18:24, 18:32, 18:72, 18:204–205, 18:344, 18:398, 19:173

and the disposition of fasting for the body (unless exempt), 2:324, 3:28, 3:115, 4:67, 4:163, 4:206, 5:96, 5:232–233, 5:342, 7:274, 8:145, 8:285–287, 9:105, 10:234, 11:263, 14:56, 14:394, 15:29, 15:96, 15:167, 16:44, 16:203, 16:269–271, 17:67–68, 17:101, 17:236–237, 18:25, 18:72–73, 18:204–205, 19:175

the Eucharist is to be kept for the sick, 3:112, 3:122, 5:341–342, 6:206, 6:219, 8:284, 12:287–288, 13:43, 13:85, 14:394, 16:270–271, 17:68, 17:260, 18:73, 18:205, 19:176

and transported with honor, 3:112, 6:219, 11:262, 13:85, 14:382, 16:283–284, 19:176–178.

In danger of death, viaticum should be received, 1:71, 3:115, 5:99, 5:233, 5:341–342, 6:206, 6:218–219, 7:242, 8:172, 8:266, 8:288, 11:265, 12:193, 12:203, 12:241, 12:287–288, 12:396–397, 13:282, 14:394, 15:89, 15:95, 15:168, 16:44, 16:270–271, 17:68, 17:260, 18:31, 18:36, 18:204, 18:207.

Frequent or even daily Communion is not necessary by divine law, 1:71, 3:118, 5:233–234, 11:265, 14:333–334

but is commendable to all who approach it with the proper dispositions, 1:71, 1:131, 2:324, 3:28, 3:114, 5:55, 5:99–100, 5:233–234, 6:207, 7:274–276, 7:606–607, 8:146, 8:289, 9:104, 10:236, 11:204, 11:266, 11:412, 11:435, 12:53, 12:183, 12:297, 14:333–334, 15:89, 15:168, 16:45, 16:271,

16:277, 17:68, 17:82, 17:101–102, 17:221, 17:237–238, 18:35, 18:60, 18:163, 18:170, 18:344, 18:399, 19:172–173
even the young, 1:71, 3:120, 12:61–62, 14:334, 18:35, 18:345.

The effects are: union with Christ, 1:70, 1:131, 3:72–73, 5:228, 6:137–138, 6:207, 7:268, 7:607, 9:89, 9:103, 10:234, 11:35, 11:55, 11:224, 11:261, 13:115, 14:56, 14:391, 15:166–167, 16:43, 16:268, 17:67, 18:204, 18:377, 18:383, 18:390, 18:397, 19:172
the increase of grace and the virtues, 1:70, 1:131, 2:31, 2:62, 2:207, 2:221, 3:72, 3:84, 4:65, 4:162, 4:205, 5:95, 5:231, 6:138, 6:207, 7:268, 7:607, 8:145, 8:285, 9:103, 11:260, 14:56, 14:391, 15:166–167, 16:26, 16:43, 16:202, 16:268, 17:67, 18:72–73, 18:206, 18:391, 18:393, 19:172
the remission of venial sins and penalties, 1:66, 2:251, 3:74, 3:128, 4:65, 4:162, 4:205, 6:207, 7:269, 8:145, 8:285, 9:104, 9:267, 11:164–165, 11:261, 13:69, 13:134, 14:391, 17:67, 18:73, 18:201, 18:206, 18:377, 18:393, 18:396
preservation from mortal sins, 1:131, 3:112, 3:120, 5:231, 7:269, 8:145, 8:285, 9:104, 11:261, 13:134, 14:391, 17:67, 17:234–235, 18:74, 18:207, 18:391, 18:396, 19:172
spiritual nourishment, 1:28, 1:56, 1:70, 1:131, 2:31, 2:158, 2:207, 2:221, 3:120, 4:64, 4:162, 4:205, 5:95, 5:222, 5:231, 6:72, 6:206–207, 7:267, 8:145, 8:285, 9:103, 9:267, 10:29, 10:236, 11:204, 11:260–262, 11:263–266, 12:53, 13:58, 13:134, 14:56, 14:112, 14:366, 14:382, 15:28, 16:43, 16:268, 17:65, 17:234–235, 18:72, 18:203–204, 18:361, 18:391, 18:396
perseverance in good, 1:70, 1:131, 5:223, 7:269, 9:103, 11:261, 14:391, 15:28, 17:67, 17:234–235, 18:74, 18:207, 18:391, 19:172
and the pledge of future glory, 1:56, 1:70, 3:72, 5:95, 5:223, 5:231, 6:54, 7:270, 7:607, 8:285, 9:103, 9:267, 10:236, 11:34–35, 11:262, 13:134, 14:391, 15:167, 16:43, 16:268, 17:65, 17:67, 18:396–397, 19:172.

XII h

The Mass is a true and proper sacrifice, 1:131, 2:222, 2:268, 2:324, 3:28, 3:124, 3:128, 4:64, 4:160, 4:204–205, 5:157–158, 5:234, 5:373–374, 7:282–283, 8:141, 8:174, 8:289, 9:95–99, 9:266, 10:239, 11:106, 11:262, 11:389, 12:72, 13:69–71, 14:54, 14:382–384, 15:29, 15:94, 15:168, 16:45,

16:272–274, 17:64, 17:69–70, 17:238–242, 18:70–71, 18:197, 18:200–203, 18:393, 19:170–171
divine, 2:222, 2:324, 3:121, 3:123, 4:64, 4:160, 4:204–205
singular, 9:95
prefigured by the sacrifices of nature and the old law, 2:222–223, 2:283, 3:128, 4:65, 4:160, 7:283, 9:96, 9:98, 10:234, 10:238–239, 11:54–55, 11:70, 11:254–255, 13:67–68, 13:125, 13:263–264, 14:105, 14:209, 14:384, 16:273, 16:317, 17:238–242, 18:391–392
external and visible, 2:222, 2:268, 2:324, 3:83, 3:89, 13:42–43, 18:200
instituted by Christ at the last supper, 2:218, 2:222, 2:268, 3:128, 4:64, 4:205, 5:159, 7:282, 8:291, 9:95, 10:238–239, 11:54–55, 11:106, 14:54, 14:384, 17:69, 17:242, 18:70, 18:197, 18:387, 18:391
by which the sacrifice of the cross is re-presented and applied, 1:131, 2:223, 2:268, 2:324, 3:127, 4:65, 4:160, 5:160, 5:234, 5:373–374, 7:283–284, 8:147–148, 8:290, 9:96–99, 10:239, 11:70, 11:106, 11:389, 13:69–70, 14:54–55, 14:385, 15:168–169, 16:45, 16:274, 17:70, 17:240–242, 18:71, 18:201, 19:65, 19:170–171.

The sacrifice does not consist in the Communion alone, 2:223, 3:123, 5:158, 5:234, 5:373–374, 14:385, 15:169, 16:274, 17:240–242, 18:204
nor is there required the presence of the faithful or the (even spiritual) Communion of those assisting, 5:271, 8:149, 18:394.

The victim at Mass is Christ himself, 1:131, 2:223, 2:292, 2:324, 3:28, 3:127, 4:63–65, 4:160, 5:159, 5:373, 7:283–284, 8:147, 8:290, 9:98, 10:239, 11:389, 13:69–70, 13:94, 14:54–55, 14:203, 14:378, 14:385, 15:168, 16:45, 16:274, 17:70, 17:241, 18:70–71, 18:200–201, 18:384, 18:392–393, 19:170–171
offered in an unbloody manner, which is different from that on the cross, 2:222, 2:268, 2:324, 3:28, 3:127, 4:65, 4:160, 5:160, 5:234, 5:373–374, 7:283–284, 8:147–148, 8:290, 9:96–97, 9:266, 10:239, 11:389, 13:69–70, 14:55, 14:384–385, 15:29, 15:169, 16:46, 16:275, 17:69–70, 17:241, 18:71, 18:200–201, 18:392–393, 19:170.

The principal one offering is Christ himself, 2:223, 2:292, 3:126, 4:65, 4:160, 5:159, 5:373, 7:284, 8:149, 8:291, 10:239, 11:389, 13:69–70, 13:94, 14:54–55, 14:203, 14:385, 15:168–169, 16:45, 16:266–267, 16:274, 17:70, 17:241, 18:71, 18:200–201, 18:384, 18:393, 19:169

through the ministration of his priests, 2:283–284, 3:126, 4:65, 4:160, 5:159, 5:373, 6:137, 7:284, 8:149, 8:291, 13:70, 13:126, 14:54, 14:384–385, 15:94, 15:168–169, 16:266–267, 17:70, 17:241, 18:71, 18:200–201, 18:393, 19:169

in which the faithful participate and co-offer in their own way, 1:131, 2:286, 3:127, 4:160, 5:162, 5:375, 8:149, 13:74, 13:95, 15:94–95, 15:169, 16:46, 16:275–277, 17:70, 18:72, 18:203.

The Mass is offered to God alone, 2:223, 2:324, 3:28, 3:124, 4:65, 4:160, 4:204, 4:205, 5:158, 5:218–219, 7:282, 8:289, 12:72, 13:70, 13:83, 14:54–55, 14:286, 14:386, 15:94–95, 15:169, 16:45, 16:272, 17:69, 17:241, 18:202

for the four ends of adoration, thanksgiving, impetration, and atonement, 3:8, 3:125, 4:65, 4:161–162, 4:205, 5:162, 5:234, 7:284, 8:148, 8:291, 9:95–99, 10:239, 10:338, 13:69–70, 14:386, 15:29, 15:95, 15:168–169, 16:46, 16:274, 17:49, 17:69, 17:240–242, 18:202, 19:171.

The Mass has power to remit sins, 2:251, 3:124, 3:128, 4:65, 4:205, 5:234, 7:284, 9:95, 9:267, 11:119, 14:386, 18:73, 18:201

and temporal punishments due to sin, 3:128, 5:160, 11:119, 14:386, 16:68, 16:373

especially for those to whom the fruit is applied, 3:131, 5:160, 8:292, 14:387, 18:202–203, 18:395

and is propitiatory for both the living and the dead, 2:324, 3:128, 3:140, 3:141–143, 3:148, 5:160, 5:274, 6:51, 7:284–285, 8:148, 8:220, 8:312, 9:95–99, 9:266, 11:119, 11:160, 12:65, 12:290, 13:72, 13:312, 14:25, 14:255–256, 14:387, 15:68, 15:203, 16:68, 16:373, 18:202–203, 18:393–394.

The ceremonies of the Mass—particularly the sacred Canon—are fitting and venerable, 1:86–87, 2:268–282, 3:28, 5:371–372, 5:378–383, 7:285,

9:79–80, 9:97, 9:265, 11:366–367, 13:7–8, 13:123–131, 14:387, 17:70–71, 18:380, 19:178–184

and contain many mystical significations in themselves, 1:97–101, 2:282–295, 5:371–372, 5:378–383, 7:285, 9:79–80, 9:97, 9:265, 10:43–44, 13:7–8, 13:94–140, 14:387–389, 17:71.

Penance

XII i

Penance is a true and proper sacrament, 1:11, 1:65, 1:130, 2:58, 2:224, 2:322, 3:26, 3:28–29, 3:154, 3:168, 3:338, 4:60, 4:67, 4:155, 4:164, 4:202, 4:206, 5:100, 5:235, 5:272, 6:72, 6:139, 6:204, 7:291, 8:151, 8:293–294, 9:106, 9:267, 11:276, 14:57, 14:396, 15:29, 15:97, 15:155, 16:33, 16:224, 17:71, 17:243, 18:23, 18:74, 18:187, 18:208, 18:361–362, 18:373, 18:400–401, 19:195

different from baptism and capable of being repeated, 1:65, 1:69, 3:29, 3:57, 4:73, 4:171, 4:206, 4:210, 5:101, 6:134, 6:207, 7:286, 7:292, 9:106, 11:434, 14:367, 15:90, 15:149, 16:222–223, 17:243–244, 18:74

called "a second plank after shipwreck," 7:286, 9:107, 9:267, 11:292, 16:222, 18:417

instituted by Christ, 1:59, 1:130, 2:62, 2:132, 2:224, 2:321, 3:15, 3:29, 3:154, 3:168, 4:68, 4:164, 5:235, 5:272, 7:308, 8:151, 8:293, 9:107, 11:276, 14:57, 14:398, 16:33–34, 16:225–226, 17:71, 17:170, 17:244–248, 18:23, 18:74, 18:208, 18:417, 19:195

in the form of a judgment, 3:338, 4:69, 4:207, 5:113, 5:273, 5:394, 6:139, 7:308–309, 7:380, 9:107, 11:276, 11:287, 14:398, 16:253, 18:208, 18:410–413, 19:196.

The sacramental form is a proper judicial sentence, 1:65, 3:28–29, 3:337, 5:113, 5:273, 5:394, 7:309, 7:380, 9:107, 13:315, 14:398, 16:253, 18:208–209, 19:196

i.e., the priest's precise words of absolution: "I absolve thee...," 1:65, 2:224, 3:155, 3:168, 3:337, 5:235, 6:139, 6:205–206, 7:293, 8:155, 8:294,

11:291, 16:33–34, 16:224–226, 17:218–219, 17:247, 18:74, 18:77, 18:216, 18:402, 19:196

which effectively forgive sins by divine power, not by the faith of the recipient, 2:224, 3:15, 3:29, 3:168, 3:337, 5:272–273, 6:74, 6:205–206, 7:293, 9:111, 11:163–164, 11:288, 14:57, 14:85, 14:397, 15:29, 15:98, 15:155, 16:33–34, 16:224–226, 17:71–72, 17:104, 17:218–219, 17:247, 18:52, 18:77, 18:148, 18:216, 18:402–403, 19:196.

The matter or quasi-matter is the acts of the penitent, 1:65, 2:224, 2:322, 3:29, 3:154, 5:235, 6:139, 7:292, 8:151, 8:294, 9:108, 11:276–277, 14:57, 14:399, 16:229–230, 17:72, 17:247–248, 18:74, 18:209, 18:402–403

which are: contrition, confession, and satisfaction (also called *parts*), 1:66, 1:131, 2:225, 2:322, 3:29, 3:156, 3:338, 5:101, 5:235, 6:72, 6:139, 6:204, 7:293, 8:151, 8:294–295, 9:108, 9:267, 11:276, 14:57, 14:399, 15:29–30, 15:155, 16:34, 16:230, 17:72, 17:102–104, 17:247–248, 18:23, 18:74–75, 18:209, 18:402–403, 19:198–199.

Contrition is a grief of soul and hatred for sins committed, with the purpose of not sinning again, 1:65, 1:124, 2:62, 2:144, 2:225, 2:322, 3:29, 3:156, 4:68, 4:166, 4:207, 5:103, 5:236, 5:389–390, 5:395–396, 6:72, 6:139, 6:204–205, 7:298, 8:152, 8:295, 9:109, 9:267, 11:278, 14:59–60, 14:73, 14:401, 14:405, 15:30, 15:101, 15:119, 15:156, 16:34, 16:36, 16:230–231, 16:234, 16:237–238, 17:73, 17:102–103, 17:248–249, 18:75, 18:212, 18:404, 19:193

it is a free and voluntary act, 2:225, 3:30, 3:337, 6:72, 6:204, 8:300, 9:109, 11:278, 16:230, 17:73, 17:248–249

it may be perfect (proceeding from charity) or imperfect (attrition), 2:225, 3:29, 3:170, 4:69, 4:166, 5:104–105, 5:236–237, 7:289–290, 7:306, 8:117, 8:152, 8:299–300, 11:279–280, 11:302, 14:403–404, 15:30, 15:101–102, 15:157–158, 16:35–36, 16:183, 16:235, 16:236–237, 17:73, 17:251–252, 18:76–77, 18:212–213, 18:404, 18:407–408, 19:193.

Confession is necessary for salvation by divine right, 1:65, 3:30, 3:156, 3:338, 4:73, 4:207, 5:101, 7:306, 9:110, 9:267, 11:286–290, 11:292, 14:57,

14:398–399, 16:226, 17:176, 18:190, 18:213–214, 18:403, 18:410–412, 19:196

it should be made in person and externally, 1:65, 2:225, 2:322, 3:30, 3:337–338, 5:107–108, 5:239, 6:204, 8:307, 9:111–112, 14:61, 14:398, 14:408, 15:97, 15:161, 16:36, 16:226, 16:239, 18:214

and ought to include the grave sins committed after baptism, 1:65, 1:131, 2:62, 2:226–227, 2:322, 3:29, 3:30, 3:338, 4:69, 4:166, 4:208, 5:108, 5:239–248, 6:204, 7:312, 8:151, 8:304, 9:110, 11:281, 11:284–286, 14:61–62, 14:406, 15:30–31, 15:99, 15:159–160, 15:161, 16:36–38, 16:39, 16:231–232, 16:239–245, 16:252–253, 17:74, 17:104, 17:253–255, 18:23, 18:77, 18:209, 18:214, 19:196

manifested to the confessor integrally, according to species and number, 1:66, 1:68, 2:226, 2:322, 3:158, 5:108, 5:244–248, 5:391–393, 6:204, 7:313, 8:305, 9:110–111, 11:284–285, 14:61–62, 14:406–407, 15:99, 15:159, 16:37, 16:231–232, 16:240–241, 17:74, 17:254, 18:77, 18:210, 18:214, 19:198

including all relevant circumstances, 1:66, 1:68, 2:226, 2:322, 3:165, 5:108, 5:244–248, 5:392–393, 6:204, 7:313, 8:305, 9:111, 11:284–285, 14:61–62, 14:406–407, 15:99, 15:159, 16:37, 16:231–232, 16:240–241, 17:74, 17:254, 18:77, 18:210, 18:214, 18:343, 18:403, 18:411, 19:198.

Venial or grave sins already directly forgiven are not necessary to confess, 3:161, 5:244, 7:312, 8:151, 11:285, 14:61, 14:407, 15:159, 15:161, 16:36, 16:39, 16:239–240, 16:252–253, 17:176, 18:23, 18:74, 18:209, 18:410, 19:196.

Salutary and appropriate satisfaction should be imposed by the confessor, 1:65, 2:227, 2:322, 3:29, 3:156, 5:114–115, 5:248, 6:139, 6:205, 7:321, 7:329, 8:154, 8:310, 9:112, 11:290, 12:187, 14:63, 14:412, 15:160, 16:38, 16:245–247, 17:75, 17:104, 17:256–257, 18:78, 18:215–216, 18:413–415, 19:196

as a medicine, 2:227, 5:115, 5:273, 6:72, 7:316, 7:328, 8:155, 9:113, 11:290–291, 14:63, 14:410, 18:79, 18:216, 18:343, 18:411

and a punishment, 2:227, 3:166, 5:115, 5:248, 5:273, 6:205, 7:325, 8:155, 8:311, 9:113, 9:267, 11:290, 14:63, 14:410, 15:160, 16:38, 16:245–247, 17:75, 17:256–257, 18:79, 18:216, 18:410–416, 19:196

and should be fulfilled by the penitent himself, 1:65, 1:131, 2:62, 3:30, 3:166, 4:70, 4:167, 4:208, 5:114, 5:249, 9:112–113, 9:267, 11:290, 14:63, 14:411–412, 15:103, 15:162, 16:245–247, 17:104, 17:257, 18:216.

XII k

The effects are: spiritual healing, 2:207, 2:226, 3:163, 5:223, 6:72, 7:324–325, 9:119, 10:29, 11:294–295, 14:366, 15:103, 17:214, 18:361, 18:409

recovery of lost justice, 4:34–35, 4:125–126, 5:222, 5:235, 7:150, 7:295, 8:94, 8:271, 9:119, 11:292, 14:49, 14:360, 14:366, 14:399, 15:103, 15:148, 16:26, 16:201–202, 17:58, 17:67, 19:196

reconciliation with God and remission of sins committed after baptism, 1:67, 2:62, 2:144, 2:224, 2:322, 3:29, 3:168, 4:34–35, 4:125–126, 4:164, 4:166, 5:100, 5:254, 6:206, 7:146, 7:293, 8:157, 8:296, 8:313, 9:119, 9:267, 11:119, 11:164, 11:292, 13:315, 14:57, 14:360, 14:399, 15:16, 15:29, 15:69, 15:103, 15:155, 16:33, 16:224, 17:71, 17:176, 17:243–244, 17:252, 18:23, 18:74, 18:208, 18:218, 18:331, 18:402, 18:408, 19:196

remission of penalty, especially eternal, 1:67, 3:163, 3:337, 5:114, 5:248, 5:254, 6:169, 8:296, 9:119, 11:119, 11:290, 11:292, 11:302, 14:63, 14:360, 14:399, 14:410, 15:103, 15:160, 16:38, 16:247, 17:165, 17:176, 17:257–258, 18:218, 18:413, 18:417, 19:196

not however of all temporal punishment due to sin, 2:228, 3:170, 4:70, 4:167, 4:208, 5:114, 5:254, 6:169, 7:323, 8:154, 8:296, 9:115, 11:119, 11:290, 11:292, 11:302, 14:63, 14:399, 14:410–411, 15:103, 16:38, 16:206–207, 16:247, 17:165, 17:257, 18:79, 18:148, 18:218, 18:417–418, 19:196

peace and consolation of soul, 2:226, 3:163, 7:295, 8:296, 8:313, 9:114–115, 9:256, 11:295, 13:315, 17:71, 18:402, 18:409

perfect revival of lost merits and grace, 3:163, 5:234, 7:150, 8:157–158, 8:296, 9:115, 9:119, 11:292, 11:448, 14:49, 14:366, 14:399, 15:103, 15:148, 16:26, 16:201–202, 17:58, 17:67, 18:218, 19:196

liberation from censures, 1:67, 3:168, 5:254, 6:206

any and all sins can be forgiven by this sacrament, 1:67, 1:130, 2:144, 2:251, 2:322, 3:29, 3:163, 3:168, 3:337, 4:166, 5:209, 6:74, 6:206, 7:146–147, 7:295, 9:112–113, 11:164, 11:292, 14:25–26, 14:257, 14:397, 16:327–328, 17:28, 17:214, 18:331, 19:196.

The necessity of the sacrament is of divine law, 1:56, 1:65, 3:163, 3:339, 4:73, 4:164, 4:171, 7:286, 7:296, 8:296, 9:110, 11:286–290, 11:292, 11:434–435, 14:57, 14:398–399, 16:226, 18:190, 18:213–214, 18:403, 18:410–412, 19:196.

The minister of penance is exclusively a priest, 1:56, 1:66, 2:62, 2:226, 2:322, 3:15, 3:28–29, 3:167, 3:339, 4:68, 4:164, 4:207, 5:108, 5:239–240, 6:74, 6:139, 7:315, 8:156, 8:294, 9:106, 11:164, 11:291, 14:57, 14:397, 15:30, 15:97, 15:159, 16:36, 16:239, 17:71, 17:253, 18:74, 18:208

who ought to have jurisdiction, 1:56, 1:68, 2:62, 5:108, 5:239, 7:315, 8:156, 8:294–295, 9:107, 11:283, 11:291, 14:333, 14:397–398, 14:422, 15:97, 15:159, 16:36, 16:239, 17:253, 18:74, 18:208

and must strictly preserve the sacramental seal, 2:226, 3:164, 5:108–109, 5:242, 7:316, 8:307, 12:301–302, 14:408, 16:223, 17:75, 17:255, 18:79, 18:217, 18:416, 19:199.

The recipient is man, baptized and fallen, 3:30, 3:154, 9:107, 11:232, 16:224, 17:222, 18:417

even someone at the point of death, 7:311, 7:316, 18:37

or unconscious, if he manifested desire for the sacrament, 3:29, 3:337.

Confession is to be made at least once a year, 1:56, 1:69, 1:127, 2:49, 2:202, 2:320, 3:25, 4:54, 4:149, 4:200, 5:53–54, 5:338–340, 6:218, 7:311, 8:154, 8:265, 9:66, 9:263, 11:434–435, 12:292, 14:44, 14:332–333, 15:26, 15:80, 15:199, 16:65, 16:228, 16:361–362, 17:31, 17:50–51, 17:214, 18:15, 18:30, 18:59, 18:169–171, 18:343–344, 18:412, 19:266

it is advisable that it be done in Lent, 1:69, 3:25, 5:339, 8:265, 18:344, 18:412

sacrilegious confession does not satisfy the precept of the Church, 1:69, 2:227, 3:162, 3:164, 4:54, 4:149, 5:340, 8:266, 18:60, 18:172–173, 18:347.

XII l

Indulgences are not pious frauds of the faithful, 2:228, 3:169, 3:368, 4:70–71, 4:167–168, 5:250, 6:169, 11:302, 12:318, 14:414–415, 16:40, 16:255–256, 17:257–260, 18:418–420, 18:453

but the remission of temporal punishments due to (previously remitted) sins, 2:228, 3:30, 3:169, 3:368–369, 4:70–71, 4:167–168, 4:209, 5:116, 5:249–250, 6:169, 8:158, 8:313, 11:302, 13:238, 14:413, 15:31, 15:104, 15:162, 16:40, 16:207, 16:255–256, 17:75, 17:258, 18:79, 18:218, 18:420–421, 19:204

to be paid before God, 3:169, 5:114, 5:249, 11:302, 16:246–247, 16:255, 17:258

through the application of the treasury of the Church (the infinite merits of Christ and the saints), 2:228, 3:14, 3:136, 3:173, 3:175, 3:361, 3:369, 4:168, 4:209, 5:118–119, 5:249–250, 6:169, 8:158, 8:313, 11:302, 11:305–306, 13:241, 14:413–414, 15:163, 16:40, 16:90, 16:256, 17:76, 18:219, 18:420, 19:204

made available through the Roman pontiff for the universal Church, 4:70, 4:167, 5:118, 5:250, 6:169, 8:158, 8:313, 11:303–304, 11:308, 12:318, 13:172–173, 13:236, 14:126, 14:414, 15:104, 18:219, 18:420

or through a bishop for his subjects, 5:118, 5:250, 6:169, 8:158, 8:313, 14:414, 15:104, 17:258, 18:219

for reasonable causes, 3:171, 5:250, 12:318, 14:416, 18:420

they have been in use from ancient times, 3:171, 3:369, 11:303–304, 14:414, 17:258, 18:418, 18:453

and may be applied to the living or the dead, 3:174, 5:253, 5:274, 8:159, 8:220, 8:314, 11:160, 11:306–309, 14:416, 16:68, 16:373, 18:147, 18:219–220, 18:421, 19:204.

Their effect depends on the reception of baptism, freedom from excommunication, the state of grace, and the fulfilling of the prescribed work,

2:229, 3:171, 4:168, 5:118, 5:251, 8:314, 11:308, 14:414, 15:104, 15:163, 16:41, 16:257–258, 17:76, 17:258–259, 18:219–220, 19:204.

Extreme Unction

XII m

Extreme unction is a true sacrament instituted by Christ and promulgated by St. James, 1:11, 1:72, 1:130, 2:59, 2:229, 2:321, 3:31, 3:175, 3:339, 4:60, 4:71–72, 4:155, 4:169–170, 4:202, 4:209, 5:121, 5:276, 6:73, 6:139–140, 6:207, 7:331, 7:334–335, 8:160, 9:119–120, 9:267, 11:312, 11:313, 12:32, 14:63, 14:416–417, 15:31–32, 15:104, 15:170, 16:46, 16:279, 17:76, 17:260–261, 18:80, 18:187, 18:220, 18:361–362, 18:373, 18:422–423, 19:206

it is variously called *anointing of the sick*, *holy anointing*, *unction of God*, and otherwise, 1:72, 2:325, 3:30, 3:335, 5:256, 7:331, 9:119, 15:31, 16:278, 17:260, 19:111–112, 19:207

it may be repeated, 3:176, 4:73, 4:171, 4:210, 6:134, 6:207, 7:336, 8:172, 9:121, 11:315, 14:367, 14:418, 15:90, 15:149, 16:278, 17:221, 18:221, 18:424, 19:206.

The matter is the anointing with oil of the infirm, 1:72, 2:230, 3:177, 5:122, 5:256, 5:276, 6:139, 7:332, 8:160, 9:120, 9:267, 11:312–313, 14:63, 14:417, 16:278, 16:296, 17:260, 18:221, 18:422–423, 19:206.

The form is either the longer (ordinary) form or the very short (extraordinary) form, 1:72, 2:230, 3:177, 5:122–123, 5:256, 7:332, 11:313, 17:260–261, 19:206.

The effect is the grace of the Holy Spirit, 1:72, 3:176, 4:169, 6:197, 8:160, 9:119–120, 11:315, 14:417, 17:77, 18:423–424

remission of sins, 1:72, 2:62, 2:230, 2:325, 3:31, 3:177, 6:73, 6:207, 7:337, 8:161, 8:315, 9:120, 11:164–165, 11:314–315, 14:417, 15:31, 15:170, 16:47, 16:282, 17:77, 17:261, 18:220, 18:424, 19:207

spiritual health, 1:72, 2:62, 2:230, 2:325, 3:177, 4:71, 4:169, 4:209, 6:73, 6:197, 6:207, 9:121, 9:268, 11:314–315, 15:104, 15:170, 16:46, 16:279, 18:80, 18:361, 18:422

arousing of confidence in divine mercy, 1:72, 2:62, 2:325, 4:169, 4:209, 7:338, 9:121, 11:315, 18:220, 18:424

comfort of soul, 1:72, 2:62, 2:230, 2:325, 3:177, 4:71, 4:169, 4:209, 7:338, 9:121, 9:268, 11:315, 14:63, 15:104, 15:170, 16:47, 16:282, 17:77, 17:261, 18:220, 18:424

cleansing of the remains of sin, 1:72, 2:62, 2:230, 3:177, 6:140, 7:338, 8:160, 9:121, 11:228, 11:314–315, 14:417, 15:170, 16:47, 16:282, 17:261, 18:220, 18:424, 19:206

strength against the temptations of the devil, 1:72, 2:62, 2:207, 2:325, 3:177, 5:121, 5:223, 7:338, 8:160, 8:315, 9:121, 10:29, 11:312, 14:366, 14:417, 15:170, 16:47, 16:282, 17:77, 17:260–261, 18:220, 18:424, 19:206

sometimes even restoration of bodily health, 1:72, 2:62, 2:230, 2:325, 3:177, 5:121, 6:73, 6:140, 6:207, 7:339, 8:161, 8:315, 9:121, 9:268, 11:315, 14:63, 14:417, 15:104, 15:170, 16:46, 16:47, 16:279, 16:282, 17:77, 17:261, 18:80, 18:220–221, 18:361, 18:422–424, 19:207.

The minister is the priest, 1:73, 2:229, 3:31, 3:177, 4:72, 4:170, 4:209, 5:122, 5:256, 6:140, 7:337, 8:160, 9:120, 11:313, 14:63, 14:417, 15:171, 16:47, 16:282, 17:76, 18:221, 18:422, 19:206.

The subject is a man gravely ill, 1:72, 2:229, 3:30, 3:31, 3:176, 4:72, 4:169, 4:209, 5:122, 5:256, 6:139, 6:196–197, 6:207, 7:334, 8:160, 8:172–173, 8:315, 9:121, 11:315–316, 12:32, 13:282, 14:64, 14:418, 15:31, 15:89, 15:104, 15:170, 16:47, 16:279–282, 17:76, 17:260–261, 18:80, 18:221, 18:422, 19:206.

The rites customarily employed by the Church are to be observed, 1:73, 6:140, 7:333, 9:120, 13:14, 18:422.

Holy Orders

XII n

Holy orders is a true and proper sacrament, 1:11, 1:73, 1:130, 2:60, 2:230, 2:325, 3:31, 3:198, 3:335, 4:73, 4:155, 4:170, 4:202, 4:209, 5:123, 5:257, 5:276, 6:73, 6:140, 6:207, 7:345, 8:161, 8:316, 9:122, 9:268, 11:321–322, 14:64, 14:419, 15:32, 15:105, 15:171, 16:47, 16:284, 17:77, 17:262–263, 18:80, 18:187, 18:222, 18:361–362, 18:373, 18:425, 19:211

instituted by Christ, 1:73, 2:62, 2:231, 2:321, 3:199, 3:339, 5:276, 8:317, 9:122, 10:282, 11:321–322, 12:10, 14:419, 17:262–263, 18:80, 18:222, 18:425–426

consisting of major and minor orders, 1:74, 2:230, 3:199, 5:257, 6:140, 6:207, 7:346, 8:162, 9:125, 11:326, 14:422, 16:284–286, 18:222, 18:426

constituting an ecclesiastical hierarchy, 1:74, 3:200, 3:339, 6:74, 6:140, 6:210, 7:346–356, 8:161–162, 8:316, 9:125, 10:338, 11:326–327, 14:22–23, 14:422, 16:191, 16:284–286, 18:141–142, 18:223, 18:426

the episcopacy, priesthood, and diaconate are of divine institution, 2:231, 3:202, 3:339, 4:170, 4:209, 5:276, 6:140, 9:125, 11:326, 12:10

the subdiaconate is a major order, 1:74, 2:230, 3:200, 5:257, 6:207, 7:346, 8:162, 9:125, 11:326, 14:422, 16:285

the minor orders are acolyte, exorcist, lector, porter, 1:74, 2:234, 3:200, 5:257, 7:346, 8:162, 9:125, 11:326, 14:422.

The form of sacramental orders is the words (prayer) of the one ordaining for the various orders, 1:74, 3:200, 5:257, 5:276, 6:140, 7:345–346, 8:162, 9:122, 11:322, 14:420, 18:223, 18:425, 19:213.

The essential matter is the imposition of hands, 1:73, 3:199, 3:201, 5:257, 5:276, 6:207, 8:162, 9:124, 11:322, 14:116, 14:420, 18:223, 19:213

to which is added the handing over of the instruments, anointing, and other ceremonies, 1:74, 3:201, 5:257, 6:140, 7:345, 9:125, 11:322, 14:420, 18:223, 18:425, 19:213.

The end is the governance and increase of the Church, 1:73, 2:207, 2:232, 5:223, 6:133, 6:207, 9:126, 9:268, 10:29, 11:217, 11:321, 12:10, 18:141–142, 18:187, 18:361, 19:210

the perpetual conservation of the mission and power of the apostles, 3:199, 3:202, 5:124, 6:74, 6:200, 9:124, 11:322, 14:239, 14:421, 15:14, 17:263, 18:51, 18:426

the ministration of divine worship, 1:73, 2:63, 2:232, 2:325, 3:134, 5:123, 6:140, 6:207, 9:126, 9:268, 10:29, 11:321, 18:51, 18:141–142.

The effects are: communication of the Holy Spirit, 3:201, 7:354, 9:126, 11:331

the indelible sacramental character (thus it cannot be repeated for the same order), 3:317, 4:73, 4:171, 4:210, 5:222, 6:134, 6:207, 7:345, 7:360, 8:163, 9:140, 9:268, 11:218–219, 11:322, 14:367, 14:421–422, 15:90, 15:149–150, 16:27–28, 16:203–205, 17:60, 17:221, 18:68, 18:189, 18:365, 19:211

with the various powers according to each order, 1:74–75, 2:63, 2:325, 3:31, 5:223, 5:257, 6:140, 6:207, 7:359, 8:161, 9:125, 9:268, 11:322, 14:64, 15:32, 15:104, 15:171, 16:47, 16:284, 17:77, 18:189, 18:425, 19:211

in the episcopacy: succession in the place of the apostles, 3:202, 4:32, 4:123, 5:271–272, 6:137, 9:127, 12:101, 14:24, 14:116, 14:421, 15:15, 16:23, 16:24, 16:181–182, 16:184–185, 17:25, 18:50, 18:135

the power of ordaining, 2:232, 3:31, 3:202, 5:257, 5:276, 9:126, 11:322, 14:421, 15:171, 16:48, 16:287–288, 18:426, 19:210

of confirming, 2:232, 3:66, 3:336, 5:257, 5:264–265, 9:126, 11:246, 14:52, 14:422, 15:28, 15:92, 16:30, 16:215, 18:426, 19:210

of blessing the holy oils, 3:62, 3:71, 5:256, 11:245, 13:31, 13:210, 15:152, 16:30, 16:215

in the priesthood: the power of celebrating Mass and absolving sins, 1:74, 2:231, 2:325, 3:199, 3:201, 3:339, 5:123, 5:159, 5:257, 5:271–272, 6:73–74, 7:147, 7:354, 9:126, 11:164, 11:322, 13:126, 14:64, 14:420, 16:36, 16:43, 16:239, 16:263–268, 17:66, 17:71, 19:210

of conferring anointing, 1:75, 2:231, 2:325, 3:62, 3:71, 5:123, 6:73, 14:63, 14:422, 15:171, 16:47, 16:282, 19:210

of baptizing, 1:75, 2:231, 2:325, 3:200, 5:123, 6:73, 11:229–230, 11:322, 14:52, 14:370, 15:150, 16:28, 16:208, 19:210
those constituted in major orders cannot again become laymen, 3:199, 3:219, 9:130
they ought to preserve celibacy, 1:75, 2:233, 3:213–221, 5:258, 5:277–279, 8:163, 14:352
they are obliged to the divine office, 1:76, 3:252, 3:258, 5:258, 5:363, 16:358–359.

The ordinary minister is the bishop alone, 1:76, 2:232, 3:200, 3:202, 5:124, 5:257, 5:276, 6:140, 6:207, 7:356, 8:162, 8:317, 9:125, 11:322, 14:421, 15:171, 16:48, 16:287, 18:224, 18:425, 19:210.

Ordinations by heretical or schismatic bishops are illicit but valid, 9:129, 14:422, 18:426–427
Anglican orders, however, are invalid, 17:263–264.

The subject is only a baptized man, 1:76, 2:234, 5:277, 9:123, 11:232, 16:224, 17:222
examined, 1:76, 5:125, 8:162, 9:123, 11:331, 15:171, 16:48, 16:286, 17:77, 19:211
rightly chosen, 5:125, 7:343, 9:122–123, 11:325, 12:10, 14:422, 15:171, 16:48, 16:126–127, 16:286, 17:77, 19:211
initiated into the previous orders, 1:74, 9:125, 11:326, 14:422, 19:212
and instructed with a due title, 1:74–75, 7:358, 8:163, 9:123, 15:171
free from irregularities, 1:76, 5:309, 7:359, 8:163, 9:122, 11:325.

Matrimony

XII o

Matrimony is the association of a man and a woman, 1:77, 2:236, 2:326, 4:72, 4:170, 4:210, 5:128, 5:258, 5:279, 6:207, 6:216, 7:362, 8:319, 9:133, 9:268, 10:148, 11:334, 11:338, 14:65, 14:101, 14:423, 15:171, 16:48, 16:288, 17:77, 17:265, 18:225

divinely instituted, 1:77, 2:62, 2:236, 2:326, 3:233, 5:279, 7:365, 8:319, 9:133, 10:148, 11:334, 14:423, 16:295, 17:265, 18:226, 18:428

subject to no merely human laws, 1:77, 2:236, 2:239, 2:320, 3:233, 7:605, 9:133, 14:424, 16:48, 16:289–291, 18:226

signifying the union of Christ with the Church, 1:77, 2:236, 3:233, 3:237, 5:36, 5:130, 5:279, 6:141, 6:207, 7:368–369, 7:374, 8:319, 9:133, 11:334, 11:337–338, 14:423, 16:291, 18:427–428, 19:214

elevated by Christ to the dignity of a sacrament, 1:77, 2:236, 2:326, 3:233, 5:277, 7:605, 8:164, 8:319, 9:133–134, 11:290, 11:334–335, 12:158–159, 14:423, 15:171, 16:48, 16:289, 17:265, 18:81, 18:224–225, 18:428–429, 19:214

so that the contract itself, among the faithful, is itself a sacrament, 1:77, 2:236, 2:326, 3:31, 3:233, 4:60, 4:72, 4:155, 4:170, 4:202, 5:258, 5:279, 6:141, 6:207, 6:216–217, 7:368, 7:605, 8:320, 9:134, 11:334–335, 12:158–159, 14:424–425, 15:105, 16:289, 17:77, 18:224–225, 18:429, 19:214.

The form of this sacrament is the consent of the spouses, 1:77, 2:236, 2:326, 3:235, 5:258, 6:207, 7:362–363, 9:133, 11:335, 14:425, 18:225, 18:427, 19:214

expressed according to the canons of the Church, 1:78, 2:203, 2:239, 3:234, 9:134, 11:335, 14:427–430, 16:49, 16:66, 16:293, 16:364–367, 18:227–229.

The end is the corporal increase of the Church, 2:208, 2:236, 2:326, 3:31, 3:233, 4:72, 4:170, 4:210, 6:133, 6:207, 7:366–367, 9:133, 9:268, 10:29, 11:217, 11:334, 17:265, 18:187, 18:361, 18:427–429.

The effect is grace sanctifying the marital union, 1:77, 2:63, 2:236, 3:31, 3:234, 4:72, 4:170, 4:210, 5:128, 5:223, 5:258, 5:279, 6:197, 8:320, 9:134, 9:268, 11:335, 14:65, 14:366, 14:424, 15:32, 15:105, 15:172, 16:48, 16:291–293, 17:265, 18:81, 18:224–225, 18:428–429, 19:214

with a right to actual graces, 2:63, 2:236, 3:31, 3:234, 4:72, 4:170, 4:210, 8:320, 9:134, 9:268, 11:336, 11:343, 14:425, 15:171–172, 16:175, 17:59, 17:265, 19:214

and the threefold good of: children, mutual fidelity, and indivisibility, 1:77, 2:236–237, 3:31, 3:233, 4:72, 4:170, 4:210, 5:128, 5:130, 5:223, 5:258, 6:141, 6:207, 7:373–374, 9:134, 9:268, 11:336–337, 15:172, 16:48, 16:291–293, 17:77–78, 17:265, 18:225, 18:427–430, 19:215

marriage is exclusively between one man and one woman (excluding polyandry and polygamy), 6:141, 6:207, 7:370, 8:164, 9:135, 9:268, 10:148, 11:338, 12:149, 14:101, 14:423–424, 15:171, 18:225, 18:373, 18:428–431

which bond endures until the death of one of the spouses, 1:77, 2:237, 4:73, 4:171, 4:210, 5:258, 5:261, 6:141, 7:371, 8:164, 8:319, 9:134–135, 11:337, 12:363, 14:101, 14:423–424, 15:172, 17:77, 17:267, 18:225, 18:373, 18:428–431, 19:215.

Impediments to marriage cannot be established or removed by the civil power, 8:323, 11:433, 15:172, 16:48, 16:49, 16:289–291, 16:293, 18:227

but only by the Church, 1:78, 2:239, 8:164, 8:322, 9:135, 11:340–343, 14:428–429, 15:172, 16:49, 16:289–291, 16:293, 16:364, 17:54, 17:216, 17:265–266, 18:227–229, 18:434

separation of spouses may be permitted in some circumstances, 1:77, 1:80, 5:261, 7:371, 9:135, 14:424, 16:289–291, 17:54–55, 18:427–428, 19:218

but civil divorce does not affect the reality of the marriage bond, 5:261, 7:371–372, 7:605, 8:323, 9:135, 10:148, 11:433, 14:424, 15:172, 16:48, 16:289–291, 17:54–55, 17:268, 18:431, 19:217.

The Sacramentals

XII p

Sacramentals are objects or actions, related to the sacraments, by which the Church obtains (especially spiritual) effects through their impetration, 2:304, 3:307, 4:81–83, 5:163–166, 5:337, 11:165, 13:31–32, 13:85–89, 14:443, 15:174, 16:50, 16:297, 17:29, 17:80–81, 18:190–191, 19:114

sacramental objects include holy water, oils, salt, candles, incense, etc., 2:178–179, 2:304, 3:27, 3:64, 3:71, 3:307–309, 4:81–83, 5:163–166,

11:165–166, 13:85–89, 13:219–220, 13:317–318, 14:443, 15:175, 16:51, 16:299–306, 17:80–81, 19:114

sacramental actions include *blessings* (of constitutive or invocative kind), 3:27, 3:46, 3:113, 3:307–308, 4:65, 4:81–82, 5:337, 11:166, 12:266, 13:29–32, 13:85–88, 14:443, 17:53, 17:80–81, 18:191, 19:113–114

with *consecrations* being the most solemn form of blessing, 3:61, 3:71, 3:308, 3:378, 4:65, 4:82, 4:161, 11:165, 13:31, 13:316–323, 14:443, 18:191, 19:113–114

and exorcisms, 3:309, 4:81, 10:155, 11:328, 13:86–88, 13:317–318, 14:443, 17:80, 18:191, 19:113.

The minister of the sacramentals is a cleric with the requisite power for each, 3:51, 11:328, 13:31–32, 13:317, 14:445

the subjects are Catholics, catechumens, and in some instances non-Catholics, 3:61, 11:165–166, 13:317–318, 14:446.

Sacramentals are rightly employed in Mass and the prescribed administration of the sacraments, 11:165–166, 11:240, 14:446–448, 16:208–210, 16:296, 16:300, 17:80–81.

Christian Perfection

XIII a

The free acts of a man are morally good or evil, 2:248, 9:141

not indifferent, 2:152, 2:248–249, 3:322, 4:14, 4:88–90, 4:97, 4:103, 4:186.

The observance of the divine commandments is necessary for all, 1:18, 1:55, 1:126–127, 2:31, 2:44, 2:52, 2:319, 3:20, 3:35, 3:76, 4:23, 4:38–40, 4:112, 4:128–129, 4:198–200, 5:7, 5:24–25, 5:46, 6:160, 7:383–384, 9:144, 9:263, 9:269, 11:93, 11:145, 11:149, 11:360, 14:28, 14:164, 14:266, 14:279, 15:36, 15:71, 15:181, 16:127–128, 17:28, 17:179–180, 17:193, 18:144, 18:150, 19:222–223

with a lifelong struggle against the world, the flesh, and the devil, 1:28, 2:155, 2:160, 3:37, 3:84, 3:352, 4:22–23, 4:89–90, 4:109, 4:111, 4:198, 5:141–142, 6:22–23, 6:161–163, 6:172–175, 7:131, 7:188, 7:580, 9:147–148, 9:256, 10:153–157, 11:146, 11:208, 12:5–6, 13:93, 13:160, 14:106, 14:196, 14:352, 14:438–439, 15:37–38, 16:87–88, 16:214, 17:131–132, 17:275–276, 19:185.

XIII b

The good works of the just make a man better, 2:46, 2:52, 2:66, 2:73, 2:148, 2:244–245, 2:328, 3:65, 4:30, 4:83–84, 4:119–120, 4:168, 4:188, 5:85, 5:262–263, 6:176–177, 9:180, 9:269, 11:39, 11:159, 11:192, 14:47–48, 14:344–355, 14:361–362, 17:182, 18:176, 18:351, 19:149

including sufferings patiently endured with faith, 2:151, 2:246, 2:328, 3:36–37, 3:72, 3:134, 4:23, 4:84, 5:77–78, 5:142, 6:31, 6:174–177, 7:327, 9:184, 10:177–181, 10:332–333, 11:39, 11:44, 11:444–445, 12:112, 12:169, 13:272, 14:192–194, 14:355, 14:368, 15:37, 15:40, 15:88, 15:104, 16:206, 17:38, 17:275, 18:183, 19:26

and, provided they are done freely in the state of grace, 4:34, 4:56, 4:125, 4:150–151, 4:200, 4:205, 8:98, 8:100, 9:181, 11:159, 11:186, 11:192, 14:48, 14:49–50, 14:353, 14:361–362, 16:201, 16:255, 17:166–167, 17:182, 18:176, 19:149

they truly merit an increase in grace and glory, 1:84, 2:150, 5:85, 5:262–263, 5:272, 5:291, 6:174–177, 7:327, 8:97, 8:98, 9:183, 10:155, 10:332–333, 11:159, 11:186, 11:192, 12:112, 12:169, 13:272, 14:47–48, 14:49–50, 14:192–194, 14:361–362, 16:79, 16:201, 16:255, 17:166–167, 17:182, 18:176, 18:351, 19:149.

Merits that have been lost, with the recovery of the state of grace, revive perfectly at the same time as the grace, 7:149–150, 8:157–158, 8:296, 9:107–108, 11:160, 11:292, 11:448, 15:103, 18:85–86, 18:218, 18:243, 19:196.

XIII c

Personal (actual) sin is a free and knowing violation of God's law, 1:128, 2:81, 2:88, 2:248, 2:329, 3:15, 4:33, 4:124, 4:196, 5:57, 5:279–280, 5:282, 8:329, 9:142, 9:269, 10:170, 11:80, 11:205, 11:445, 14:45, 14:335, 15:16, 15:68, 15:134, 16:14, 16:127–128, 17:33, 17:36, 17:173–174, 18:85, 18:242, 19:188

divided by gravity as either mortal or venial, 1:66, 2:80, 2:249, 2:329, 3:15, 4:33, 4:124, 4:196, 5:58, 5:280–281, 6:204, 8:329, 9:142, 11:446, 14:46, 14:335, 15:16, 15:69, 15:134, 16:15, 16:128, 17:36, 17:174, 18:85, 18:243, 18:447, 19:188–192

but not passed on through the generations like original sin, 2:80, 2:329, 3:15, 6:204, 9:143.

Mortal sins are those by which God is always offended, 1:66, 1:128, 2:80, 2:249, 2:330–331, 3:161–162, 4:33, 4:124, 4:196, 6:43–44, 9:143, 9:269, 11:447, 14:336–337, 16:15, 16:128, 17:37, 17:174

and man is made an enemy of God, 1:66, 2:144, 3:114, 4:33, 4:124, 4:196, 5:57, 7:569, 8:42, 9:143, 10:174, 11:35, 11:166, 11:448, 14:262, 14:337, 15:103, 15:134, 16:175, 16:255, 17:37, 17:175, 19:188

losing the divine life of grace in the soul, 1:66, 1:128, 2:80, 2:249, 2:330, 3:15, 3:353, 4:33, 4:124, 4:196, 5:58, 5:281, 7:569, 8:329, 9:143, 10:170, 11:446, 14:49, 14:335, 15:16, 15:69, 15:134, 15:143, 16:15, 16:128–129, 17:37, 17:58, 17:158, 17:175, 18:85, 18:176, 18:243, 18:444, 19:188

made a servant of sin, 2:330, 9:146, 11:24

even a member of the devil, 3:62, 3:114, 5:30, 7:568, 9:145, 10:170, 10:250, 11:24, 17:37

and merits eternal damnation, 1:66, 1:128, 2:80, 2:250, 2:330–331, 3:62, 4:33, 4:37, 4:124, 4:126, 4:196, 4:197, 5:25, 5:58–59, 6:44, 7:149, 8:330, 9:143, 10:170, 11:80, 11:302, 11:448, 14:20, 14:46, 14:229, 14:262, 14:335, 15:16, 15:69, 15:71, 15:103, 15:134, 15:203, 16:15, 16:129, 16:327, 17:37, 17:161, 17:164, 17:176, 18:85, 18:243, 19:188

even one who is justified can sin mortally, 1:65, 1:75, 3:369, 9:145, 11:285–286, 16:361–362, 17:182.

Venial sins are less grave offenses, 1:67, 2:80, 2:250, 2:330, 3:14, 3:15, 3:51–52, 3:161–162, 3:355, 4:33, 4:124–125, 4:196–197, 5:59, 5:281, 8:330, 9:143, 9:269, 11:164–165, 13:301, 14:46, 14:336, 15:16, 15:69, 15:134, 16:15, 16:128, 16:130, 17:37, 17:164, 17:176–177, 18:86, 18:243, 18:448, 19:190

by which justifying grace is not destroyed in the soul, 1:67, 1:128, 2:80, 2:250, 2:330, 3:161, 3:355, 4:33, 4:124–125, 4:196–197, 5:59, 5:281, 8:330, 9:143, 11:164–165, 11:446, 15:16, 15:69, 16:131, 18:86, 18:244

but which nonetheless weakens the soul's charity and adherence to God, 1:67, 1:128, 2:80, 2:250, 2:330, 3:62, 4:33, 4:124–125, 4:196–197, 5:59, 5:281, 8:330, 9:145, 9:177, 11:164–165, 11:455, 14:270, 14:337, 15:135, 16:15, 16:128, 16:131, 17:38, 18:86, 18:244, 19:190

without a special privilege, they cannot be entirely avoided in this life, 3:352, 6:167–168, 7:146, 8:90–91, 9:145, 9:147, 9:177, 11:446, 13:153.

XIII d

It is possible to increase the justice received through the grace of Christ, 4:19, 4:71, 4:168, 5:85, 5:262–263, 8:97, 8:98, 8:123–124, 9:141, 9:203, 11:159, 16:26, 16:201–202, 17:17, 17:59, 17:182, 18:176, 18:351, 19:149

and the virtues ought to be increased, 2:64–65, 2:150, 2:327, 3:27, 3:31, 3:47, 3:60, 3:72, 4:54, 4:90, 4:130–131, 4:135, 9:141, 9:180, 9:203, 13:187–189, 14:47, 14:344, 18:182, 18:300

by observance of the commandments, 2:44, 2:169, 2:319, 3:20, 3:30, 4:10, 4:38–39, 4:99, 4:128–129, 4:198–200, 7:385, 9:183, 9:203.

The way of spiritual perfection is the imitation of Jesus Christ, "master and example of all sanctity," 3:35, 3:37, 3:224, 4:100, 5:71, 5:89, 6:45–47, 7:94, 9:20, 9:180, 10:33, 11:27, 11:112–113, 11:380–381, 11:437–445, 12:47–52, 13:249, 13:295, 14:19, 14:48, 14:217–218, 14:272, 14:350–355, 15:37, 15:139, 16:18, 16:147, 16:252, 17:275, 18:350, 19:148–149.

In the threefold way of the spiritual life—purgative, illuminative, and unitive, 5:354–361

there is required also the exercise of external good works, 2:66, 2:73, 2:150, 2:326, 3:34, 3:232, 5:57–58, 5:74–75, 5:85, 5:351–354, 7:541–542,

9:180–181, 11:30, 11:159, 12:32, 12:48–50, 13:159–161, 13:238, 14:50, 14:184, 14:276, 14:362, 15:17, 15:160–161, 16:125–126, 17:18, 17:28, 17:179–180, 18:150, 18:236, 19:149

and positive resistance against temptation, 1:28–29, 1:49, 1:56–58, 1:108–109, 2:160, 3:38, 4:58, 4:88, 4:151, 4:154, 4:195, 4:201, 5:84, 5:142–143, 5:327–330, 5:367–369, 6:22–23, 6:54, 6:128–130, 6:174–175, 7:455–457, 7:541–542, 7:576, 8:235–236, 9:256, 10:155, 11:20, 11:207–208, 11:408–412, 11:446–447, 12:124, 12:185, 12:202, 13:159–161, 14:38, 14:196–197, 14:405–406, 14:438–439, 15:37–38, 15:40, 15:88, 15:136, 15:158, 16:79, 16:124, 16:135, 16:237–238, 17:18, 17:74, 17:103, 17:213–214, 17:274–276, 18:162–163, 18:183, 18:247, 19:186

so that no one advances spiritually through Quietism (Molinism), 11:30, 11:192, 11:446–447, 14:438–439, 16:135, 17:213–214, 17:274–276, 19:186.

XIII e

Alone or in community, the vowed religious life, (also called the *consecrated life*) is especially commended by the Church, 2:205, 2:206, 3:221–232, 7:366, 7:452, 9:213, 11:343, 11:380–381, 12:113, 12:125–126, 17:56, 18:174, 18:348–349, 19:219

consecrated celibacy (perpetual chastity, virginity) is superior to marriage, 2:205, 3:32, 3:34, 3:215, 3:218–219, 6:141, 7:366, 9:217–218, 11:343, 11:380, 11:444, 12:51, 13:318, 14:351, 17:56

the solemn vow of chastity prevents a valid marriage, 1:80, 2:205, 3:213, 3:219, 3:340, 5:128, 5:277–278, 8:322, 9:136–137, 11:341, 11:379, 16:290, 18:227–228.

The Last Things

XIV a

Death is the separation of the human soul from the body, 3:10, 3:284, 3:345, 5:204, 6:42, 6:47, 7:86, 8:81, 8:201, 10:335, 11:115, 11:168, 14:26, 14:218, 14:258, 15:63, 16:91, 17:177, 18:45, 18:126, 19:296

it is a penalty for sin, 2:248, 2:329, 4:21, 4:111, 5:57, 5:280, 6:44–45, 6:161, 6:184, 8:62, 8:193, 9:222, 10:165, 11:39, 11:83, 11:167, 13:66, 14:12, 14:199–200, 14:258, 15:133, 16:13, 16:91, 16:121, 17:35, 18:45, 18:87, 18:117, 18:247, 19:41

the (particular) judgment of each soul follows immediately after death, 2:127, 2:129, 2:266, 3:11, 4:14, 4:75, 4:103, 4:173, 5:71, 5:207, 7:114, 8:204, 9:222, 9:276, 11:128–129, 11:454, 14:20, 14:26, 14:227–228, 14:258, 15:12, 15:65, 15:202–203, 16:67, 16:367–369, 17:29, 17:38, 17:119, 17:145, 18:87, 18:130, 18:247–248, 18:449, 19:296

before the redemption, no souls dwelt in heaven with God, 2:125, 3:10, 4:25, 4:115, 5:204–205, 6:44–49, 6:199, 7:96–98, 8:84, 11:72, 11:116, 13:250–251, 13:318–319, 14:18–19, 14:222, 15:11, 15:64, 15:140, 16:85–86, 16:142, 17:138–139, 18:47, 18:96, 18:127–128, 19:67.

Souls of the baptized who die without sin, temporal penalty, or attachment to sin, immediately attain heaven, 1:60, 2:129, 3:11, 3:192, 3:284, 3:380, 5:198, 5:207, 6:71, 6:135, 9:222, 11:116, 14:20, 14:229, 15:71, 15:204, 16:206–207, 16:256, 17:29, 17:100, 17:145, 18:87, 18:150, 18:248, 18:274, 18:450, 19:298

to enter which the state of grace is required, 2:147, 3:14, 3:84, 4:34, 4:125, 5:71, 5:198, 5:207, 7:326, 9:222, 10:170–171, 11:116, 11:119, 14:199–200, 14:229, 15:144, 16:201, 16:374, 17:145, 18:248, 18:276, 19:298.

Heaven is the place and supernatural state of perfect happiness with God, 1:118, 2:157, 2:267, 3:16, 3:380, 4:13, 4:75, 4:102–103, 4:173–174, 4:212, 5:22, 5:210, 6:21, 6:79–81, 6:150, 7:166, 8:64, 9:228, 9:255, 10:182, 11:116,

11:175–176, 11:202, 13:332, 14:27, 14:162, 14:195, 14:261–262, 15:17, 15:71, 15:204, 16:68, 16:375, 17:9, 17:100, 17:118, 17:178–179, 18:52, 18:88, 18:114, 18:274–275, 18:450, 19:298

which cannot be investigated by reason alone, 2:267, 4:103, 6:80–81, 6:156–157, 7:167, 9:228, 13:338–340, 14:100, 14:261–262, 17:178–179

nor attained in this life, 6:153, 8:46–47, 9:228, 11:201, 13:332, 13:338–340, 17:8, 18:114

it consists in the immediate, intuitive, face-to-face vision and enjoyment of God (beatific vision), 1:118, 2:146, 2:149, 3:284, 4:10, 4:13, 4:75, 4:102, 4:174, 4:212, 5:22, 5:198, 5:199, 5:210, 6:21, 6:79, 7:98, 7:167, 8:46, 8:224, 9:228, 10:147, 10:170–171, 10:182, 11:116, 11:175–176, 13:251, 13:338–340, 14:195, 14:261, 15:204, 16:68, 16:375, 17:9, 17:178–179, 18:88, 18:114, 18:250, 18:274–275, 18:450, 19:298

where faith and hope are done away with, 3:359, 8:48, 8:102, 9:228, 10:47, 11:348, 18:274, 19:314.

The vision takes place through the *lumen gloriae*—light of glory, 3:281, 3:363, 4:13, 4:102, 5:198, 7:166–167, 8:47, 10:335, 16:375, 18:114, 18:250, 18:455

and it is eternal, 3:284, 4:9–10, 4:99, 4:188, 5:72, 5:198, 6:79–81, 7:163, 8:65, 9:24–25, 9:228–229, 9:253, 10:335, 11:175, 11:455, 13:338–340, 14:26, 14:195, 14:261, 15:17, 15:71, 15:204, 16:68, 16:375, 17:9, 17:29, 17:100, 17:119, 17:178–179, 18:52, 18:88, 18:114, 18:250, 18:451, 19:298

it is the reward of good works, 1:10, 1:24, 1:132, 2:147, 2:150, 4:9–10, 4:13, 4:99, 4:102, 4:188, 4:190, 5:72, 5:75, 5:133, 5:207, 5:291, 6:5, 6:76, 7:117, 7:162, 7:326, 8:98–99, 9:23–24, 9:253, 11:128, 11:180, 14:49, 14:226–227, 14:262, 14:361–362, 15:12, 15:15, 15:65, 15:204, 16:68, 16:125–126, 16:375, 17:9, 17:99–100, 17:118, 17:178–179, 18:250, 18:450, 18:455–456

it admits of degrees, 3:285, 5:200, 7:170, 8:48, 8:225, 11:175–176, 11:202, 13:339, 14:262, 18:250, 18:450–452, 18:455–457, 19:298.

Souls of those who die in the state of grace, but with venial faults or temporal penalties not yet satisfied are detained in purgatory, 1:67, 1:118, 2:251, 2:318, 3:14, 3:51, 3:196–197, 3:317, 3:355, 4:37, 4:124–125,

4:126–128, 4:197–198, 5:22, 5:198, 5:274, 6:169, 7:96, 8:65–66, 8:312, 9:178, 9:252, 11:116, 11:119, 11:306, 14:21, 14:229, 15:15, 15:203, 16:67, 16:88, 16:206–207, 16:372–373, 17:29, 17:38, 17:164–166, 17:260, 18:87, 18:148, 18:248, 18:418, 18:447–454, 18:466, 19:299

the existence of which is certain from scripture, 2:252, 3:14, 3:52, 3:193–195, 4:37, 4:127, 4:197, 5:275–276, 7:96, 9:178, 11:119–120, 14:228, 15:15, 17:167–168, 18:452–454

consisting in a state of satisfactory penalties which the souls suffer, 2:251, 2:318, 3:14, 3:197, 3:355, 4:37, 4:70, 4:127, 4:197–198, 5:22, 5:200, 5:274, 6:51, 6:169, 8:65–66, 9:178, 9:252, 11:116, 11:119, 11:159, 11:302–303, 13:314, 14:21, 14:229, 15:15, 15:68, 15:203, 16:67, 16:88, 16:372–373, 17:38, 17:165–166, 18:87–88, 18:249, 19:299

while tormented by a mysterious fire, 2:252, 3:14, 3:194, 3:353, 5:199, 5:274, 5:275–276, 7:96, 8:66, 9:178, 11:116, 15:15, 16:373, 17:168, 18:447–448, 18:452, 18:466–467

secure in their salvation, but awaiting final deliverance into heaven, 1:118, 2:251, 3:10, 3:14, 3:197–198, 3:352, 4:37, 4:127, 5:274, 6:169, 7:96, 8:67, 9:178, 11:116, 11:119, 13:314, 14:229, 15:68, 16:88, 16:372–373, 17:165, 18:88, 18:453, 19:299–300

they are unable to merit further, 3:196–197, 4:127, 5:274, 8:99, 9:178, 11:159, 13:314, 14:412, 16:373, 18:87, 18:247–248, 18:453, 19:300

and are helped by the prayers, good acts, and alms of the living, 1:7–8, 1:24, 2:151, 2:318, 3:14, 3:112, 3:197, 3:351, 4:37, 4:127–128, 5:21, 5:274, 6:51, 7:505, 8:67, 8:174, 8:220, 8:312, 9:252, 11:119, 11:120–121, 11:159–160, 12:65, 12:113, 12:338, 13:312, 13:314, 14:25, 14:75, 14:255–256, 15:68, 15:186, 15:203, 16:68, 16:90, 16:373, 17:29, 17:80, 17:166–167, 18:14, 18:147–148, 18:250, 18:330, 18:450–453, 18:466, 19:300

by indulgences, 3:317, 3:368, 5:274, 8:67, 8:220, 8:312, 9:252, 11:160, 11:306–309, 14:255, 14:416, 15:203, 16:68, 16:373, 18:147, 18:219–220, 18:450–452, 19:204

and especially by the Sacrifice of the Mass, 1:24, 2:292, 3:84, 3:112, 3:130, 3:143, 3:148, 3:351, 5:21, 5:274, 6:51, 7:284–285, 8:67, 8:148, 8:312, 9:95–99, 9:252, 11:119, 11:120–121, 11:160, 12:65, 12:290, 13:72, 13:312, 14:25,

14:255–256, 15:68, 15:203, 16:68, 16:373, 18:147, 18:202–203, 18:330, 18:450–452.

Souls of those who die in original sin or grave personal sin (or outside the Church), 2:251, 5:71, 5:198, 5:207, 6:49–50, 8:67, 9:25, 9:222, 9:226, 11:132, 14:20, 14:262, 15:62, 15:71, 15:134, 15:203, 16:121–123, 16:129–130, 16:327, 17:37, 17:161, 17:176, 18:87, 18:136, 18:194, 18:248, 18:275, 18:450, 19:301

immediately descend into hell, 1:66, 1:118, 2:80, 2:129, 2:251, 2:267, 3:192, 3:196, 4:21, 4:37, 4:110, 4:126, 4:196, 4:197, 5:22, 5:198, 5:207, 6:49–50, 6:192, 9:222, 11:132, 14:20, 14:262, 15:12, 15:62, 15:71, 15:134, 15:203, 16:67, 16:129–130, 16:371–372, 17:9, 17:29, 17:100, 17:143–144, 17:176, 18:21, 18:52, 18:87, 18:150, 18:248, 18:275, 18:450, 18:465, 19:301

where they are punished by different punishments, 2:267, 3:196, 3:355, 4:9, 4:75, 4:173, 4:197, 4:212, 5:71–72, 5:200, 6:49, 6:81–82, 7:117–118, 8:68, 9:224, 9:227, 11:134, 14:27, 14:263–264, 15:71, 15:203, 16:67, 16:371–372, 17:37, 17:178–179, 17:251, 18:87, 18:248, 18:275, 18:450–457, 18:465, 19:301

chiefly by exclusion from the vision and enjoyment of God, 2:80, 5:71, 5:199, 6:49, 6:81, 7:118, 8:68, 8:224, 9:226, 10:153, 10:170, 11:134, 11:455, 13:251, 14:263, 15:203, 16:67, 16:371–372, 17:179, 18:87, 18:194, 18:249, 18:465, 19:301

and by pain of sense in a mysterious fire, 3:11, 3:181, 3:194, 3:198, 4:75, 4:173, 4:212, 5:22, 5:71–72, 5:199, 6:78, 6:81–82, 6:200, 7:96, 7:118, 8:68, 9:227, 10:153, 10:170, 10:335, 11:116, 11:134, 11:455, 12:92, 14:263, 15:12, 15:17, 16:371–372, 17:37, 17:179, 18:87, 18:249, 18:447, 18:450–456, 18:466, 19:301.

The punishments of hell are eternal, 1:48, 1:81, 1:128, 2:80, 2:267, 3:11, 3:16, 3:193, 3:196, 3:355, 4:9, 4:74–75, 4:173, 4:211, 4:212, 5:22, 5:71–72, 5:199, 5:210, 6:38, 6:50, 6:78, 6:81–82, 6:192, 6:200, 7:96, 7:118, 8:68, 9:227, 10:153, 10:335, 11:116, 11:132–134, 11:455, 12:88, 12:92, 14:27, 14:263–264, 15:17, 15:71, 15:203, 16:67, 16:371–372, 17:9, 17:29, 17:100, 17:144, 17:176, 17:179, 18:52, 18:87, 18:248, 18:450–452, 18:465, 19:301

but little children (in limbo) who die without baptism do not suffer the punishment of fire, 2:80, 2:248, 5:198, 5:199–200, 5:205–206, 8:63–64, 10:171–173, 11:116, 14:368, 16:153, 16:207–208, 17:171–172, 18:194, 18:372, 18:461–463

but go to a place different from that of the other damned, 2:80, 2:248, 3:10, 3:198, 4:25, 4:115, 4:193, 5:198, 5:205–206, 11:116, 14:368, 16:153, 16:207–208, 17:171–172, 18:194, 18:461–463

their fate is ultimately a mystery of divine providence, 8:42, 10:171–173, 14:368, 17:171–172.

XIV b

At the end and consummation of the world, there will be a general resurrection of all the dead, 1:20, 1:24, 1:118, 2:22, 2:126, 2:127, 2:145, 2:314, 3:6, 3:16, 3:186, 3:309, 3:316, 5:22, 5:207, 5:209–210, 6:5, 6:54, 6:76–77, 7:155, 8:70, 8:223, 9:23, 9:252, 10:335, 11:7, 11:100, 11:131, 11:167–174, 12:125, 13:34–35, 14:26, 14:258–260, 15:16, 15:70, 15:203–204, 16:91, 16:369–370, 17:29, 17:39, 17:177–178, 18:52, 18:149, 18:288, 18:331–332, 18:449–450, 19:76–78, 19:307–309

even of the damned, 1:118, 3:11, 3:16, 4:74, 4:172, 4:211, 4:212, 5:22, 5:207, 6:54, 6:77–78, 7:155, 8:71, 9:23, 11:131, 11:171–172, 14:26, 14:259–260, 15:70, 15:204, 16:91, 16:369–370, 18:149, 18:288, 18:331–332, 18:449, 19:77, 19:308

with their own proper bodies, 1:24, 1:118, 2:127, 2:145, 2:146, 3:16, 3:102, 4:7, 4:74–75, 4:172–173, 4:211, 4:212, 5:22, 5:198, 5:209, 6:5, 6:54, 6:76–77, 7:156, 8:60, 8:71, 8:223, 9:23, 10:335, 11:168, 12:125, 14:26, 14:258–260, 15:16, 15:70, 15:203–204, 16:68, 16:91, 16:374–375, 17:39, 17:178, 18:52, 18:149, 18:288, 18:331–333, 18:449–450, 19:308

miraculously reconstituted, 1:24, 2:145, 2:147, 3:102, 4:75, 4:172–173, 4:211, 4:212, 6:54, 6:76–77, 7:156, 9:24, 11:168, 12:125, 14:259–260, 16:91, 17:178, 18:332–333.

Then there will follow a general (universal) judgment, 1:24, 2:21, 2:127–129, 2:266, 2:273, 3:11, 3:186–187, 4:74–75, 4:172–173, 4:211, 5:71, 5:198, 5:207, 6:57–59, 7:114, 8:71, 8:204, 8:223, 9:23, 9:252, 10:286, 10:335,

11:129–135, 11:454–455, 12:20, 12:91, 13:268, 14:20, 14:226–227, 15:12, 15:65, 15:70, 15:202–204, 16:67, 16:87, 16:91, 16:369–370, 17:29, 17:38, 17:142–145, 18:52, 18:129, 18:149, 18:248, 18:275, 18:331, 18:449–450, 19:76–78, 19:309–311

carried out through Jesus Christ as supreme judge, 1:24, 2:21, 2:127, 2:273, 3:6, 3:11, 3:64, 3:309, 3:316, 4:74–75, 4:172–173, 4:211, 5:207, 6:57–59, 6:192, 6:200, 7:116–117, 8:71–72, 8:204, 9:23, 10:286, 11:96, 11:129, 11:131–135, 12:20, 12:186, 13:251, 13:268, 14:20, 14:204–205, 14:226–227, 15:12, 15:65, 15:202, 16:67–68, 16:87, 16:369–370, 17:29, 17:39, 17:142–145, 18:48, 18:129, 18:149, 18:275, 18:331, 18:448–450, 19:77, 19:309

who will render to each according to his works, 1:24, 2:21, 2:127–129, 3:11, 3:16, 3:193–194, 4:75, 4:172–173, 4:211, 4:212, 5:207, 5:272, 5:291, 6:5, 6:57–59, 6:76, 6:200, 7:117–118, 8:72, 9:23–24, 9:252, 10:335, 11:128–129, 11:132, 14:184, 14:226–227, 14:264, 15:12, 15:15, 15:65, 15:70, 15:202–204, 16:67, 16:91, 16:370, 17:39, 17:99–100, 17:142–145, 17:177, 18:16, 18:43, 18:48, 18:129, 18:288–289, 18:300, 18:456, 19:310

when this is done, then the Church will reign with him forever, 3:13, 6:57–59, 9:24, 10:338–339, 11:132, 12:186, 14:207, 18:450

there will never be a final restoration of the demons or the damned, 4:21, 4:74, 4:110, 4:172, 4:211, 4:212, 5:71, 5:198, 6:38, 6:50, 6:57–59, 6:78, 8:68, 9:25, 10:153, 11:132–133, 14:263–264, 15:17, 16:67, 16:371, 17:29, 17:144, 18:451.

Catholic Memory Lists

XV

Select Prayers

Every Catholic should commit the following prayers to memory:

Sign of the Cross

✠ In nomine Patris, et Filii, et Spiritus Sancti. Amen.

✠ In the name of the Father, and of the Son, and of the Holy Ghost. Amen.

Apostles' Creed

The Apostles' Creed summarizes the chief truths of the Catholic faith:

Credo in Deum Patrem omnipotentem, creatorem coeli et terrae.

I believe in God the Father Almighty, Creator of heaven and earth.

Et in Jesum Christum Filium ejus unicum, Dominum nostrum.

And in Jesus Christ, his only Son, our Lord.

Qui conceptus est de Spiritu Sancto, natus ex Maria Virgine.

Who was conceived by the Holy Ghost, born of the Virgin Mary.

Passus sub Pontio Pilato, crucifixus, mortuus, et sepultus.

Suffered under Pontius Pilate, was crucified, dead, and buried.

Descendit ad inferos; tertia die resurrexit a mortuis.

He descended into hell; the third day he rose again from the dead.

Ascendit ad coelos, sedet ad dexteram Dei Patris omnipotentis.

He ascended into heaven, sitteth at the right hand of God the Father Almighty.

Inde venturus est judicare vivos et mortuos.

From thence he shall come to judge the living and the dead.

Credo in Spiritum Sanctum.

I believe in the Holy Ghost.

Sanctam ecclesiam catholicam, sanctorum communionem.

The holy Catholic Church, the communion of saints.

Remissionem peccatorum.

The forgiveness of sins.

Carnis resurrectionem.

The resurrection of the body.

Et vitam aeternam. Amen.

And life everlasting. Amen.

Pater Noster

Pater Noster, qui es in coelis, sanctificetur nomen tuum. Adveniat regnum tuum. Fiat voluntas tua, sicut in coelo, et in terra. Panem nostrum quotidianum da nobis hodie. Et dimitte nobis debita nostra sicut et nos dimittimus debitoribus nostris. Et ne nos inducas in tentationem, sed libera nos a malo. Amen.

Our Father, who art in heaven, hallowed be thy name. Thy kingdom come. Thy will be done, on earth, as it is in heaven. Give us this day our daily bread. And forgive us our trespasses as we forgive those who trespass against us. And lead us not into temptation, but deliver us from evil. Amen.

Ave Maria

Ave Maria, gratia plena, Dominus tecum; benedicta tu in mulieribus, et benedictus fructus ventris tui, Jesus. Sancta Maria, Mater Dei, ora pro nobis peccatoribus, nunc et in hora mortis nostrae. Amen.

Hail, Mary, full of grace, the Lord is with thee; blessed art thou amongst women, and blessed is the fruit of thy womb, Jesus. Holy Mary, Mother of God, pray for us sinners, now and at the hour of our death. Amen.

Gloria Patri

Gloria Patri, et Filio, et Spiritui Sancto. Sicut erat in principio, et nunc, et semper, et in saecula saeculorum. Amen.

Glory be to the Father, and to the Son, and to the Holy Ghost, as it was in the beginning, is now, and ever shall be, world without end. Amen.

Confiteor

Confiteor Deo omnipotenti, Beatae Mariae semper Virgini, beato Michaeli archangelo, beato Joanni Baptistae, sanctis apostolis Petro et Paulo, omnibus sanctis, (et tibi, Pater,) quia peccavi nimis cogitatione, verbo et opere, mea culpa, mea culpa, mea maxima culpa. Ideo precor Beatam Mariam semper Virginem, beatum Michaelem archangelum, beatum Joannem Baptistam, sanctos apostolos Petrum et Paulum, omnes sanctos (et te, Pater) orare pro me ad Dominum Deum nostrum.

I confess to Almighty God, to Blessed Mary ever Virgin, to blessed Michael the archangel, to blessed John the Baptist, to the holy apostles Peter and Paul, to all the saints, (and to you, Father,) that I have sinned exceedingly, in thought, word, and deed, through my fault, through my fault, through my most grievous fault. Therefore, I beseech Blessed Mary ever Virgin, blessed Michael the archangel, blessed John the Baptist, the holy apostles Peter and Paul, all the saints, (and you, O Father,) to pray to the Lord our God for me.

Misereatur nostri omnipotens Deus, et, dimissis peccatis nostris, perducat nos ad vitam aeternam.

May the Almighty God have mercy on us, forgive us our sins, and bring us to everlasting life. Amen.

Indulgentiam, absolutionem, et remissionem peccatorum nostrorum, tribuat nobis omnipotens et misericors Dominus.

May the Almighty and merciful Lord grant us pardon, absolution, and remission of all our sins. Amen.

Acts of Faith

O my God! I firmly believe that thou art one God in three divine Persons, the Father, the Son, and the Holy Ghost. I believe that thy divine Son became man, and died for our sins, and that he will come to judge the living and the dead. I believe these and all the truths which the holy Catholic Church teaches, because thou hast revealed them, who canst neither deceive nor be deceived.

Act of Hope

O my God! relying on thy infinite goodness and promises, I hope to obtain pardon of my sins, the help of thy grace, and life everlasting, through the merits of Jesus Christ, my Lord and Redeemer.

Act of Charity

O my God! I love thee above all things, with my whole heart and soul, because thou art all-good and worthy of all love. I love my neighbor as myself for the love of thee. I forgive all who have injured me, and ask pardon of all whom I have injured.

Act of Contrition

O my God! I am heartily sorry for having offended thee, and I detest all my sins, because I dread the loss of heaven and the pains of hell, but most of all because they offend thee, my God, who art all-good and deserving of all my love. I firmly resolve, with the help of thy grace, to confess my sins, to do penance, and to amend my life.

Grace before Meals

Benedic, Domine, nos et haec tua dona quae de tua largitate sumus sumpturi, per Christum Dominum nostrum. Amen.

Bless us, O Lord, and these thy gifts which we are about to receive from thy bounty, through Christ our Lord. Amen.

Grace after Meals

Agimus tibi gratias, omnipotens Deus, pro universis beneficiis tuis, qui vivis et regnas in saecula saeculorum. Amen.

Fidelium animae, per misericordiam Dei, requiescant in pace. Amen.

We give thee thanks, O Almighty God, for all thy benefits, who livest and reignest forever. Amen.

May the souls of the faithful departed, through the mercy of God, rest in peace. Amen.

Eternal Rest Prayer

℣. Requiem aeternam dona eis, Domine.

℟. Et lux perpetua luceat eis.

Fidelium animae, per misericordiam Dei, requiescant in pace. Amen.

℣. Eternal rest grant unto them, O Lord.

℟. And let perpetual light shine upon them.

May the souls of the faithful departed, through the mercy of God, rest in peace. Amen.

Prayer to Guardian Angel

Angele Dei, qui custos es mei, me tibi commissum pietate superna; hodie (hac nocte) illumina, custodi, rege, et guberna. Amen.

Angel of God, my guardian dear, to whom his love commits me here; ever this day (this night) be at my side, to light and guard, to rule and guide. Amen.

Prayer to St. Michael

Sancte Michael archangele, defende nos in proelio, contra nequitiam et insidias diaboli esto praesidium. Imperet illi Deus, supplices deprecamur: tuque, Princeps militiae caelestis, Satanam aliosque spiritus malignos, qui ad perditionem animarum pervagantur in mundo, divina virtute, in infernum detrude. Amen.

Saint Michael the archangel, defend us in battle, be our protection against the wickedness and snares of the devil. May God rebuke him, we humbly pray; and do thou, O Prince of the heavenly host, by the power of God, thrust into hell Satan and all the evil spirits who wander through the world seeking the ruin of souls. Amen.

Angelus

V. Angelus Domini nuntiavit Mariae.
℟. Et concepit de Spiritu Sancto.

Ave Maria, etc.

℣. Ecce ancilla Domini,

℟. Fiat mihi secundum verbum tuum.

Ave Maria, etc.

℣. Et Verbum caro factum est,
℟. Et habitavit in nobis.
Ave Maria, etc.

℣. Ora pro nobis, sancta Dei Genitrix,
℟. Ut digni efficiamur promissionibus Christi.

Oremus.

Gratiam tuam, quaesumus, Domine, mentibus nostris infunde; ut qui, Angelo nuntiante, Christi Filii tui incarnationem cognovimus, per passionem eius et crucem ad resurrectionis gloriam perducamur. Per eumdem Christum Dominum nostrum. Amen.

℣. The angel of the Lord declared unto Mary.
℟. And she conceived of the Holy Ghost.

Hail Mary, etc.

℣. Behold the handmaid of the Lord,

℟. Be it done unto me according to thy word.

Hail Mary, etc.

℣. And the Word was made flesh,
℟. And dwelt amongst us.
Hail Mary, etc.

℣. Pray for us, O holy Mother of God,
℟. That we may be made worthy of the promises of Christ.

Let us pray.

Pour forth, we beseech thee, O Lord, thy grace into our hearts; that we, to whom the incarnation of Christ, thy Son, was made known by the message of an angel, may, by his passion and cross, be brought to the glory of his resurrection, through the same Christ our Lord. Amen.

Mysteries of the Rosary

Joyful Mysteries

1. The Annunciation of our Lady when the Son of God was conceived.
2. The Visitation of St. Elizabeth.
3. The Nativity of our Lord Jesus Christ.
4. The Presentation of our Lord in the Temple.
5. The Finding of our Lord in the Temple among the doctors.

Sorrowful Mysteries

1. The Agony of our Lord in the garden.
2. The Scourging at the pillar.
3. The Crowning with thorns.
4. The Carrying of the cross to Mount Calvary.
5. The Crucifixion and death on the cross.

Glorious Mysteries

1. The Resurrection of our Lord.
2. The Ascension into heaven.
3. The Coming of the Holy Ghost.
4. The Assumption of our Lady into heaven.
5. The Coronation of our Lady above all angels and saints.

Salve Regina

Salve Regina, Mater misericordiae; vita, dulcedo, et spes nostra, salve. Ad te clamamus exsules filii Hevae. Ad te suspiramus, gementes et flentes in hac lacrimarum valle. Eia ergo, advocata nostra, illos tuos misericordes oculos ad nos converte. Et Iesum, benedictum fructum ventris tui, nobis post hoc exsilium ostende. O clemens, o pia, o dulcis Virgo Maria.

℣. Ora pro nobis, sancta Dei Genitrix.

℟. Ut digni efficiamur promissionibus Christi.

Hail, holy Queen, Mother of mercy; our life, our sweetness, and our hope. To thee do we cry, poor banished children of Eve. To thee do we send up our sighs, mourning and weeping in this valley of tears. Turn then, most gracious advocate, thine eyes of mercy toward us. And after this our exile, show unto us the blessed fruit of thy womb, Jesus. O clement, O loving, O sweet Virgin Mary.

℣. Pray for us, O holy Mother of God.

℟. That we may be made worthy of the promises of Christ.

Prayer before Catechism

✠ In nomine Patris, et Filii, et Spiritus Sancti. Amen.

✠ In the name of the Father, and of the Son, and of the Holy Ghost. Amen.

Veni, Sancte Spiritus, reple tuorum corda fidelium, et tui amoris in eis ignem accende.

Come, O Holy Ghost! fill the hearts of thy faithful, and kindle in them the fire of thy love.

℣. Emitte Spiritum tuum et creabuntur.

℟. Et renovabis faciem terrae.

℣. Send forth thy Spirit and they shall be created.

℟. And thou shalt renew the face of the earth.

Oremus.

Let us pray.

Deus, qui corda fidelium Sancti Spiritus illustratione docuisti. Da nobis in eodem Spiritu recta sapere, et de eius semper consolatione gaudere. Per Christum Dominum nostrum. Amen.

O God, who didst instruct the hearts of the faithful by the light of the Holy Spirit, grant us in the same Spirit to be truly wise, and ever to rejoice in his consolation. Through Christ our Lord. Amen.

Actiones nostras quaesumus, Domine, aspirando praeveni, et adjuvando prosequere: ut cuncta nostra oratio et operatio a te semper incipiat, et per te caepta finiatur.

Direct, we beseech thee, O Lord, our actions by thy holy inspiration, and carry them on by thy gracious assistance, so that every prayer and work of ours may begin always from thee and by thee be happily ended. Through Christ our Lord. Amen.

Prayer after Catechism

Grant us, we beseech thee, O Lord, the help of thy grace, that what by thy instructions we know is to be done, by thy assistance we may perfectly accomplish, through Jesus Christ our Lord. Amen.

On the Church

Sacraments

The seven sacraments of the Catholic Church are:

1. Baptism
2. Confirmation
3. Holy Eucharist
4. Penance (Confession)
5. Extreme Unction (Anointing of the Sick)
6. Holy Orders
7. Matrimony

The Manner in Which a Lay Person Is to Baptize in Case of Necessity

Pour common water on the head or face of the person to be baptized, and say while pouring it: "I baptize thee, in the name of the Father, and of the Son, and of the Holy Ghost."

Twelve Apostles

1. Peter
2. James (son of Zebedee)
3. John
4. Andrew
5. Philip
6. Bartholomew
7. Matthew
8. Thomas
9. James (son of Alpheus)
10. Judas (named Thaddeus)
11. Simon (surnamed the Zealot)
12. Matthias (chosen to replace Judas Iscariot)

Four Marks of the Church

1. One
2. Holy
3. Catholic
4. Apostolic

Three Parts of the Church

1. Church Triumphant—in heaven
2. Church Suffering—in purgatory
3. Church Militant—on earth

Nine Choirs of Angels

First Hierarchy

1. Seraphim
2. Cherubim
3. Thrones

Second Hierarchy

4. Dominations
5. Virtues
6. Powers

Third Hierarchy

7. Principalities
8. Archangels
9. Angels

Commandments and Precepts

Two Great Commandments

1. Thou shalt love the Lord thy God with thy whole heart, and with thy whole soul, and with all thy mind, and with all thy strength. This is the greatest and first commandment.

2. Thou shalt love thy neighbor as thyself. This commandment is like the first, and on these two commandments depend all the law and the prophets.

Ten Commandments

1. I am the Lord thy God; thou shalt not have strange gods before me.
2. Thou shalt not take the name of the Lord thy God in vain.
3. Remember to keep holy the sabbath day.
4. Honor thy father and thy mother.
5. Thou shalt not kill.
6. Thou shalt not commit adultery.
7. Thou shalt not steal.
8. Thou shalt not bear false witness against thy neighbor.
9. Thou shalt not covet thy neighbor's wife.
10. Thou shalt not covet thy neighbor's goods.

Precepts of the Church

The precepts of the Church outline the basic obligations of Catholics:

1. To hear Mass on Sundays and holy days of obligation.
2. To fast and abstain on the days appointed.
3. To confess one's sins at least once a year.
4. To receive the Holy Eucharist at least during the Easter season.
5. To contribute to the support of the Church and her clergy.
6. To observe the marriage laws of the Church.

Sin

Seven Deadly Sins and Opposing Virtues

The seven deadly sins, also known as capital sins, are the vices or evil habits that are considered the root of all other sins. Each sin has a corresponding virtue that opposes it, helping us to combat and overcome sin. Here is a brief description of each sin, with its opposing virtue:

1. Pride: Inordinate love of one's own greatness.
   —Opposed by Humility
2. Covetousness: Inordinate desire for earthly goods.
   —Opposed by Liberality
3. Lust: Inordinate desire for illicit sexual pleasure.
   —Opposed by Chastity
4. Anger: Inordinate desire for vengeance against others.
   —Opposed by Meekness
5. Gluttony: Excessive love of food and drink.
   —Opposed by Temperance
6. Envy: Undue sorrow at another's good fortune.
   —Opposed by Brotherly Love
7. Sloth: Lethargy towards spiritual goods and duties.
   —Opposed by Diligence

Sins against the Holy Ghost

These are sins considered particularly grave, and "unforgivable" insofar as those who commit them do not repent before death. They are as follows:

1. Presumption of God's mercy: Foolish confidence that one can be saved without a good life or without keeping the commandments.

2. Despair of salvation: Distrust in the mercy and power of God, doubting that one can be saved.

3. Resisting the known truth: Arguing obstinately against known points of faith or perverting the truth of the gospel.

4. Envy of another's spiritual good: Sadness or resentment at another's advancement in virtue and grace.

5. Obstinacy in sin: Willfully persisting in wickedness despite sufficient instruction and admonition.

6. Final impenitence: Dying without confession or contrition for one's sins, remaining unrepentant.

Sins that Cry to Heaven for Vengeance

The sins that cry to heaven for vengeance are considered especially heinous, such that they invoke God's wrath due to their manifest evil. They are as follows:

1. Willful murder: The voluntary and unjust taking away of another's life.

2. The sin of Sodom: Unnatural sexual sin, particularly lustful acts with one of the same sex.

3. Oppression of the poor: Cruel and unjust dealing with the poor, widows, and orphans.

4. Defrauding laborers of their wages: Withholding or lessening the wages due to workers.

Nine Ways of Being Accessory to Another's Sin

1. By counsel.
2. By command.
3. By consent.
4. By provocation.
5. By praise or flattery.
6. By concealment.
7. By partaking.
8. By silence.
9. By defense of the ill done.

Virtues

Theological Virtues

1. Faith
2. Hope
3. Charity

Cardinal Virtues

The cardinal virtues are four in number, called "cardinal" because they are considered the "hinges" upon which all other moral virtues depend. They form the four principal good habits or personal capacities that dispose us to good actions. They are as follows:

1. Prudence: The virtue that helps us make appropriate judgments and decisions.
2. Justice: The virtue that compels us to give each person what is their due.
3. Fortitude: The virtue that strengthens us to endure hardship for the sake of the good.
4. Temperance: The virtue that helps us use pleasurable things within reason, moderating appetites and desires.

Gifts, Fruits, Beatitudes, and Counsels

GIFTS OF THE HOLY GHOST

The gifts of the Holy Ghost are seven in number, helping the faithful further respond to the promptings and inspirations of the Holy Ghost and better enabling them to do good and avoid evil. They are as follows:

1. Wisdom: A gift that moves us to direct our lives and actions to God's honor and eternal salvation.

2. Understanding: A gift enabling us to better comprehend the high mysteries of our faith.

3. Counsel: A gift that helps us receive and share greater insight and discernment in making good decisions.

4. Knowledge: A gift that helps us better know and analyze things and events in themselves.

5. Piety: A gift that instills in us a devout and zealous spirit in our service of God, parents, and superiors.

6. Fortitude: A gift that provides us with the strength to endure and overcome dangers for the sake of our faith.

7. Fear of God: A gift that curbs our rashness, keeps us from sin, and fosters obedience to God's law.

Fruits of the Holy Ghost

The fruits of the Holy Ghost are twelve in number, serving as both manifestations of the work of the Holy Ghost in the faithful, and prompting them to further reflect his love and goodness in the world. They are as follows:

1. Charity: The love of God and neighbor, which is the root of all goodness.
2. Joy: The ability to serve God with a cheerful heart.
3. Peace: The tranquility of mind that remains steadfast amidst the storms of life.
4. Patience: The capacity to endure adversities for the love of God.
5. Longanimity: An unwearied confidence in expecting good things to come.
6. Goodness: A disposition that wishes well to all.
7. Benignity: A sweet and affable manner in speech and conduct.
8. Mildness: The quality that mitigates anger and passion.
9. Faith: Fidelity in observing covenants and promises made to others.
10. Modesty: A humble demeanor that excludes arrogance and haughtiness.
11. Continency: The ability to abstain from excesses and maintain self-control.
12. Chastity: The preservation of purity in both mind and body.

Eight Beatitudes

1. Blessed are the poor in spirit, for theirs is the kingdom of heaven.
2. Blessed are the meek, for they shall possess the land.
3. Blessed are they that mourn, for they shall be comforted.
4. Blessed are they that hunger and thirst after justice, for they shall be filled.
5. Blessed are the merciful, for they shall obtain mercy.
6. Blessed are the clean of heart, for they shall see God.
7. Blessed are the peacemakers, for they shall be called the children of God.
8. Blessed are they that suffer persecution for justice' sake, for theirs is the kingdom of heaven.

Evangelical Counsels

The evangelical counsels are three specific counsels given by Jesus Christ in order to guide individuals toward higher spiritual perfection. While not mandatory for salvation, they help individuals overcome the primary obstacles to holiness. They are as follows:

1. Voluntary Poverty: Forsaking all worldly possessions or the direct control thereof, in order to follow Christ more closely.

2. Perpetual Chastity: Living in inviolable chastity (celibacy) and renouncing all sexual pleasure, for the sake of the kingdom of heaven.

3. Entire Obedience: Submitting one's personal will to a spiritual superior in all things not sinful, to better follow God's will.

Works of Mercy

The works of mercy are divided into two categories: corporal works of mercy and spiritual works of mercy.

Corporal Works of Mercy

1. To feed the hungry.
2. To give drink to the thirsty.
3. To clothe the naked.
4. To harbor the harborless (shelter the homeless).
5. To visit the sick.
6. To visit the imprisoned.
7. To bury the dead.

Spiritual Works of Mercy

1. To give counsel to the doubtful.
2. To instruct the ignorant.
3. To admonish sinners.
4. To comfort the afflicted.
5. To forgive offenses.
6. To bear patiently those who are troublesome.
7. To pray for the living and the dead.

Four Last Things

The four last things concern the end of each man's earthly life, encouraging reflection on one's actions and promoting a life of virtue and preparation for heaven. They are as follows:

1. Death: The final separation of man's body and soul, indicating the end of man's earthly life, when one is no longer able to sin or merit grace.

2. Judgment: The decree of God regarding our eternal destiny, issued immediately after our own death (particular judgment), and publicly confirmed at the end of the world (general judgment).

3. Hell: The eternal state of punishment for those who die in a state of mortal sin, deprived of the presence of God and subjected to unending torment.

4. Heaven: The eternal state of bliss for the righteous, where they enjoy the beatific vision of God and eternal happiness in his presence.

TRADIVOX

Alphabetic Index

A

Aaron, 5:267, 5:277, 7:231, 7:341, 7:344, 10:233, 10:243–244, 11:448, 13:83, 13:316, 14:420, 16:164; type of Christ, 10:43, 13:125, 16:273, 18:294

Abba, 6:65, 7:54, 7:511, 11:103, 19:85, 19:151

Abel, 1:81, 6:69, 9:52, 9:152, 10:207–208, 11:451, 12:79, 14:103, 16:176, 16:313, 16:363, 17:238, 18:91, 19:275; type of Christ, 7:85, 7:449, 8:196, 10:208–209, 10:301, 11:254, 13:125, 13:128, 14:209, 16:272

Abortion, 1:45–46, 2:191, 5:310, 6:110, 6:217, 7:367, 7:441, 11:243, 11:386, 11:401, 12:42, 12:358, 14:307, 16:273

Abraham, 1:95, 2:143, 3:283, 5:198, 5:220, 5:302, 6:171–172, 7:66, 7:174, 7:583, 8:13, 9:52, 9:115, 9:195, 10:215–221, 11:193, 12:126, 13:221, 17:161, 19:300–301; calling of, 7:385, 10:215, 10:317–318, 13:237, 14:103, 16:176, 18:91, 19:18; divine promises made to, 2:278, 7:66, 7:78, 10:215–216, 10:263, 13:170, 13:254, 14:103, 16:141, 16:177, 18:91–92, 19:13, 19:18; faith of, 6:48, 6:179, 10:218–219, 10:221, 11:208, 12:360, 13:128, 13:228, 14:104, 14:176, 16:86, 19:138, 19:142

Absolution. *See* SI.XII i

Abstinence, 1:49, 1:91, 1:103, 1:127, 2:85, 2:200–201, 2:259, 2:320, 3:25, 3:238, 3:245–251, 3:256–258, 3:334, 4:53–54, 4:87, 4:147–148, 5:46–53, 5:342–345, 5:348–349, 6:224, 7:274, 7:378, 7:382, 8:331, 8:264–265, 9:149, 9:243, 9:245, 10:150, 10:291, 11:398, 11:460, 12:204, 12:309–310, 13:143–144, 13:146–147, 13:168, 13:188–189, 13:196, 13:247, 14:43–44, 14:328–332, 15:81, 15:108, 15:124–126, 15:201, 16:64–65, 16:216, 16:228, 16:270, 16:359–360, 17:49–50, 17:90, 17:212–213, 18:15, 18:58–59, 18:168–169, 19:254

Acceptance, 3:129, 3:349, 18:50, 18:138–140, 18:321, 18:459; of divine revelation (*see* SI.I c)

Accidents, 7:441, 10:147, 11:176, 11:198, 11:268, 12:22, 13:238, 13:266; of the Eucharist (*see* SI.XII f)

Accomplice, 10:156, 11:224, 12:153, 13:156; naming in sacramental confession, 5:394, 8:307, 11:284, 14:407, 16:231; in sin, 1:45–46, 1:48, 1:51–52, 1:53–54, 2:196, 2:252–253, 2:331, 3:34, 5:70, 5:255, 5:285, 5:312–313,

6:109, 7:114, 7:465, 9:156–163, 9:246–247, 9:271, 10:164, 11:139, 11:402, 11:421, 11:428, 12:67, 12:127, 12:255, 14:197, 14:316, 14:343–344, 15:35, 15:77, 15:192, 16:350–351, 17:45, 17:272, 18:55, 18:161, 18:163, 18:415, 19:277 (*see also* SI.XV)

Accusation. *See* SI.XII i

Acedia. *See* SI.XV

Acolyte, 1:74, 2:234, 3:200, 5:257, 6:140, 6:207, 7:346, 7:349, 8:162, 9:125, 11:326–327, 11:328–329, 13:113, 13:318, 14:422

Action: Catholic, 19:98; of Christ (*see* SI.VIII a–h); civil, 6:224, 18:327; moral (*see* SI.VII d; and XIII); *in Persona Christi,* 3:171, 3:369–370, 9:93, 18:80, 18:188, 18:200, 18:223, 18:390

Act(s), 1:33, 1:51, 1:67, 7:218, 7:445, 15:39; carnal (*see* SI.XI r); of charity (*see* SI.XV); of contrition (*see* SI.XV); exterior (*see* SI.XI; and XIII); of faith (*see* SI.XV); of hope (*see* SI.XV); of penance necessary, 1:65–66, 1:90, 1:92, 1:131, 2:224, 2:299, 3:169–172, 5:88, 5:112, 5:115–117, 5:248–254, 6:205, 7:288–290, 8:154–155, 8:310–311, 9:108, 10:213, 10:272–275, 11:19, 11:86, 11:113, 12:20, 12:380, 13:36, 13:158–159, 14:57–58, 14:399, 15:101, 16:360, 18:23, 18:30, 18:75, 18:77, 18:190, 18:214, 18:343, 18:402–404

Adam, 4:20, 4:109, 4:196, 8:60–62, 8:192–194, 10:145, 10:201, 12:179, 13:55, 13:219, 15:132, 18:44–45, 18:90–91, 18:115–117, 18:278; Christ as new, 7:79, 10:25–26, 10:175, 11:84, 11:88, 11:128, 12:37, 13:56, 13:324, 14:201, 14:219, 14:444; sin of (*see* SI.VII c)

Adherence, 2:116, 11:409, 11:446, 12:290, 13:147; of faith to revelation (*see* SI.I c; and XI b)

Adoption, 1:18, 1:27, 1:60, 5:82, 5:222, 6:146, 7:54, 7:77, 7:521–523, 9:13, 9:265, 10:232, 10:319, 11:69, 12:73, 12:342, 13:242, 14:13, 14:204, 16:85, 16:205, 18:62, 18:67, 18:181, 18:370, 18:435, 19:85

Adoration, 1:33, 1:99, 2:222, 2:333–334, 3:121–123, 3:280–281, 3:301–306, 3:357, 4:39, 4:129, 5:13, 5:26–30, 5:98, 5:152–153, 5:162–163, 5:295, 5:331–336, 6:27, 6:63, 6:206, 6:219–220, 7:259, 7:266, 7:395, 8:85, 8:245, 9:189, 9:266, 10:101, 10:336, 11:12–13, 11:362–363, 12:72, 12:230, 12:363–364, 13:85, 13:127, 13:215–216, 13:271, 14:31, 14:382, 14:393, 15:51, 15:73, 15:118, 16:266, 17:68, 17:69, 17:229, 17:280, 18:25, 18:53, 18:152–154, 18:207, 18:268, 18:334, 19:177, 19:228, 19:324

Adultery, 1:9, 1:47–48, 1:53–54, 1:78, 1:126, 2:45, 2:191–192, 2:197, 3:23, 3:218–220, 4:48, 4:141, 4:198, 5:38–39, 5:246, 5:261, 5:288, 5:310, 6:114–117, 6:193, 6:202–203, 6:217, 7:371–372, 7:449, 8:254, 9:49, 9:261, 11:337–338, 11:412, 12:42, 13:192, 13:200, 14:310, 14:425–426, 15:23, 15:53, 15:77,

15:120, 15:182, 16:61–62, 16:227, 16:346–349, 17:46, 17:89, 17:106, 17:204, 17:268, 18:15, 18:54–55, 18:162, 18:430–433, 19:215, 19:224, 19:279

Adults, baptism of, 3:53–54, 3:56, 3:59–65, 5:224, 7:208, 8:139, 8:274–275, 10:60, 11:165, 11:232–233, 12:12, 12:201–202, 16:211, 17:223, 18:193–194, 18:369, 18:438, 19:127

Advent, 1:79, 2:51, 2:298–299, 2:320, 3:238–239, 3:267, 4:86, 7:44, 8:264, 8:267, 10:44, 11:342, 12:259, 12:301, 13:146–162, 15:108–109, 15:124, 19:179, 19:249; of Christ in history (*see* SI.VIII g; and VIII h); of grace in the soul (*see* SI.X; and XII c); of the last judgment (*see* SI.XIV b)

Advocate, 1:33, 1:121, 7:114, 7:392, 11:215, 11:367, 13:153, 13:157; Christ before the Father as, 6:142–143, 7:110, 7:510, 8:203, 10:35, 11:56, 11:127, 11:464, 13:171, 13:252, 14:225, 19:75; Holy Spirit (Paraclete) (*see* SI.V d)

Affliction, 2:31, 5:142, 5:203–204, 6:31, 6:175–176, 7:597, 8:37, 8:78, 8:236, 10:179, 10:213, 11:44, 11:202, 11:208–209, 12:68, 12:357, 13:172, 13:235, 14:355, 18:83, 18:112, 18:234, 18:270, 18:416

Africans, 10:212, 11:242, 11:345, 12:42, 12:188–190, 12:350–351, 13:178

Age, 1:76, 1:78, 6:77, 10:187, 10:340, 11:168, 11:227, 12:68, 13:93, 13:194; advanced in (*see* Elderly); for confirmation, 2:217, 3:68, 4:62, 4:157, 5:227, 6:215, 7:236, 8:140, 8:280, 11:246, 11:250, 18:69, 18:196; of discretion necessary for penance, 1:66, 1:91, 3:25–26, 4:54, 4:149, 5:54, 5:344–345, 6:218, 7:311, 8:265, 11:287, 11:434, 12:292, 14:44, 14:333, 15:80, 15:199, 16:65, 16:361, 16:362, 17:51, 17:214, 18:32, 18:59, 18:169, 18:343–345, 18:412; for receiving Eucharist, 1:71, 3:26, 3:85, 3:120, 4:55, 4:149–150, 5:54, 5:233, 5:340, 6:218, 7:276–277, 8:144–145, 8:266, 8:289, 9:268, 11:265, 11:435, 12:292, 14:44, 14:333, 15:95, 15:199–200, 17:215, 18:29–36, 18:60, 18:170–171, 18:343–345, 19:175

Agnosticism, 16:323

Albigensianism, 12:281–282, 12:285–286, 12:292, 13:242

Almsgiving, 1:66, 1:82–83, 2:229, 2:238, 2:251, 2:255, 2:326, 3:34, 3:166, 3:250, 3:351, 4:71, 4:83, 4:168, 5:74–75, 5:115, 5:117, 5:351–353, 6:51, 6:61, 6:99, 6:139, 6:167, 6:205, 7:466–467, 7:577, 8:100, 8:311–312, 9:175, 9:193–196, 9:273–274, 10:314, 10:341, 11:29, 11:355–357, 12:63, 12:209–215, 13:118, 13:160–161, 14:255, 14:274, 14:362, 15:35, 15:104, 15:160, 15:203, 16:38, 16:248, 16:257, 17:38, 17:87, 17:257, 17:272, 18:147, 18:312–313, 18:452, 19:193

Altar, 1:74, 1:88, 1:92, 1:95–97, 3:129–130, 3:135, 7:342, 7:444, 10:219, 10:268, 11:190, 11:237, 13:22–23, 13:83, 13:210–211,

17:264, 19:178, 19:240; blessing of the, 2:307, 3:307, 13:83, 13:319–322, 14:444, 16:179, 16:296, 16:301; Christ's cross as, 2:124, 3:127, 5:377, 5:384, 7:284, 11:305, 13:68, 13:71, 13:211, 14:203, 16:151, 16:266, 16:274, 17:241, 18:386, 18:393, 18:419; most Holy Sacrament of the, 1:11, 1:31, 1:69–71, 1:131, 2:294, 2:323, 5:95, 5:274, 5:374, 5:383, 7:360, 8:147, 8:161, 8:234, 8:290, 9:95, 11:126, 11:254, 13:268, 14:378, 14:396, 15:29, 15:168–169, 16:265–268, 16:274–275, 16:300, 17:66, 17:134, 18:384–385, 18:391, 19:168, 19:178, 19:240

Ambo. *See* Pulpit

Amen, 2:285, 5:375–377; meaning of, 1:28, 2:22, 2:149, 4:75, 4:174, 4:212, 5:143, 6:177, 7:601, 8:237, 9:32, 9:256, 10:248, 11:177, 11:209–210, 13:43, 13:105, 13:137, 14:68, 14:265, 14:439, 15:178, 16:80, 18:150, 18:183, 19:181

Analogy of faith, 8:338. *See also* Typology

Angel(s), 4:20–21, 4:110, 7:61, 7:392, 8:86, 13:237, 15:131, 15:132; Gabriel, 1:4, 1:29, 1:31, 1:121, 2:32, 2:163, 2:300, 2:317, 3:19, 3:332, 3:268, 3:285, 4:23, 4:59, 4:113, 4:154, 5:143–145, 5:369, 6:180, 6:183, 8:195, 8:237–238, 9:33, 9:257, 10:295, 11:10–11, 11:210–213, 12:219, 13:171, 13:228–229, 13:279, 14:440, 15:86, 15:138, 16:17, 16:80, 16:115, 16:142, 16:301, 17:16, 17:87, 17:188–189, 18:66, 18:95, 18:184, 18:271, 19:38, 19:55, 19:236; in general (*see* SI.VI c; and VII a); guardian, 1:122, 2:33, 2:117–118, 2:317, 2:335, 3:273, 3:281, 3:356, 3:364, 4:88, 4:91, 4:110, 4:221–222, 5:153–155, 5:395, 7:516–517, 8:58–59, 8:191, 10:161–162, 11:128, 11:195, 12:182, 13:143, 13:299–301, 14:10, 14:75, 14:76, 14:195, 15:54, 15:131, 15:132, 16:92, 16:109, 16:115, 16:117, 16:328, 17:27, 17:34, 17:280, 18:44, 18:113, 18:183, 19:37–38, 19:321; nine choirs of (*see* SI.XV); sin of, 2:118, 2:180, 3:283–284, 4:21, 4:110, 5:59–60, 5:81, 6:27, 6:55, 7:62, 8:57, 8:190, 10:153–154, 10:156, 13:291, 13:298, 13:338, 14:10, 15:132, 16:118, 16:121, 17:27, 17:33–34, 17:131, 17:174, 18:44, 18:112, 18:270–272, 19:36

Anger, 1:44, 1:109, 2:259–260, 15:70, 15:136; as a capital sin (*see* SI.XV); passion of, 2:84, 2:244, 5:36, 5:59, 5:65–66, 5:247, 5:289, 5:301, 6:111–114, 11:22, 13:91

Anglican, 11:300, 12:401; orders not valid, 9:129–130, 17:221, 17:263–264; sect, 5:216–217, 5:376–377, 8:21, 12:322–323, 13:232, 13:329, 17:158, 17:212–213

Animals, 2:123, 10:30, 11:5; creation of, 10:110–134, 11:104, 14:102, 16:99, 16:101–102, 16:114, 19:16; man and stewardship of, 6:32, 6:107–108, 7:62, 10:135, 10:141–146, 16:119, 16:140, 19:275; sacrifice of, 3:129,

7:281, 8:9, 8:147, 10:207, 10:234, 11:52, 13:126, 13:264, 14:103, 14:209, 16:140–141, 16:272–273, 16:317, 17:238–239, 19:93

Anniversaries, 3:190–191, 11:238, 13:312; in Catholic liturgy (*see* Feasts)

Annunciation, 1:134, 3:290, 17:87, 17:281; feast of, 2:300, 3:268, 4:23, 4:86, 4:113, 4:192, 13:227–230, 15:106, 15:123, 15:138, 16:142–143, 19:57; by Gabriel to Mary (*see* SI.VIII b; and VIII h)

Anointing: in baptism (*see* SI.XII c); in confirmation (*see* SI.XII e); in holy orders (*see* SI.XII n); of the sick (*see* SI.XII m); symbolic meaning of, 2:313–314, 3:71, 5:15, 5:123, 5:276, 6:68, 7:68–70, 9:87–88, 11:105–106, 11:241–242, 11:244–245, 11:312–313, 13:73, 15:153, 16:30, 16:215, 16:278–279, 18:375

Antichrist, 1:104, 6:209, 7:117, 8:69–70, 11:129, 11:130–131, 14:284, 17:148, 18:450, 19:306

Apocrypha, 5:193

Apollinarism, 8:49, 12:182

Apostasy, 1:25, 1:55, 2:141, 3:228, 4:41, 4:133, 5:297, 8:104, 8:220–221, 9:262, 10:202, 11:93, 11:130, 11:148, 12:7, 12:95, 12:179–180, 12:318, 13:192, 13:215, 14:129, 15:183, 16:338, 17:258, 18:233–234

Apostle(s), 1:18–19, 1:23, 1:116, 2:142, 2:315, 7:533, 8:206, 8:210, 8:317, 10:27, 10:63, 12:6–34, 13:14, 13:256–257; authoritative teaching of (*see* SI.I f; II a; II c–d; II e–f; III a; and III e–f); choosing and calling of, 3:203–204, 3:216, 11:21, 11:22, 11:26–27, 12:6–7, 12:11–12, 14:110–111, 15:110, 18:95, 18:302; holy orders and (*see* SI.II e; and XII n); successors of (*see* SI.I f; II e; III a; and XII n)

Apostolate, 12:402

Apostolic, 1:22–23, 15:14, 15:147; mark of the Church (*see* SI.II a); succession necessary, 1:23, 2:142, 2:315, 3:155, 3:204–205, 3:328, 3:371–372, 6:69, 7:139, 9:129–130, 9:132, 11:154, 11:158, 12:101, 13:331, 14:139, 14:239, 14:243, 14:397, 14:421, 16:182, 16:195, 16:198, 18:49–50, 18:106, 18:133–135, 18:137, 18:257, 18:305, 19:119–120

Arianism, 5:193–194, 5:216, 6:34, 6:35, 6:39, 6:141, 8:221, 9:186, 11:100, 12:172–175, 12:177, 12:187, 13:328, 13:331, 14:118–119

Ark of the Covenant, 3:298, 3:366, 5:28–29, 7:272, 7:597, 8:243, 10:240, 10:247–248, 10:261–262, 10:268–269, 13:7, 13:85, 14:107, 14:392; as a Marian symbol, 4:219, 4:223, 13:157, 13:228, 13:280

Arms, 7:338, 10:237, 10:248, 10:260–261; and legitimate defense, 5:308–309, 8:252–253, 11:401–402, 12:259–261, 12:271–273, 12:313–314, 13:285–286, 13:289–290, 14:307, 18:342, 19:275. *See also* SI.XI q

Art, 7:395, 7:503, 13:13–14; sacred, 3:297, 3:365, 12:46–47,

13:25–27, 14:127, 14:288–289 (*see also* SI.XI e)

Ascension, 1:98, 1:100, 1:135, 2:132, 12:211, 13:242, 13:250; of Christ (*see* SI.VIII h); feast of, 1:87, 2:297, 3:262, 3:271, 4:26, 4:86, 4:116, 4:193, 5:19, 5:340, 5:387, 12:241, 12:302, 13:219, 13:252–253, 14:326, 15:106, 15:123, 15:125, 17:49, 17:89, 17:140, 17:146, 18:167, 19:73

Asceticism, 12:48–50, 12:185, 12:246–247, 12:310–312, 17:49, 17:68, 17:274; spiritual growth and, 6:129–130, 7:457, 12:60, 15:37. *See also* Penance

Assent to Church teaching, 2:133–134, 3:316–318, 3:322, 3:373, 5:183, 7:45, 8:103–108, 8:337–338, 9:10, 11:89–94, 11:148, 14:5–6, 14:73, 14:168–169, 14:248, 14:251–252, 14:345, 16:55, 16:94, 16:321, 16:323, 17:12, 17:84, 17:90–92, 17:121–122, 17:159, 18:107–108, 18:255, 18:321, 18:458–459

Assistance, 1:105, 15:82; of angels (*see* angels); of deacons, 5:257, 8:135, 8:144, 10:160, 11:270, 11:304, 11:330–332, 12:10–11, 12:64, 12:103, 13:117, 13:219–220, 14:422, 16:285

Assumption, 1:135, 3:291, 8:70, 13:242, 17:49, 17:89, 17:210; feast of, 2:300, 3:272, 4:86, 11:216, 12:258, 13:91, 13:162, 13:279–282, 14:326, 15:200, 18:18, 18:59, 18:167–168, 19:126; privilege of Mary's (*see* SI.VIII k)

Astrology, 6:26–28, 6:84–85, 13:339, 19:229

Athanasian Creed. *See* Creed

Atheism, 2:114, 3:379, 8:5, 10:69–70, 11:153, 11:430, 12:374, 12:398, 13:10, 13:18, 14:339, 16:323

Atonement, 4:37, 4:127, 6:47, 6:205, 7:115, 7:323, 10:168, 10:174–175, 10:344–345, 11:13, 11:80–83, 11:96, 11:112, 11:119, 12:125–129, 12:243–244, 13:130, 13:170, 14:21, 14:396, 15:88, 16:274–275, 17:17, 18:329, 19:26

Attribute, divine. *See* SI.IV b

Attrition. *See* SI.IX b; and XII i

Author of scripture. *See* SI.IV c; and V d

Authority, 1:25, 2:186, 3:239–240, 7:28, 11:190, 11:336–338, 15:146, 15:191; of the apostles (*see* SI.I f; II a; II c–d; and II e–f); of the Church (*see* SI.II); of Church councils (*see* SI.II d); of Church fathers (*see* SI.I e–f); of clergy (*see* SI.XI m; and XII n); of scripture (*see* SI.I f); of the state (*see* SI.XI g); of the supreme pontiff (*see* SI.III); of tradition (*see* SI.I e–f)

Autonomy, mistaken notions of, 11:180–181, 11:185, 12:190, 13:199

Avarice, 6:128, 6:202; as a capital sin (*see* SI.XV)

Ave Maria. See SI.XV

Azymus (unleavened bread), Eucharistic matter. *See* SI.XII f

B

Babel, Tower of, 10:214–215, 13:111, 13:256, 14:103

Babylon, 3:211, 5:376, 7:68, 7:139, 10:286, 10:318, 12:159, 13:51, 13:221, 14:107–108, 18:94

Balsam, oil, 2:214, 2:215, 6:136, 7:230–231, 8:269, 8:278, 9:86, 11:244–245, 14:375, 15:92, 15:152, 17:227, 18:195, 18:373. *See also* Chrism

Banns, marriage, 1:79, 3:234, 6:217, 11:340–341, 13:111, 17:52–53, 18:229

Baptism. *See* SI.XII c–d

Baptistry, 11:236–237, 16:209

Battle, spiritual, 2:30, 2:114, 2:301, 7:229, 10:153–155, 10:163, 11:246–247, 11:253, 11:319–320, 11:323–324, 12:120, 12:169–170, 12:185, 12:316–317, 13:14, 13:235, 13:298, 15:37–38, 16:79, 16:88–89, 16:115, 16:124–125, 17:160, 19:164, 19:201. *See also* War

Beatific vision. *See* SI.XIV a

Beatitude, eternal. *See* SI.XIV a

Beatitudes. *See* SI.XV

Beauty, 11:172–173, 11:261–262, 13:14, 13:39, 13:45; artistic, 10:163, 12:46, 12:204, 13:13–14, 13:64; divine, 6:29, 8:64, 10:151, 11:36, 11:175, 11:266, 12:361, 13:153, 13:337–339, 16:103, 16:107, 16:115, 16:375, 17:118, 17:179, 18:255, 19:16; natural, 6:28–29, 7:167, 8:73, 10:133–134, 10:145, 10:151, 11:168, 11:214, 12:143, 12:262, 13:235–236, 13:280–281, 13:287, 13:325, 13:333–338, 16:132, 18:90, 18:350

Belief, 1:99, 1:110, 3:73, 3:352, 7:125, 14:165; as merely natural assent, 3:196, 5:183, 8:5–8, 10:65–66, 10:192, 11:90–91, 11:424–432, 13:239–240, 14:168, 17:120–121, 18:103, 18:252–254, 18:437 (*see also* SI.I d); as supernatural response to revelation (*see* SI.I c; IX b; and XI b)

Benedictines, 3:228, 12:202–208, 12:221–224, 12:230–231, 12:238–239, 12:245–246, 13:197, 13:269, 14:120–121

Benediction. *See* Blessing

Benevolence, 7:434; of God, 8:231, 18:115; virtue of, 11:436

Benignity, as a fruit of the Holy Ghost. *See* SI.XV

Berengarianism, 5:194, 5:216, 6:138, 7:258, 12:256–257, 12:261, 12:263, 13:85, 13:127

Bestiality, 5:310–311, 6:217–218, 7:450–451

Bible. *See* SI.I f

Bigamy, 2:191–192, 5:279, 7:371, 8:164, 12:319

Birth of Christ, 1:97, 1:134, 7:80; feast of, 2:199, 2:295, 3:257, 3:266–267, 4:86–87, 4:113, 4:192, 5:17, 5:304, 5:348, 5:350, 5:388, 10:338, 12:201, 12:230, 12:342, 13:36–37, 13:143, 13:163–169, 14:326, 14:329–330, 16:143, 18:59, 18:167, 19:57, 19:97, 19:249; in history (*see* SI.VIII h)

Bishop, 1:22–23, 3:27, 3:202, 7:202, 8:215–218, 18:50–51, 18:80, 18:135, 18:316–317; office of (*see* SI.II d–f; and XII n); of Rome (*see* SI.III a–i)

Blasphemy, 1:39–40, 2:44, 2:157, 2:182, 2:260, 3:21, 3:87, 3:289, 3:344, 3:361–362, 4:45, 4:136–137, 4:218–219, 5:190, 5:246, 5:288, 6:91, 6:193, 6:201, 7:414, 8:246, 9:166–167, 10:73, 10:291, 11:376–378, 11:398, 11:424, 12:297, 12:375, 13:85, 14:33, 14:67, 14:291–292, 14:303–304, 15:75, 15:188, 16:59, 16:337–338, 17:43, 18:155, 18:439, 18:454, 19:238–239, 19:241

Blessing, 1:3, 1:75, 3:307, 13:29–32, 17:81; after meals, 1:6–7, 2:336, 4:8, 4:97, 4:186, 5:156, 11:98, 11:188, 12:54, 12:121, 14:77, 14:354, 15:55, 15:88, 15:121, 16:96, 17:86, 17:108, 17:278, 19:157, 19:160, 19:322 (*see also* SI.XV); before meals, 1:6–7, 2:336, 4:8, 4:97, 4:185, 5:156, 11:98, 11:188, 12:54, 12:121, 14:77, 14:354, 15:55, 15:88, 15:121, 16:96, 17:86, 17:107, 17:278, 19:157, 19:160, 19:322, (*see also* SI.XV); nature of (*see* SI.XII p); nuptial, 2:238–239, 3:236–239, 4:72, 4:170, 4:210, 5:260, 7:373, 8:267, 8:320, 11:339, 11:343–344, 14:428, 15:173, 16:66, 16:366, 17:53, 19:213; official (*see* SI.XII p)

Blindness: disability, 10:124, 10:313–314, 10:316, 11:39–41, 12:11–12, 12:16, 16:156, 16:209; of sin, 3:163, 6:81, 6:153, 6:213, 7:454, 9:151, 10:61, 11:13, 11:25, 11:141, 11:450, 12:16, 13:340, 14:207, 14:392, 16:236, 18:163, 18:272, 18:439

Blood: baptism of, 2:210, 2:212, 3:56, 5:225, 8:135, 8:276, 11:146, 11:229, 13:169, 14:373, 15:150–151, 16:29, 16:212, 17:61–62, 17:225–226, 18:194, 18:372, 19:135–136; Eucharistic, of Christ (*see* SI.XII f–g); "of martyrs, seed of Christians," 10:332, 12:10, 12:232, 12:258, 12:303, 12:400, 12:403, 13:25, 14:117

Body of Christ, 1:21, 3:73, 8:81, 11:77–78, 11:127, 18:149, 19:67; Church as (*see* SI.II a); Eucharistic, of Christ (*see* SI.XII f–g)

Body, human, 1:56–58, 11:127, 17:118; creation of (*see* SI.VI b; VI d; and VII b); respect for, 1:45, 1:54, 2:207–208, 5:8, 6:32, 7:453, 8:245, 9:49, 9:261, 10:136–137, 11:107, 11:408, 13:32, 14:289–290, 16:57, 16:132, 16:330–331, 16:333, 16:374, 19:303; resurrection of (*see* SI.XIV b); temple of the Holy Ghost, 3:60, 3:70, 3:292–293, 4:43, 4:135, 7:123, 7:443, 7:453, 8:245, 9:151, 10:137, 11:240, 11:369, 11:408, 11:411, 12:57, 13:84, 13:260, 13:322, 14:289–290, 19:85–86, 19:134–135, 19:303; unity of soul and (*see* SI.VI d; and VII b)

Bond, marital. *See* SI.XII o

Books, canonical. *See* SI.I f

Bread, 1:28, 2:31, 2:158, 3:18, 7:554, 8:141–144, 8:233–234; miracle of multiplying, 3:82, 11:34; Eucharistic (*see* SI.XII f)

Breviary. *See* Divine office

Brother(s), 5:344, 5:351–353, 6:40–41, 7:443, 7:548, 8:89, 8:231, 12:295, 12:366–367, 12:399–400, 13:120, 14:275, 18:67, 18:91, 18:181, 18:185, 19:259–260

Burial, 2:294, 2:306, 4:55, 4:87, 5:54, 5:195, 5:298, 5:308, 5:382–385, 7:88, 7:95, 8:221, 8:253, 8:265, 9:197, 9:274, 10:168, 11:71, 11:404–405, 12:65–66, 12:294–295, 13:32–35, 14:273, 16:365, 18:36, 18:84, 18:237, 18:282, 18:329, 18:343, 19:115, 19:302–303

Business, 3:266, 5:147, 5:175–177, 5:361, 5:364, 6:59, 6:104, 6:224, 7:420, 7:467, 10:54, 14:314, 16:206, 17:187, 18:33, 18:54, 18:155, 18:166, 18:341, 19:91

C

Cadaver. *See* Corpse

Call: to chastity universal (*see* SI.XI r); to enter Catholic Church universal (*see* SI.I c; and II b); to holiness universal (*see* SI.XIII); to holy orders (*see* Vocation)

Calumny, 1:51, 2:195–196, 4:49, 4:143, 5:318, 5:326–327, 5:391, 6:193, 6:202, 8:258–259, 10:199, 11:428–429, 12:69–70, 13:302, 14:40, 14:319, 15:78, 15:195, 16:223, 16:353, 17:47, 17:203, 17:206–207, 18:164, 18:242, 18:411, 19:293

Canon, 2:289, 3:242, 13:83; of Mass, 2:276–282, 3:147, 5:380–381, 6:206, 8:149, 8:150, 12:107, 13:85, 13:123–131, 16:265–267, 19:168–170, 19:181–184; of Scripture (*see* SI.I f)

Canonization. *See* Saint(s)

Capital. *See* Money

Capital punishment. *See* Execution

Capital (Deadly) sins. *See* SI.XV

Cardinal: office of, 5:250, 8:27, 16:287, 19:99–100; virtues (*see* SI.XV)

Cataphrygians, liturgical abuse of, 6:138

Catechesis, 19:8; nature and purpose of, 5:5–6, 5:181–182, 6:191, 6:199, 6:213, 7:35–44, 8:165–171, 10:14–61, 18:27–28, 18:172, 18:346; use of catechisms in, 5:6, 5:54, 5:181–182, 7:35–44, 8:166, 8:183, 10:58–61, 14:97

Catechism, Roman, 7:38–44, 7:607, 8:146, 19:7, 19:138

Catechumenate, 10:60–61

Catechumen(s), 1:98, 2:297, 2:300, 3:59–65, 3:124, 5:378, 5:387, 7:209, 8:17, 8:104, 8:123, 10:60–61, 11:234–239, 13:101–102, 13:112, 13:254, 16:212, 16:296, 18:317, 18:366, 19:108

Cathedra, speaking *ex*. See SI.III f

Catholic: Church (*see* SI.II); literal meaning of, 2:21, 2:138, 4:31, 4:121, 5:183, 6:68, 8:19, 8:210, 9:21, 9:252, 12:235, 14:24, 15:14, 16:25, 16:193, 17:157, 18:49, 18:132, 19:119; mark of the Church (*see* SI.II a); name of the true Christian, 1:17–18, 1:25, 1:110, 4:29, 4:119, 9:249, 12:235, 18:40, 18:101, 18:251

Celibacy, 1:75–76, 2:205, 2:233–234, 3:213–221, 3:340, 5:56, 5:258, 5:277–279, 5:392–393, 7:413, 7:452, 8:162–163, 8:164–165, 11:329–330, 11:380, 13:240, 14:351, 19:219–221

Cemetery, 6:224, 11:85–86, 11:364, 13:32–35, 14:444, 16:154, 19:240, 19:304

Censure, 2:138, 3:379, 5:190, 5:239, 5:255, 5:309, 6:221, 8:162–163, 8:315, 9:68, 12:197, 12:205, 12:376, 14:370, 18:140, 18:143, 18:321. *See also* Excommunication; and Interdict

Ceremonies, 2:155, 2:304–307, 13:6–9, 14:291, 14:446–450, 19:110–112: of Mass, 1:97–101, 2:282–295, 3:133–145, 5:181, 5:228, 5:371–388, 7:285, 8:150, 11:366–367, 13:94–140, 14:387–388, 17:70–71, 18:58, 18:167, 19:121, 19:170 (*see also* SI.XII h); of sacraments, 1:61, 1:64, 1:85–87, 2:213–214, 2:217, 3:57–65, 3:71–72, 3:317, 3:341, 4:60, 4:155, 5:194, 5:220–221, 5:260, 5:371–372, 7:181, 8:279, 8:307–308, 9:79–80, 9:265, 11:220–221, 11:333, 13:11, 14:367, 14:371–372, 14:375–376, 15:27, 15:92, 17:80, 17:92–93, 18:69, 18:192, 18:374, 19:112 (*see also* SI.XI e). *See also* SI.VIII h; and X i

Certitude: of faith (*see* SI.I c; and XI b); of justification or predestination (*see* SI.IX c; and X h); natural, 5:209, 6:23, 8:5, 8:55–56, 11:89, 14:100, 17:7, 18:103, 18:253

Character, sacramental. *See* Sacramental character

Charism, 8:339

Charity, 2:166–169, 2:319, 7:445, 7:528, 19:117; act of (*see* SI.XV); as a fruit of the Holy Ghost (*see* SI.XV); God is, 6:63, 7:51, 10:46–47, 10:54, 11:347, 11:362, 14:9, 14:185, 19:144; supernatural (theological) (*see* SI.XI d)

Chastity, 1:53, 1:133, 2:164, 2:244, 3:32, 3:34, 3:213–221, 7:457, 11:380; as an evangelical counsel (*see* Evangelical counsels; SI.XIII e; and XV); as a fruit of the Holy Ghost (*see* SI.XV); within marriage, 1:76, 1:80, 3:237–238, 3:240, 5:261, 5:278, 6:115, 6:224, 7:274, 7:378, 7:382, 7:452, 8:322, 9:261, 11:412, 12:59, 12:297, 13:240, 16:61, 16:346, 17:284, 18:430; virtue of, 2:204–205, 2:233–234, 2:257–258, 2:328, 2:330, 3:33, 4:48, 4:50, 4:141, 4:144, 5:63, 5:126, 5:311, 7:438, 7:452, 8:136, 8:254, 8:331, 9:217, 10:336, 11:408–417, 12:50–51, 12:143–145, 13:240, 14:347–348, 15:34, 16:221, 17:284, 18:55–56, 18:162–163, 18:246, 18:445, 19:283

Children: admitted to Holy Communion, 2:141, 3:26, 3:85, 3:120, 4:55, 4:149–150, 5:233, 5:340, 6:206, 6:218, 7:276–277, 8:144–145, 8:289, 9:68, 11:265, 11:267–268, 12:61–62, 12:386–387, 14:44, 14:333, 15:95, 15:199–200, 17:215, 18:29–36, 18:60, 18:170–171, 18:343–345, 19:175; baptism of, 1:61, 1:130, 2:141, 2:212,

3:51–53, 3:59–65, 3:332, 5:88, 5:224, 5:226, 6:135, 7:207, 8:130, 8:275, 9:55, 9:81, 10:172, 11:116, 11:232, 12:17, 12:258, 13:15, 14:368, 15:42, 15:109, 15:151–152, 16:208, 16:211, 16:213, 17:222, 18:193, 18:282, 18:370, 19:131–134; duties of, 1:43–45, 2:185–187, 3:22, 3:234, 4:54–55, 4:149–150, 5:35–36, 5:42, 5:127, 5:261, 5:306, 5:344, 6:103–104, 7:427–437, 8:250, 9:48, 11:393–396, 11:434, 12:54, 12:58–59, 12:232, 13:331, 14:36, 14:298, 15:190–191, 15:199, 16:291–292, 16:342–343, 17:44, 17:202, 18:55, 18:157, 18:159, 18:172, 19:258; duties toward, 1:45–47, 2:238, 3:22, 3:65, 3:241–242, 4:46, 4:139, 5:35–36, 5:57–58, 5:111, 5:126–131, 5:307–308, 6:102, 6:214–215, 7:205, 7:437–439, 8:183, 8:250, 9:7–8, 9:161, 11:230, 11:337, 11:396–399, 11:434–435, 12:54, 12:57–58, 12:59–62, 13:331, 14:304–305, 15:23, 15:191, 16:220, 16:292, 16:294, 16:324, 16:343, 17:44, 17:202, 18:55, 18:157–158, 18:171–172, 18:229, 18:346, 19:128, 19:262; dying without baptism, 2:248, 3:52–53, 3:57, 5:199, 6:110, 7:208, 8:42–44, 8:63–64, 8:135, 8:275, 9:81, 11:116, 11:230, 14:368, 16:153, 16:207–208, 17:171–172, 17:218, 18:372, 18:461–463; as primary end of marriage (*see* SI.XII o)

Choice. *See* Will

Chrism, 1:63–65, 2:214, 2:215, 3:64, 3:70–71, 3:307, 3:336, 4:61, 4:82, 4:157, 5:150, 5:227, 5:265, 6:136, 6:204, 7:130, 7:224, 7:227, 7:230–231, 8:278–279, 9:85–88, 9:265, 11:221, 11:244–245, 11:250, 13:27–28, 13:210, 13:222, 13:320–321, 14:375, 15:28, 15:92, 15:152–153, 16:30, 16:215, 17:227, 18:195–196, 18:373–375, 19:162–163

Christ. *See* SI.VIII a–h

Christian, 2:313, 3:35, 3:266, 19:128–132; meaning of the name, 1:17–18, 1:63, 1:114–115, 2:4, 2:111, 2:311, 5:148–149, 6:21, 6:68, 7:73, 7:225, 9:9, 9:249, 11:113, 14:344, 18:40, 18:101, 18:103; sign of the cross and, 1:110–111, 1:114, 2:312, 3:9, 3:38, 3:40, 3:46–48, 3:308, 4:28, 4:118, 4:194, 5:149–151, 6:136, 7:239, 11:97–99, 12:52–53, 13:31, 14:375, 15:38, 15:49, 15:57, 16:50, 16:210, 16:215, 16:298–299, 17:12, 17:83, 18:40–41, 18:101–102

Christmas. *See* Birth of Christ

Church. *See* SI.II

Circumcision, 2:295–296, 3:267, 4:76, 4:86, 7:207, 11:12, 13:173; sign of the old covenant, 3:52, 5:388, 7:174, 9:81, 10:217, 13:170–171; superstitious after coming of Christ, 3:264, 5:189, 6:94, 14:177, 18:370

Citizens, 7:163, 10:158; duties of, 3:22, 4:47, 4:140, 7:433–435, 8:251–252, 11:399, 12:53, 12:65, 13:331, 18:157, 18:159–160, 18:339, 19:264; rights of, 5:318, 18:55, 18:226

Clandestine marriages, 4:52, 4:147, 4:150, 4:200, 5:130, 5:259–260,

5:262, 6:217, 11:342, 16:66, 16:365

Clandestine societies, 8:24, 16:336–337, 17:203, 19:267

Clergy, 1:93, 2:209, 3:340, 19:212; attire of, 1:96, 2:283, 3:133–135, 5:377, 6:223, 8:150, 11:251, 12:64, 13:15, 13:32, 13:73–81, 14:388–389, 16:305, 19:178; ranks of (*see* SI.XII n)

Clerics. *See* Clergy

Clothing, 1:28, 1:34, 1:57, 3:64, 3:133–135, 3:230–231, 7:118, 11:67, 12:129, 12:204, 12:380, 13:18–19, 13:73–81; of clerics (*see* Clergy); and modesty, 2:324, 2:336, 3:38, 3:41, 4:67, 4:88, 4:163, 4:206, 5:96, 5:152, 5:312, 7:456, 8:292, 10:225, 11:190, 11:263, 11:406–407, 11:411, 12:48, 12:50–51, 12:58, 12:106, 12:145, 12:192, 13:287, 14:309, 14:311, 14:394, 15:38, 15:88, 15:96, 15:193, 16:33, 16:61, 16:221, 16:347, 17:276

Cloud of glory, 11:36

Cognition (knowledge). *See* SI.I a–e; IV a; and VIII f

Collaboration: of citizens for common good, 8:251, 12:53, 19:255; of laity in mission of the Church (*see* Laity)

Commandment(s), 7:379, 10:31; of the Church (*see* SI.XI m; XII g; and XII k); of conscience, 2:169, 4:55, 4:140, 4:150, 6:106, 14:58, 16:174–175, 16:183, 16:218, 17:40–41, 19:222; of God (*see* SI.XI e–t); of parents and superiors, 2:185–190, 2:254, 3:22, 3:234, 3:249, 4:46, 4:139, 5:35, 5:261, 5:306–307, 5:391, 6:103, 6:106, 6:210, 8:250–252, 9:48, 9:260, 11:394, 11:399–400, 12:54, 12:58–59, 12:232, 14:36–37, 14:298–304, 16:342–345, 17:202, 19:227; as a way of being accessory to sin (*see* SI.XV)

Commending the departing soul, 3:180–185, 9:117, 11:318–319, 12:65, 12:294–295, 13:313–316

Commitment of spouses within marriage (*see* SI.XII o)

Common good. *See* Good

Communication: in sacred things (*communicatio in sacris*), 2:172–173, 2:307, 3:150, 3:242, 5:255, 14:391, 14:429, 16:126, 16:317, 17:42, 17:195 (*see also* XI e); of spiritual goods (*see* SI.II b; and XII l); with those outside the Church, 2:139, 2:173, 5:255, 5:273, 8:222, 8:229, 9:16, 9:253–254, 12:68, 14:128, 18:51, 18:142–143

Communion, 1:127, 7:242, 7:274, 14:389; daily, 2:159, 2:207, 2:324, 5:99–100, 5:233–234, 7:274, 7:606, 8:146, 8:289, 9:267, 11:266, 11:435, 12:53, 12:183, 15:168, 16:45, 16:271, 17:68, 17:101–102, 18:35, 18:60, 18:170, 18:344–345, 18:399, 19:173, 19:174; between the divine Persons (*see* SI.V e); first, 5:54, 5:233, 10:55, 10:57, 11:272–273, 12:386–387, 13:135, 15:27, 15:95, 16:240, 16:244, 17:97, 17:215, 18:31, 18:34–35, 18:171–172, 18:345–346, 19:175; received by children, 2:141, 3:26, 3:85, 3:120, 4:55, 4:149–150,

5:233, 5:340, 6:206, 6:218, 7:276–277, 8:144, 8:289, 9:268, 11:265, 11:267–268, 12:61–62, 12:386–387, 14:44, 14:333, 15:95, 15:199–200, 17:215, 18:29–36, 18:60, 18:170–171, 18:343–345, 19:175; sacramental (*see* SI.XII g); of saints (*see* SI.II b); spiritual (acts of), 3:149, 5:100, 7:271, 8:292–293, 16:277, 19:172

Communism, inherently evil, 19:122

Compassion, 1:28, 1:83, 5:37, 5:141, 5:351–353, 7:586, 9:196, 9:273, 12:292–293, 13:202–203, 14:17, 18:268, 19:145

Concealment, as a way of being accessory to sin. *See* SI.XV

Conception, 2:247, 7:76–77, 7:367; of Christ (*see* SI.VIII b; and VIII h); of Mary Immaculate (*see* SI.VIII k); and the right to life, 1:46–47

Concomitance, 2:220, 2:223, 3:85, 3:106–110, 3:345–348, 4:63, 4:159, 5:230–231, 6:137, 6:219, 7:260–261, 8:142, 8:147, 8:290–291, 9:101–102, 11:257–258, 11:269, 14:56, 14:381, 15:94, 15:165, 16:42, 16:263–265, 17:65–66, 17:235–236, 18:201, 18:388, 19:175

Concordats, 14:134–135

Concupiscence, 1:47–48, 1:53, 1:72, 2:197, 2:248, 3:36, 3:37–38, 3:62–63, 3:120, 3:233, 3:247, 4:22–23, 4:111–112, 4:196, 5:231, 5:258, 5:280, 5:367–368, 6:128–129, 6:203, 7:213, 7:483, 8:61–62, 8:285, 8:329, 9:83–84, 10:170–171, 10:201, 11:82, 11:85, 11:452–453, 12:130–131, 13:159–161, 13:166–167, 14:200, 14:368, 14:390, 15:37, 15:133, 15:170, 16:14, 16:47, 16:88, 16:123–124, 16:282, 17:27, 17:36, 17:56, 17:213–214, 17:274–276, 18:45, 18:74, 18:117, 18:282–283, 18:449, 19:41–43, 19:185. *See also* SI.VII d

Condemnation, 1:31, 4:21–22, 4:110–111, 5:16, 5:43, 5:177, 5:188, 5:216–217, 5:274, 5:384, 6:58–60, 7:224, 10:171, 10:205, 12:197, 12:205, 12:292, 14:201, 16:370, 17:143, 18:282, 18:376. *See also* SI.X g–h; and XIV

Confession: sacrament (*see* SI.XII i); of St. Peter the Apostle, 2:131, 7:135–136, 10:34–35, 11:146, 14:210, 18:303, 19:53; of St. Thomas the Apostle, 11:77–78, 14:210, 16:157–158

Confirmation. *See* SI.XII e

Congregations, Pontifical, 1:22, 1:118, 18:322

Conjugal act. *See* SI.XI r

Conscience: examination of (*see* Examen); in general (*see* SI.II g)

Consecrated life, 3:221–232, 3:339, 5:39, 5:297, 5:310, 5:361, 5:363, 6:15, 7:341–343, 7:357–359, 7:366, 7:452, 8:164–165, 9:135, 9:136–139, 9:213–221, 9:276, 10:38, 10:40–41, 11:380–381, 12:122–132, 12:170, 13:241, 14:119–120, 14:124–125, 14:130–132, 14:133, 14:135, 14:352, 16:251, 17:56–57, 18:227,

18:347–349, 19:218–221. *See also* SI.XIII e

Consecration, 11:105, 12:258, 12:327–328, 13:84, 13:181–186, 13:259–260; of bishops, 1:73, 14:420; Eucharistic (*see* SI.XII f; and XII h); official (*see* SI.XII p)

Consent, 1:20, 1:28, 1:47–49, 1:53, 1:67, 1:80, 1:108, 2:252, 3:34, 8:92, 8:105, 9:157–158, 9:270, 9:271, 11:409–410, 11:446–447, 19:140, 19:186–190; doctrinal, of fathers and theologians (*see* SI.I f); in marriage (*see* SI.XII o); as a way of being accessory to sin (*see* SI.XV)

Constitution, 19:97–100; of the Church (*see* SI.II a); of states (*see* SI.XI o)

Constitutions, Apostolic, 2:199, 3:308, 4:82, 10:5, 11:120, 12:248, 13:44, 18:320–321

Consubstantial, 2:121, 2:220, 2:272, 3:316, 5:193–194, 5:196, 6:34, 6:63, 7:71, 8:173, 9:14, 9:20, 9:250, 10:39, 11:96, 11:97, 11:106, 12:173, 13:129, 13:260, 14:204, 15:61, 18:42, 18:110, 18:267, 18:287

Consummation, 1:111, 2:294, 7:137, 19:94, 19:305; of all things at the end of time (*see* SI.XIV b); of divine revelation in Christ (*see* SI.I b; VIII g–h; and X i); of marriage vows (*see* SI.XII o)

Contemplation, 3:222, 5:355–356, 5:359–361, 5:369, 5:371, 6:100–101, 7:50, 10:30, 10:43, 12:125–132, 14:446, 18:239, 18:286, 18:299, 19:59

Continence, 2:244, 2:328, 7:452, 19:243; binding on Roman clergy, 1:75–76, 2:233–234, 3:213–221, 3:340–341, 5:258, 5:277–279, 5:310, 5:392–393, 8:162–163, 11:329, 19:220; and divorce, 5:261, 5:278; as a fruit of the Holy Ghost (*see* SI.XV)

Contraception, sinfulness of. *See* SI.XI r

Contract: matrimonial (*see* SI.XII o); of property, 5:42, 5:391, 8:256–258

Contrition, 1:66, 1:92, 2:210, 2:224–225, 2:263, 2:322, 4:34–35, 4:68–69, 4:126, 4:165–166, 4:207, 5:103–105, 5:235–238, 7:298–306, 8:152–156, 8:295–296, 9:109, 11:280–282, 18:75–77, 18:194, 18:205, 18:212–213, 18:406–408, 19:193; act of (*see* SI.XV); necessary for sacramental absolution (*see* SI.IX b; and XII i)

Conversion, 3:163–164, 3:175, 4:41, 4:77, 4:133, 5:37, 6:54, 6:168, 7:208, 7:539, 8:91–94, 10:216, 10:346, 11:124–125, 11:131, 11:160, 12:157–158, 12:188–189, 12:201–202, 12:299–300, 12:370–372, 13:215, 14:245, 14:253, 14:361, 16:152, 16:248, 16:257, 16:276, 19:127–128

Cooperation: in abortion, 5:310, 14:307; in evil, 1:45–46, 1:48, 1:51–52, 1:53–54, 2:196, 2:252–253, 2:331, 3:34, 5:70, 5:255, 5:285, 5:312–313, 6:109, 6:201, 7:114, 7:465, 8:38, 9:156–163, 9:246–247, 9:271, 10:164, 11:139, 11:402, 11:421, 11:428, 12:67, 12:255, 14:197, 14:316,

14:343–344, 15:35, 15:77, 15:192, 16:350–351, 17:45, 17:272, 18:55, 18:161, 18:163, 18:415, 19:277 (*see also* SI.XV); with grace, 5:80, 5:84, 5:114, 5:165, 6:161, 7:179, 7:541–542, 8:78–79, 8:91–94, 9:270, 10:26, 10:202, 11:88–89, 11:113, 11:183–184, 14:325, 14:358–359, 15:144, 16:314, 17:182, 17:237, 19:84; of Mary in the redemption (*see* SI.VIII i–k)

Corpse: cremation ordinarily illicit, 13:32, 14:260, 18:166, 19:267, 19:303; rites for burying, 3:185–190, 16:365, 19:302

Corpus Christi, feast of, 2:298, 3:272, 4:86, 6:15, 7:607, 13:85, 13:263–269, 16:284, 16:339, 17:210, 18:167, 19:52, 19:177

Correction, 1:10, 4:37, 4:47, 4:140, 6:147, 8:250, 8:303, 14:300, 14:304, 15:37, 15:191; fraternal, 1:46–47, 1:83, 2:75, 2:245, 2:326, 3:210, 5:74, 5:320, 5:354, 8:28, 9:161, 11:354–355, 14:274–275, 14:343, 16:38, 16:248; of superiors, 1:46–47, 2:196, 3:210, 11:354, 11:397, 11:400–401

Council(s): binding pronouncements of (*see* SI.II d); general (ecumenical, universal), 1:78–79, 1:87, 2:137, 3:207, 3:317–318, 3:373, 5:181, 5:190, 5:194, 5:213–217, 7:262, 8:26–27, 8:29–31, 9:260, 11:100, 11:136, 11:147, 11:287, 12:172, 12:186, 12:197, 12:205, 12:220–221, 12:230, 12:234, 12:292, 12:305, 12:312, 12:329, 13:111, 13:230, 14:238, 16:24, 16:185, 17:91, 18:26, 18:51, 18:139, 18:306–307, 19:98, 19:101; particular (local, regional), 7:258, 8:26, 14:204, 18:33–34, 18:260

Counsel(s), 1:10, 1:45–46, 1:48, 1:51, 1:81, 1:83, 1:133, 2:73, 2:204–206, 2:242, 2:252, 2:326, 2:331, 3:34, 4:84, 4:87, 5:40, 5:70, 6:109, 6:201, 9:156–157, 10:314, 17:55; evangelical (*see* Evangelical counsels; SI.XIII e; and XV); as a gift of the Holy Ghost (*see* SI.XV); as a way of being accessory to sin (*see* SI.XV)

Covenant, new, 5:221, 5:373, 6:206, 10:246, 10:295, 17:232, 18:67–70, 18:93, 18:129, 18:198, 18:361–363, 19:13, 19:65; old, 5:49, 5:221, 5:302, 5:343, 7:66, 10:246, 10:277, 13:170, 18:93, 18:96, 18:119, 18:361, 19:13, 19:44

Covetousness, as a capital sin. *See* SI.XV

Craniotomy. *See* Abortion

Creation. *See* SI.VI

Creator. *See* SI.V b; and VI a

Creature(s). *See* SI.VI

Creed: Apostles' (*see* SI.XV); Athanasian, 1:24, 3:261, 6:4–5, 6:199, 7:59–60, 8:51, 9:25, 11:100, 13:54, 18:251; NicenoConstantinopolitan, 2:272–273, 3:55, 3:139, 3:319, 5:193–194, 5:214–216, 6:29–30, 6:34, 6:38, 6:53, 6:62–64, 6:71, 7:53, 8:173–174, 11:100, 12:186, 13:111–112, 14:213, 14:242; profession of, 2:8, 2:313–314, 8:173–175, 13:111–112, 17:92,

19:81; of Trent, 3:316–318, 3:373, 8:173–175

Cremation, 19:303; ordinarily illicit, 13:32, 14:260, 18:166, 19:267

Cross, 1:89, 2:304, 13:290–292; of Christ, 1:110–111, 1:114, 2:124, 3:9, 3:127, 3:270, 5:377, 5:379–382, 5:384–385, 6:45–47, 6:136, 7:192, 7:354, 8:72, 8:147–148, 8:199–200, 8:290, 9:16, 10:167, 11:67, 12:158, 12:209, 12:216, 13:201–202, 13:215–216, 13:292–294, 15:139, 16:18, 16:77, 16:150, 18:22, 18:47, 18:127, 18:296; of the Christian, 2:305, 2:312, 3:37, 9:113, 9:219, 15:37, 15:40, 17:275, 17:278, 18:40, 18:102; Eucharist as perpetual sacrifice of (*see* SI.XII h); sign of the, 1:3, 1:110, 1:114, 1:123, 2:6–7, 2:114, 2:312, 3:9, 3:46–48, 3:306, 4:28, 4:61, 4:82, 4:118, 4:194–195, 5:149–152, 6:136, 7:223, 7:239, 8:307–308, 9:16–17, 11:97–99, 12:52–53, 12:147, 13:31–32, 13:103, 13:259–260, 14:6, 14:178–179, 15:10, 15:38, 15:49, 15:57, 15:115, 15:174–175, 16:50–51, 16:257, 16:298–299, 17:138, 18:13, 18:40–41, 18:101–103, 18:251–252, 19:88, 19:113–115, 19:318

Cult: freedom of (*see* SI.XI o); in general (*see* SI.XI e)

Culture, 13:15, 19:332. *See also* SI.II i

Cup, 7:92, 7:325, 13:84, 16:41, 16:259, 16:261, 19:175

Custom, 1:29, 1:41, 3:254, 4:90, 6:215, 6:220–221, 7:243, 7:351, 19:114, 19:304; having force of law, 1:82, 1:91, 2:201, 2:216, 5:350, 8:150, 9:54–55, 10:44, 11:121, 13:23, 18:29, 18:167–168

D

Daily bread, 1:3, 1:26, 1:28, 1:119, 2:31, 2:159, 3:18, 4:58, 4:153, 5:140, 5:185, 6:163–165, 7:554, 7:564, 8:233, 8:234, 9:30, 9:255, 10:236, 11:204–205, 14:68, 14:437, 15:19, 15:84, 16:78, 17:186, 18:65, 18:182, 19:151–152, 19:318

Damnation. *See* SI.X g–h; and XIV a

Darkness, 2:303, 7:580, 16:109, 16:166; of intellect, result of the fall (*see* SI.VII d); powers of, 16:51, 16:299, 18:182, 18:249, 18:316, 18:448–449, 19:63, 19:244

Davidian psalter, 13:45, 13:48–49, 18:257

Day, 1:79, 1:82, 2:298, 3:8–11, 3:258, 3:263–273, 13:43–45; holy (*see* Feast); of the Lord (Judgment) (*see* SI.XIV b)

Deacon(s), 1:60, 1:74–75, 7:351, 18:192, 18:368, 19:180–184, 19:211; order of (*see* SI.XII n)

Deadly (Capital) sins. *See* SI.XV

Death, 1:4, 1:44–46, 1:70, 1:100–109, 1:131, 2:98, 2:265, 2:329, 3:10, 3:196, 6:75, 7:79, 7:86–87, 9:222–224, 11:454, 13:32, 13:66; end of earthly life (*see* SI.XIV); as one of the four last things (*see* SI.XV); penalty in civil law (*see* Execution); remember thy (*memento mori*), 6:82, 11:454, 12:296, 13:34, 14:27, 14:258, 16:369–370,

17:280, 18:87, 18:100, 18:183, 18:247

Decalogue. *See* SI.XI e–t

Deceased: indulgences for (*see* SI.XII l); Mass offered for (*see* SI.XII h; and XIV a)

Decision, binding in faith (*see* SI.II c; II h; and III f)

Defense, 14:307, 19:292; of the Church, 5:185–186, 12:191, 12:259–261, 12:281, 18:326; of country, 5:308–309, 10:161, 14:303, 14:307, 16:246, 19:268, 19:275; duty of those responsible for the lives of others, 5:299–300, 5:308–309, 5:323; of evil, as a way of being accessory to sin (*see* SI.XV); of the faith, 3:231, 5:185–186, 8:12, 8:32, 8:136–137, 9:58, 10:40, 12:170–172, 12:328, 16:216, 17:147, 18:27, 18:444, 19:266; of self, 1:53, 2:190, 4:45, 4:137, 5:299–300, 5:308–309, 5:323, 6:98, 7:442, 8:252, 11:402, 14:321, 14:598, 18:342, 19:275

Definition, dogmatic. *See* SI.II c; and III f

Defunct. *See* SI.XIV a

Deity: one true (*see* SI.IV–V); triune (*see* SI.V)

Demon, 1:88–89, 2:162, 7:494, 7:582, 8:57–58, 8:67–68, 18:44, 18:112–113, 18:261, 18:448; existence, action in the world (*see* SI.VI c); exorcism removes influence of, 1:62, 1:74, 2:180, 3:60–61, 3:306–307, 4:81, 5:257, 6:214, 8:58, 11:25, 11:37, 11:328, 12:17–18, 13:86–88, 14:371, 19:113; idolatry, a worship of, 2:44, 3:303–304, 5:296–297, 6:27–28, 11:364, 12:140, 18:272, 19:127, 19:229

Deposition of clerics, 3:207–209, 3:213–216, 11:148, 12:248, 12:251, 18:335, 18:416

Deposit of faith. *See* SI.I b

Desert, 5:348, 5:386, 7:86, 7:160, 10:160, 11:19–21, 16:137, 16:251, 18:93, 19:47

Desire, 1:29, 1:83, 1:108, 3:18, 3:360, 6:134, 6:144–145, 7:139, 7:485, 7:528, 19:42; baptism of (*see* SI.XII d); involuntary not sinful, 2:197, 5:142–143, 5:282, 5:328–330, 5:367–368, 6:112, 6:174–175, 6:203, 7:487–488, 8:254, 11:408–410, 12:202, 14:311, 16:63, 16:127, 16:132, 16:221, 16:227, 16:355, 19:282; moderation of (*see* SI.XV); when sinful, 1:36, 1:48, 1:53–54, 2:197, 2:255–256, 2:329, 4:50–51, 4:143–144, 5:38–39, 5:52, 5:60, 5:62–64, 5:287–290, 5:312, 5:327–330, 5:368–369, 6:128–129, 6:203–204, 7:487–488, 8:254, 8:260, 9:261, 11:408–410, 11:446–447, 12:153, 14:41, 14:311, 15:196, 16:63, 16:121, 16:132–134, 16:346, 16:355, 17:207, 18:76, 18:165

Despair, 1:37, 2:88, 2:152, 2:261, 2:330, 3:33, 4:35, 4:41, 4:133, 5:31, 5:67–68, 5:133, 5:283, 5:292, 5:310, 6:82, 6:168, 7:302, 7:570, 8:68, 8:93, 8:157, 8:310, 8:326, 8:331, 9:164, 9:246, 9:252, 11:181–182, 14:280, 14:342, 15:34, 15:184, 16:56, 16:326–328, 17:195, 18:234–235, 18:244, 18:406, 19:141–142, 19:301; as a

sin against the Holy Ghost (*see* SI.XV)

Destiny, 16:368, 16:370, 19:296; worship of sinful, 5:296–297, 18:313, 19:229

Detraction, 1:52, 2:45, 2:188, 2:195–196, 3:24, 4:49, 4:143, 5:44–45, 5:318–327, 6:123, 6:202, 7:475, 8:258, 9:152, 11:427–428, 12:190–191, 12:290, 14:40, 14:318–319, 15:25, 15:195, 16:353, 17:47, 17:203, 17:207, 18:164, 18:386, 19:292–293

Development, legitimate of doctrine. *See* SI.I f

Devil. *See* Demon

Devotion, 1:34, 1:71, 1:89, 1:122, 1:131, 3:115, 3:117, 3:284–285, 4:43, 4:135, 5:67, 5:97, 5:342, 5:350, 5:354, 6:144, 7:40, 7:191, 8:86, 8:169, 8:226, 8:292, 9:149, 9:245, 10:345, 11:191, 11:362, 11:390, 13:235–243, 13:275–276, 14:65–66, 14:432–433, 15:106, 15:181, 16:275, 16:277, 16:284, 16:297, 16:304, 16:320, 17:81, 17:82, 18:33, 18:35, 18:44, 18:67, 18:163, 18:178, 18:257, 18:399, 19:156, 19:176

Diaconate. *See* SI.XII n

Dignity, 1:44, 1:54, 7:81, 19:58, 19:282–283; of man as God's creature, 6:32, 6:35, 7:65, 10:144–145, 10:161, 11:107, 13:29–30, 13:227–228, 13:262–263, 13:291, 18:271, 19:256; of married state, 7:368–372, 8:164, 8:319, 10:102, 11:335–339, 12:158–159, 14:423–424, 15:171, 16:48, 16:289, 16:366–367, 18:81, 18:224–225, 18:428–429; of the ordained, 5:255, 6:140, 7:68, 7:341, 8:317, 9:128, 11:322–324, 12:169–170, 12:246, 16:287, 18:80, 18:223, 18:427

Diocese, 5:239, 5:350, 7:355, 8:210, 14:240, 16:181, 16:288, 18:51, 18:141, 19:98–101

Discernment, 15:27, 15:109; of spirits, 11:366; of vocation, 3:223–224, 5:124–128, 7:341–343, 7:357–359, 8:162–163, 8:318, 11:325, 11:338, 11:381, 14:422–423, 14:430, 16:126–127, 16:286, 17:56–57, 18:224, 19:211–212, 19:271

Disciples, 3:86–87, 3:209; of Jesus Christ, 1:21–22, 1:94, 1:114, 1:120, 6:53, 7:110, 7:341, 8:81, 8:206, 8:284, 11:21, 11:26–27, 12:159–160, 13:176, 14:111, 14:270, 16:20, 16:83, 16:303, 18:70, 18:197, 18:391, 19:71–72, 19:78–80; of John the Baptist, 11:33, 13:148–149, 16:197, 16:302, 19:48; Christians called to be, 15:37, 16:77, 19:79, 19:93

Discipline, ecclesiastical, 1:56, 1:73, 3:107, 3:331, 12:246, 18:134, 18:306, 18:418. *See also* SI.II b; and III d

Discrimination, when unjust, 19:146

Dispensation, 1:41, 1:82, 1:91, 2:239, 3:265, 3:350–351, 5:129, 5:297–298, 5:301–302, 7:259, 8:247, 8:287, 10:60, 11:379–380, 14:32, 14:198, 15:173, 15:201, 16:214, 16:359, 16:364, 17:54, 17:68, 18:58, 18:168, 18:226, 18:374, 19:243

Disposition, 3:56, 3:132, 3:234, 19:282; for frequent Communion (*see* SI.XII g); for justification (*see* SI.IX b); for reception of the sacraments in general (*see* SI.XII b)

Divination, 1:32, 4:44, 4:135, 5:30, 5:296–297, 6:84, 6:86, 7:414, 9:42, 10:155–156, 11:364, 16:317–319, 19:229

Divine office, 1:76, 2:154–155, 3:258–261, 5:383–384, 6:201, 6:212, 10:43, 10:44, 11:366–367, 12:204, 13:43–62, 16:285, 16:309, 16:358–359

Divinity: of the Church (*see* SI.II a); false, 2:172, 3:301, 3:366, 5:27, 5:190, 5:296, 10:69, 10:291, 11:5, 12:38, 19:229; of Jesus Christ (*see* SI.VIII a); participation of man in God's (*see* SI.XIV a); of the three Persons (*see* SI.V)

Divisions, 1:22, 1:67, 6:66, 7:476, 8:21, 10:44, 10:337–338, 12:302–303, 18:322

Divorce. *See* SI.XII o

Doctrine, 1:18, 1:102–104, 2:311, 3:324, 3:338, 7:44, 7:387; of Christ perfect, 4:31, 4:121, 8:50, 8:52–53, 8:82, 8:183, 8:184, 9:9, 9:211, 12:237, 14:115, 14:168, 16:24, 16:189–190, 18:46, 18:120; of the Church (*see* SI.II c); legitimate development of (*see* SI.I f). *See also* Dogma

Dogma: binding definition of (*see* SI.I c; II c–d; and III f); does not evolve, 8:337, 10:186–189 (*see also* SI.I b; and I f)

Donatism, 1:95, 3:206–207, 5:192–193, 6:68, 6:135–136

Doubt: heretical (*see* SI.XI b); positive (*see* SI.I c)

Dove, 2:130, 3:100, 3:301, 3:368, 5:333, 7:187, 7:397, 10:211, 11:19, 11:137, 11:271, 13:176, 14:21, 16:140, 16:160

Doxology, 2:285, 3:137, 3:138, 3:146, 11:12, 11:136, 13:47, 13:52, 13:102–103, 13:260, 14:72, 14:86, 14:387, 15:120, 17:279, 19:318–320

Dualism, 6:29, 12:281–282, 13:30

Duel. *See* SI.XI q

Dulia, 1:33, 2:178, 5:26, 5:31, 5:218–220, 5:302, 5:335–336, 7:391–395, 8:85–86, 8:245, 11:189, 11:367–369, 12:72, 12:230, 13:6, 14:33, 14:285–286, 15:21, 15:74, 15:185–186, 16:105, 17:79, 17:263, 18:153

Duty, 1:38, 5:35–36, 5:57–58, 5:149, 5:190–191, 5:252, 5:286, 17:239; of children, 1:43–45, 2:185–187, 3:22, 3:234, 4:54–55, 4:149–150, 5:35, 5:58, 5:127, 5:261, 5:306–308, 6:103–104, 7:427–437, 8:250, 9:48, 11:393–396, 11:434, 12:54, 12:58–59, 12:232, 13:331, 14:36, 14:298, 15:190–191, 15:199, 16:291–292, 16:342, 16:394, 17:44, 17:202, 18:33, 18:55, 19:258; of citizens, 2:189, 3:22, 4:47, 4:140, 5:307, 7:433–435, 8:252, 9:48, 11:399, 12:53, 13:331, 14:303–304, 15:76, 16:221, 16:292, 18:15, 18:69, 18:167–169, 19:263, 19:267; of civil authorities, 1:45, 2:207, 3:22, 4:47, 4:140,

5:307, 7:440–441, 11:399–400, 13:331, 14:306, 16:185, 18:158; of clergy, 1:76, 2:207, 3:22, 4:80, 5:307, 6:191, 6:199, 6:209–211, 7:40, 8:316–317, 11:28–30, 11:399–400, 14:99, 16:271, 16:342–343, 17:216, 19:101, 19:109; of defense (*see* Defense); of ecclesiastical superiors, 1:45, 2:207, 3:22, 4:46–47, 4:139, 5:217, 5:307, 7:350–352, 11:399–400, 14:304, 16:187, 16:342–343, 17:203, 18:50, 18:138, 18:159, 18:308, 18:320; of parents, 1:45–47, 2:238, 3:22, 3:65, 3:241–242, 4:46, 4:139, 5:35–36, 5:57–58, 5:126–128, 5:261, 5:307–308, 6:102, 6:214–216, 7:437–439, 8:183, 8:250, 9:7–8, 9:161, 11:230, 11:337, 11:396–399, 11:434–435, 12:54, 12:57–58, 12:59–62, 13:331, 14:304, 15:23, 15:191, 16:214, 16:291, 16:342–343, 16:351, 17:44, 17:202, 18:35, 18:55, 18:158, 18:172, 19:128, 19:261; to resist unjust commands, 2:54, 2:186, 2:189, 2:206, 3:210, 5:307, 5:309, 6:103, 7:435, 10:330, 11:394, 12:8–10, 12:58, 12:232, 14:304, 17:202, 18:341–342

E

Earth, 1:22–23, 1:81, 1:116, 1:121, 2:158, 5:198, 7:48, 18:21, 18:43, 18:108; creation of (*see* SI.VI)

Easter, 1:71, 1:92–94, 1:127, 2:202, 3:10, 3:238–239, 19:70–74, 19:79; feast of, 1:93, 2:296–297, 3:252, 3:262, 3:270–271, 4:55, 4:146, 4:149, 4:200, 5:18, 5:384–387, 6:218, 7:222, 7:276, 8:264, 8:266, 9:66, 9:243, 10:338, 13:223–227, 14:44, 14:329, 14:332–334, 15:200, 16:166, 16:362, 17:51, 18:59–60, 18:170, 18:172, 18:343–344, 19:70, 19:179, 19:248–250; first, 4:26, 4:115, 4:193, 5:18, 5:206, 5:382, 11:72–73, 14:222, 15:11, 15:64, 16:19, 17:140. *See also* SI.VIII h

Eastern Church(es), 3:153, 3:213–215, 5:224, 5:376, 8:21, 11:138, 11:222, 12:257, 12:312–313, 12:398–399, 13:223–224, 14:122, 18:29, 18:466, 19:121–122, 19:175, 19:179

Economy of salvation. *See* SI.X i

Ecumenical councils. *See* Council(s)

Education. *See* SI.XI p

Elderly, 5:345, 6:103, 6:107, 7:352, 7:392, 10:331, 11:399, 14:304, 15:191, 18:94, 18:221, 19:206

Election, 7:537; of clerics, 5:323, 10:244, 11:331, 12:247–249, 18:425–426; not the source of civil authority (*see* SI.XI a; and XI o); papal (*see* SI.III h)

Elevation: of man (*see* SI.VII a–b); of sacred Host at Mass, 2:277, 2:292, 3:142–143, 3:148, 5:162–163, 5:381, 6:219, 13:85, 13:126–127, 13:269, 14:89, 14:388, 15:95, 16:264, 19:183–184

Emmanuel, 10:334, 14:216, 17:66, 18:290, 19:45–46

End, 1:33, 1:89, 1:115, 18:21, 18:42, 18:50, 18:108, 18:261; of creatures (*see* SI.VI f); of human life (*see* SI.XIV a); supernatural, of men (*see* SI.VII a); of the world (*see* SI.XIV b)

Enemy, 7:131, 7:159, 7:306; hatred of, 2:167, 5:141, 5:281, 5:293–294, 16:354; love of, 2:167–168, 3:36, 3:42, 4:52, 4:58, 4:146, 4:154, 4:199–200, 5:35, 5:293, 7:505, 8:119–120, 8:253, 8:328, 11:28–29, 11:206–207, 11:353–354, 12:243, 12:297, 13:202, 13:215–217, 14:29, 14:271–273, 15:37, 15:42, 15:144, 15:176, 16:173–174, 17:192, 17:274, 18:84, 18:237, 19:147

Enjoyment: of creatures, 7:163, 11:21, 11:86–87, 13:325; inordinate, 5:51, 5:76, 5:288, 7:585, 11:21, 11:86, 11:452–453, 12:319–320, 13:258–259, 14:277, 16:339. *See also* SI.XV

Envy, 2:258, 2:262, 7:447, 9:167, 9:271, 18:95, 18:162, 18:245, 18:272, 19:43, 19:147; as a capital sin (*see* SI.XV); as a sin against the Holy Ghost (*see* SI.XV)

Epiphany, 19:59, 19:179; feast of, 1:79, 2:296, 3:238–239, 3:262, 3:267, 4:86, 5:386, 13:175–180, 14:428, 15:125, 16:146, 17:210, 18:167, 19:249

Episcopacy. *See* Bishop

Error(s), 1:25, 1:80, 3:324–326, 7:140, 14:24, 14:246–251, 17:90–92, 19:101–104; defense against by right doctrine, 2:140, 3:331, 4:123, 5:214–216, 12:170–172, 12:191, 14:251, 19:54, 19:101; invincible (inculpable), 3:323, 5:184, 5:285, 5:333, 7:323, 7:441, 11:150–151, 12:349, 14:253, 16:182–184, 17:21, 18:144, 18:314, 18:323, 19:120; in judgment, 5:43, 5:192, 5:324–326, 10:196, 16:244–245, 17:40–41, 19:227; of non-Catholics (*see under proper names*); philosophical (*see* SI.I e); vincible (culpable), 1:101, 3:323, 5:56, 5:191, 5:285, 5:311, 5:341, 6:93, 6:191, 6:199, 6:209–213, 6:220, 8:104, 8:244, 11:93, 11:457, 14:253, 14:332, 16:182, 17:40–41, 17:42, 17:194–195, 18:438

Eschaton. *See* SI.XIV

Eternity: of God (*see* SI.IV b); of man's reward (*see* SI.XIV b)

Ethics, natural, 8:93, 8:105, 18:463

Eucharist. *See* SI.XII f–h

Euthanasia, 5:291

Evangelical counsels, 3:34, 5:56, 7:366, 7:413, 9:213–214, 9:221, 11:361, 11:380–381, 15:35, 17:55–56, 17:87, 17:273, 18:173–175, 18:348–349, 19:220–221. *See also* SI.XIII e; and XV

Evangelization, 5:78, 5:194, 12:350–353, 12:370–372

Eve, 1:31, 4:20, 4:109, 4:196, 8:60–62, 8:192–193, 16:120, 19:39, 19:271; creation of miraculous, 8:60, 10:147–149, 13:283, 16:13, 16:118–119, 18:44, 18:90, 18:115; Mary as new, 6:184–186, 7:79, 9:34–36, 10:169, 11:111–112, 13:229, 13:283, 14:440, 16:141

Evil, 1:29, 1:82, 1:118, 1:127, 7:448, 8:37–38, 19:263; leading another to (*see* SI.XI d; and XV); minister of the sacraments (*see* SI.XII b); moral, 1:67, 5:44–45, 5:104, 5:142–143, 5:300–301, 6:82, 8:37, 11:206–209, 14:439, 16:153, 16:171, 16:187, 17:37, 17:56,

19:277; origin not of God (*see* SI.V b; and VI g); physical, 5:57, 8:37, 11:208–209, 18:112, 18:270

Evil one. *See* Demon

Evolution of dogma, erroneous, 8:337, 10:186–189. *See also* SI.I b; and I f

Examen, 13:174; daily, 1:108–110, 1:123–124, 2:155, 2:335, 3:40–41, 4:89–90, 5:154, 5:177, 7:305, 8:298, 11:278, 12:61, 14:58, 14:78–79, 14:400, 14:413, 15:41, 15:88, 15:109, 16:362, 17:108, 17:279, 19:159, 19:194, 19:321; prior to sacramental confession (examination of conscience), 2:322, 3:30, 3:157–158, 4:68, 4:165, 4:207, 5:102–103, 5:242–244, 5:390–393, 7:314, 8:297–298, 9:110, 11:277–278, 14:58–59, 14:81–83, 14:400–401, 15:31, 15:100–101, 15:156, 16:34, 16:227–234, 17:256, 18:75, 18:210, 19:198, 19:202

Example, 1:29, 1:89–90, 5:17–18, 5:29, 5:89, 5:131, 5:392, 6:45–46, 10:33, 10:38, 11:398, 12:130–131, 12:169–170, 14:217, 14:354, 15:23, 15:92, 15:139, 15:192–193, 16:18, 16:61, 16:372, 17:45, 17:203–204, 18:97, 18:123, 19:279–280

Excommunication, 1:45, 1:68, 2:138, 2:190, 2:202, 2:227, 3:119, 3:167–168, 3:219, 5:54–55, 5:255–256, 5:273, 5:340, 6:206, 6:225, 7:133, 7:274, 8:18, 8:221, 9:22, 9:68, 9:187, 9:253, 10:5, 11:148–149, 11:161–162, 12:172, 12:227, 14:213, 14:252, 14:285, 14:307, 16:365, 18:51, 18:142–143, 18:219, 18:335, 18:460, 19:115, 19:217

Execution, 1:107; of criminals by civil authority licit, 1:45, 2:45, 2:190, 5:308–309, 5:342, 6:108–109, 7:440–441, 8:252, 9:160–161, 11:401–402, 12:295, 12:305, 14:307, 19:275

Exercises, spiritual, 1:107, 2:102, 2:333, 2:335, 3:38–42, 3:252, 4:46, 5:170, 5:173, 5:360–361, 12:52–54, 12:61, 12:332, 14:393, 14:415, 15:88, 17:80, 19:276

Existence of God. *See* SI.IV a

Exodus, 5:334, 7:420, 7:483, 10:62, 18:257

Exorcism, 1:61–62, 2:180, 3:306–307, 4:81, 5:257, 6:214, 7:223, 8:58, 10:155, 11:25, 11:37, 11:328, 12:17–18, 13:86–88, 14:371–372, 14:443, 18:190–191, 19:113, 19:131–132

Exorcist, 1:74, 2:234, 3:200, 5:257, 6:140, 7:349, 8:162, 9:125, 11:27, 11:328, 12:178, 14:422

Expectation of the last things. *See* SI.XIV; and XV

Experience, 9:100, 19:27, 19:261; religious, not determining truth (*see* Modernism)

Expiation, 5:302, 7:150, 7:572, 8:295, 8:314, 10:17, 10:283, 11:13, 14:410, 18:279, 18:282

External perceptibility of revelation. *See* SI.I a–b

Extreme unction. *See* SI.XII m

F

Facts, 19:73; dogmatic (*see* SI.I e–f; and II c–d); juridical necessary for trial, 16:289

Faith, 1:18–19, 1:34–37, 1:115–116, 1:132–133, 2:64, 2:114, 2:180, 2:313, 2:323, 3:16, 3:41, 3:331, 7:45–46; act of (*see* SI.XV); as a fruit of the Holy Ghost (*see* SI.XV); supernatural (theological) (*see* SI.I c–f; IX b; and XI b). *See also* Creed

Fall: of the angels (*see* SI.VI c); of man (*see* SI.VII c)

Fallen man: recipient of baptism (*see* SI.XII k); state of (*see* SI.VII d)

Family, 7:130, 7:336, 7:373, 8:251, 18:94, 18:125, 18:190, 18:336–337; rights and duties within (*see* SI.XI). *See also* SI.XII o

Fasting, 1:82, 1:91, 3:34, 3:249, 3:334, 8:263–265, 13:143–144, 19:193, 19:253–254; before Communion, 2:324, 3:28, 3:115, 4:67, 4:163, 4:206, 5:96, 5:232, 5:304, 5:342, 7:243, 8:145, 8:173, 8:285–287, 11:263, 14:56, 14:394, 15:29, 15:167, 16:44, 16:203, 16:269–270, 17:67, 17:101, 17:236, 18:25, 18:72–73, 18:204–205, 19:175; ecclesiastical (*see* SI.XI h); as a form of penance, 1:34, 1:49, 1:82, 2:200–201, 3:25, 3:245–248, 5:47–53, 5:117, 5:278, 5:343–349, 5:386, 6:99, 6:205, 6:220–221, 8:311, 9:183–184, 9:188–189, 9:273, 10:298, 12:48–50, 12:310–311, 13:158–162, 14:332, 15:160, 16:38, 16:206, 16:248, 17:49–50, 17:257, 18:169, 18:237, 18:417, 18:463, 19:193

Father, 1:26–27, 1:44, 1:116–117, 7:66, 7:431; first Person of the Trinity (*see* SI.VI a); head of the family (*see* SI.XI k); priests rightly called, 2:187, 6:106, 6:193, 6:201, 7:431, 11:293, 12:358–359, 13:98

Fathers of the Church, 3:308, 7:180, 8:31–33, 10:15, 12:171–172, 14:119, 18:251, 18:411; authority of (*see* SI.I f)

Fatherland, love of. *See* SI.XI m

Fault(s), 1:109, 2:331, 5:120, 5:130, 5:154, 5:318–323, 6:31, 6:168–169, 7:158, 7:294, 8:250, 9:144, 9:164, 14:319, 14:400, 15:109, 15:162, 15:195, 18:51, 18:144, 18:331, 18:409, 19:293

Fear, 1:10, 1:38–39, 1:132, 7:59, 8:96, 8:112–113, 19:31, 19:68; as a gift of the Holy Ghost (*see* SI.XV); as imperfect sorrow for sin (*see* SI.IX b; and XII i); passion of, 3:162, 5:108, 5:241, 5:321, 6:22, 9:205–206, 10:200, 14:427, 16:180, 16:182, 18:88, 18:250, 18:407

Feast(s), 1:42, 2:183–184, 2:199, 5:302, 6:93–101, 6:193, 8:263, 8:265, 10:45–46, 13:37–41, 13:140–141, 15:123–125, 15:198, 16:339, 16:358, 18:15, 18:57–58, 18:166–168, 19:177–179; Easter the greatest, 3:270, 13:224, 16:161, 16:166, 19:245, 19:250; ecclesiastical (*see* SI.XI h); Sunday as, 2:183, 3:262–265, 5:386, 6:96, 13:41, 13:142, 14:298, 16:339, 18:57–58, 18:166, 19:245

Fecundity, 7:57, 7:78, 18:348, 18:430; frustrated in conjugal act sinful (*see* SI.XI r)

Fermented bread, used in Eucharist, 5:228, 7:246–247

Fidelity, 7:503, 7:592, 8:105, 8:236, 8:254, 18:92, 19:290–291; in marriage (*see* SI.XI k)

"Filioque." *See* SI.V d

Fire, 1:90, 16:196, 19:301–312; eternal (*see* SI.XIV a); New (ceremonial), 1:93, 13:218–219, 19:251; as a symbol of the Holy Ghost, 2:130, 2:199, 2:297, 3:271, 4:27, 4:117, 5:387, 11:137, 13:81, 13:255–256, 15:142, 16:20, 16:168, 17:146, 19:79

Flattery, as a way of being accessory to sin. *See* SI.XV

Flesh, 1:20, 1:80, 1:118, 3:37; of Christ received in Eucharist (*see* SI.XII f–h); of Christ that of the Son of God (*see* SI.VIII b); resurrection of all (*see* SI.XIV b); works of, 1:47–49, 1:53–54, 2:256, 3:322, 5:63, 5:287–288, 6:22, 6:128–130, 6:172, 6:204, 7:549, 9:209, 9:272, 11:142–143, 12:314–315, 12:319–320, 12:323–325, 12:385–386, 14:438, 15:25, 15:37–38, 15:78, 16:88, 16:132, 16:214, 17:275

Flock, 2:131, 3:371, 3:377, 4:32, 4:122, 5:53, 5:211, 8:31, 10:124, 16:191, 16:288, 17:156, 17:216, 18:135, 18:303, 19:94, 19:115

Flood, 3:325–326, 7:194–195, 7:439, 8:211, 10:210–213, 11:149, 14:103, 14:312, 16:139, 17:238, 18:91, 18:314–315, 19:14

Fonts (sources), 8:12–33; of moral action, 5:282–286, 11:446–447, 16:130, 19:189; of revelation (*see* SI.I f)

Foreigner, 5:161, 10:332, 12:64, 12:314–315

Foreknowledge, divine. *See* SI.IV c

Forgiveness, 1:24, 7:446, 8:222, 8:235, 11:353–354; exercised in the Church (*see* SI.XII); impossible to the unrepentant, 2:263, 3:34, 3:192–193, 3:196–198, 4:36, 4:49–50, 4:58, 4:142–143, 4:154, 5:69, 5:101, 5:116, 8:309, 11:164, 11:181–182, 11:451–452, 14:257, 16:234, 16:253, 16:352, 17:72, 17:247, 18:75, 18:77, 18:213, 18:410, 19:192, 19:198; of sin a divine power, 1:28, 1:65–66, 2:144, 3:14, 3:156, 4:68, 4:164, 5:21, 5:101, 5:209, 5:272, 6:74, 7:145, 9:252, 11:163, 14:280, 15:67, 16:90, 17:168, 17:245, 18:52, 18:148, 18:213, 19:193

Form, 3:243, 18:22, 18:110, 19:121, 19:123; and matter in the sacraments (*see* SI.XII a); sacramental (*see individual sacraments*); substantial, of man (*see* SI.VI d)

Formation, 5:126–128, 6:209–210, 7:35, 7:62, 17:41

Formula(s): of absolution, 1:65, 2:224, 3:155, 3:167–168, 5:272, 6:139, 7:293, 8:155–156, 8:294, 15:98, 16:224–225, 17:218–219, 17:247, 18:402, 19:196, 19:197; of faith (*see* Creed)

Fornication. *See* SI.XI r

Fortitude: as a cardinal virtue (*see* SI.XV); as a gift of the Holy Ghost (*see* SI.XV)

Fortune-telling, 2:173, 3:20, 4:44, 4:135–136, 5:30, 5:296, 6:84, 7:391, 14:283, 15:21, 15:183, 16:177, 16:318–321, 17:42, 17:197, 19:229

Fraternal: charity, 3:33, 5:217, 7:511, 7:524, 8:119–120, 8:328, 9:51–52, 10:225, 11:28–29, 11:38, 11:351–357, 13:211, 13:262, 14:347, 14:349, 18:322, 19:147–149, 19:286, 19:323; correction, 1:46–47, 1:83, 2:75, 2:245, 2:326, 3:210, 5:74, 5:320, 5:354, 8:28, 9:161, 11:354–355, 14:274–275, 14:343, 16:38, 16:248

Fraticelli, 11:382–383

Fraud, 1:49–50, 2:256, 4:36, 5:70, 5:259, 5:287, 5:315–316, 6:120, 6:194–195, 6:202–203, 7:461, 8:256, 8:331, 9:150, 9:261, 11:420, 14:314, 18:245, 18:420

Freedom, 7:509, 9:220, 19:24–25, 19:273; of God (*see* SI.VI a); of man (*see* SI.II g; II i; III e; and VIII g); to marry (*see* SI.XII o); necessarily limited (*see* SI.I d–e; and XI o)

Freemasonry, 8:244, 12:374, 16:336–337, 17:203, 18:166

Friend, 1:33, 1:38, 1:108, 1:112, 2:257, 3:75–76, 4:88, 5:26, 5:41, 5:137, 5:188, 5:298, 6:45, 7:168, 7:394, 8:119–120, 13:314, 16:223, 18:62, 18:175, 18:334, 18:359, 19:143, 19:148

Friendship, 2:62, 2:195, 4:34–35, 4:125, 5:41, 5:298, 7:305, 10:201, 12:181, 17:9, 18:24, 19:188, 19:277, 19:280

Fruits of the Holy Ghost. *See* SI.XV

Fulfillment: of all time (*see* SI.XIV); of Messianic prophecies in Christ (*see* SI.VIII h; and X i); of the old law in the new, 2:126, 4:65, 4:78, 4:160, 5:221, 5:379, 7:78, 8:241, 10:31, 13:255, 14:209, 19:44

Funerals, 5:298, 7:433, 12:309, 13:314–316, 19:160, 19:303–305

Future, 7:317, 7:576, 19:197–205, 19:229; divine knowledge of (*see* SI.IV c); superstitious inquiry into, 4:44, 4:135, 5:30, 5:296, 6:28, 6:84, 6:86, 11:98, 11:364, 11:366, 14:283, 15:21, 15:183, 16:127, 18:152 (*see also* Astrology; and Fortune-telling)

G

Gambling, 14:315, 16:349

Genesis, historicity of. *See* SI.I f

Genitrix (Mother of God). *See* SI.VIII i

Gentleness. *See* Meekness

Gestures, 1:33, 1:57, 11:189–190, 11:389–390; liturgical (*see* Ceremonies)

Ghost, Holy: fruits of (*see* SI.XV); in general (*see* SI.V d); gifts of (*see* SI.XV); sins against (*see* SI.XV)

Gifts of the Holy Ghost. *See* SI.XV

Glory, 1:92, 1:110, 1:120, 1:128, 2:150, 6:141, 7:168, 8:47–48,

8:120, 8:204–205, 8:232, 9:255, 13:339, 18:64, 18:179, 18:267, 19:9–17; of God the end of all creatures (*see* SI.VI f)

Gluttony, as a capital sin (*see* SI.XV)

Gnosticism, 3:218, 3:280–281, 5:277

God. *See* SI.IV–V

Good: common, 5:306–309, 5:323, 6:133, 7:143, 8:251, 12:62–66, 12:203–205, 13:327, 13:331, 18:203, 18:241, 19:255; God alone able to draw from evil, 5:267, 6:31, 6:176–177, 8:37, 10:312, 13:277, 14:192–194, 18:270, 19:24; God as author and source of all, 2:30, 3:308, 5:145, 5:174, 6:31, 6:86, 7:166, 7:495, 8:34–35, 9:13, 9:30, 9:163, 9:275, 11:87, 13:50, 14:28, 14:181, 16:36, 16:106, 16:109, 17:118, 17:192, 18:43, 18:72, 18:245, 18:356, 19:22, 19:144; moral, 5:172, 6:209, 9:272–273, 16:125, 16:171, 17:41, 18:237–238, 18:463–464; works (*see* SI.X f; X g; XII j; XIII a; XIII b; and XIV a)

Good news. *See* Gospel(s)

Goodness, 1:127, 1:133, 2:328, 3:32, 18:242, 19:109–114; of creatures, 3:249, 3:308, 3:334, 4:82, 5:48, 5:164, 5:337, 6:28–32, 8:54, 10:80–164, 13:29–30, 13:324, 14:191, 15:132, 19:34; as a fruit of the Holy Ghost (*see* SI.XV); of God (*see* SI.IV b; and VI a); of marriage, 5:223, 5:258, 6:141, 7:365–374, 9:218, 12:158–159, 15:171, 16:295–296

Goods. *See* Property

Gospel(s), 1:9, 1:98, 3:200, 3:230, 7:352, 8:12, 8:14, 12:35–36, 19:105–106; authors of, 1:116, 2:295, 12:15, 12:28–31, 12:32, 12:34–36, 13:110, 14:171; canonical (*see* SI.I f); proclaimed at Mass, 2:272, 2:282, 2:287, 3:139, 3:145, 3:146–147, 5:374, 5:379–380, 5:383, 8:262, 13:108–111, 13:138–139, 14:327, 14:387, 16:179, 16:267

Grace, 1:18, 1:59–60, 1:118–119, 1:128–131, 2:209, 3:17, 3:26, 3:234, 3:335, 18:61–62, 18:175–177, 18:351–357; for fallen man (*see* SI.X); for the first man (*see* SI.VII b); Mary full of, mediates all (*see* SI.VIII a; and VIII b); after meals, 1:6–7, 2:336, 4:8, 4:97, 4:186, 5:156, 11:98, 11:188, 12:54, 12:121, 14:77, 14:354, 15:55, 15:88, 15:121, 16:96, 17:86, 17:108, 17:278, 19:157, 19:160, 19:322 (*see also* SI.XV); before meals, 1:6–7, 2:336, 4:8, 4:97, 4:185, 5:156, 11:98, 11:188, 12:54, 12:121, 14:77, 14:354, 15:55, 15:88, 15:121, 16:96, 17:86, 17:107, 17:278, 19:157, 19:160, 19:322 (*see also* SI.XV)

Gratitude, 5:331, 6:31, 7:50, 8:6, 8:191, 9:84, 12:53, 13:136–140, 14:431, 15:40, 15:96–97, 16:293, 16:363, 17:50, 18:73, 18:206, 18:399, 19:159, 19:232

Gratuitousness, 7:60, 7:144, 7:543–544, 8:93, 8:183, 10:199–203, 11:183, 14:359–360

Greed, as a capital sin. *See* SI.XV

Greeks, 7:172, 7:253, 19:57; schismatic, 5:216, 8:21, 11:138, 11:222, 12:312–313, 14:122, 14:380, 18:309–310; united, 3:153, 3:213–215, 5:228, 5:376, 14:388

Guardian angel(s). *See* Angel(s)

Guilt, 2:252–253, 3:170, 3:352, 7:65, 8:154, 18:79, 18:282, 19:146–147, 19:206–207; state of (sin) (*see* SI.VII c; X f; and XIII c)

H

Habitual grace. *See* SI.IX a; and X f

Habit: bad (*see* Vice); good (*see* Virtue)

"Hail Mary." *See* SI.XV

Happiness, 3:26, 4:22, 4:75, 4:111, 4:174, 4:212, 7:98, 7:166, 8:54, 8:112, 8:224, 8:328, 8:334, 19:94–95; beatitudes bring, 3:16, 6:157, 6:162, 8:333–334, 9:211–212, 9:275, 11:28, 11:143, 13:302, 14:353, 16:13, 16:120, 16:220, 18:52, 18:250; desire for universal, 5:191, 11:143, 13:333, 13:340, 14:261, 17:8

Harmony, 13:39; of old and new testament, 3:90, 3:329, 4:78, 5:350, 5:379

Hatred, 8:136, 8:190, 8:301, 11:351, 19:144–147; related to murder (*see* SI.XI q); of sin and evil necessary, 3:35, 3:42, 3:270, 4:24, 4:114, 4:193, 5:65, 5:101, 5:104, 6:81, 7:299, 7:301, 7:305, 8:96, 8:137, 8:152–153, 8:294, 8:299, 9:113, 9:144–146, 11:278–281, 15:156, 15:158, 16:34, 16:234, 17:73, 17:249, 17:250, 18:75–76, 18:126, 18:212–213, 18:352, 18:404, 19:23

Head, 3:186, 3:239, 5:130, 6:116, 7:43, 7:47, 12:54, 12:59, 13:288, 13:331, 17:171, 18:125, 18:158, 19:261; of the Church on earth, the pope (*see* SI.III); of the Church universal, Jesus Christ (*see* SI.II a)

Healing: blessed oil signifies, 3:62–63, 3:71, 5:265, 9:75, 11:244–245, 17:260, 19:163, 19:207; sacraments of (*see* SI.XII m; and XII i); supernatural gift of, 5:223, 7:144, 8:56, 12:25, 16:310–311, 16:319, 17:214, 18:407, 19:206

Health, bodily, 1:10, 1:83, 7:336, 7:502, 13:193–194, 16:308, 19:107; effected by sacrament or sacramental, 1:72, 2:62, 2:230, 2:325, 3:177, 5:121, 6:72–73, 6:133, 6:206, 7:339, 8:161, 8:315, 9:98, 9:119–121, 9:267–268, 12:356, 14:64, 14:417, 15:170, 16:279, 16:282, 17:76, 17:261, 18:424; as an idol, 1:36, 14:283

Heart: hardness of, 2:256, 3:163, 5:62, 5:75, 5:83–84, 6:50, 7:454–455, 7:585, 8:80, 8:93, 8:216, 8:221, 8:331, 9:150, 9:168–169, 10:332, 11:278, 11:450, 14:392, 16:78–79, 18:94, 18:163, 18:430–431; of Jesus, 1:70, 5:81, 6:95, 12:366, 13:270–276, 16:277, 17:82, 18:377, 19:52, 19:149; of Mary, 11:12, 11:14, 11:215; purity of, 1:10, 1:57, 1:132, 2:246, 2:328, 3:33, 4:84, 5:77, 5:176, 5:378, 6:175, 7:485, 8:333, 9:211, 9:275, 10:234, 11:28, 12:50–51,

12:144, 13:302, 14:396, 15:34, 17:88, 17:271, 18:241, 19:182

Heaven: in general (*see* SI.VII a; and XIV a); as one of the four last things (*see* SI.XV)

Hebrews. *See* Israel

Hell: in general (*see* SI.XIV a); as one of the four last things (*see* SI.XV)

Heresy. *See* SI.II b; and XI b

Hermit(s), 3:224–225, 3:228, 3:230, 12:120–125, 12:189, 12:246–247, 12:255–256, 12:282. *See also* Consecrated life

Hierarchy, 11:351–352, 13:318; of the Church (*see* SI.II a); of creatures, 5:207, 6:28–29, 10:150

History, 1:88, 1:97, 18:90, 19:34–35; creation begins (*see* SI.VI a); to end in victory (*see* SI.XIV b); providence guides (*see* SI.VI g)

Holiness: of angels (*see* SI.VI c; VII a; XI e; and XI g); of Christ (*see* SI.VII c; and VIII f); of God (*see* SI.IV b–c); loss of (*see* SI.VII c–d); mark of the Church (*see* SI.II a); of Mary (*see* SI.VII c; and VIII k); original (*see* SI.VII b); state of (grace) (*see* SI.X f; XIII b; and XIV a); universal call to, 9:64, 11:161, 12:52–56, 12:66, 14:185, 14:255, 18:158

Holy orders. *See* SI.XII n

Holy Spirit. *See* SI.V d

Homeland, patriotism and. *See* SI.XI m; and XI o

Homily, 4:79, 5:34, 5:149, 8:248, 14:327, 16:292, 16:321, 19:101, 19:168

Homosexual: acts (*see* Sodomy); attraction (*see* Perversion, sexual)

Honor, 3:367, 11:393, 11:452; of clergy, 2:187–188, 4:44, 4:136, 5:35, 5:391, 6:106, 6:212, 7:433–434, 8:218, 8:318, 8:319, 9:48, 9:260, 11:322–323, 13:299, 14:37, 14:301–303, 15:191, 16:60, 16:343, 18:224, 19:212; of God, 1:27, 1:33–34, 1:126, 2:172, 3:20, 3:28, 3:121, 3:341, 3:351, 4:41–43, 4:45, 4:65, 4:134–135, 4:137, 4:161, 4:205, 5:13–15, 5:134, 5:139, 5:187, 5:290–292, 5:330, 6:146, 6:201, 6:207, 7:321, 7:343, 8:242, 8:265, 8:291, 9:51, 9:262, 10:269, 11:362, 13:6, 13:299, 14:217, 14:279–285, 15:18, 15:29, 15:54, 15:75, 15:183, 15:185, 16:46, 16:54, 16:104–105, 16:274, 16:300, 16:315–319, 16:325, 16:328, 17:242, 18:156, 18:200, 18:341, 19:81, 19:229–233, 19:239–243 (*see also* SI.XI e; and XI g); of parents, 1:9, 1:33, 1:43–44, 1:56, 1:126, 2:45, 2:185–186, 3:22, 4:46, 4:139, 5:35–36, 5:261, 5:306–307, 5:391, 6:101–105, 6:193, 6:201, 7:427–437, 8:250, 9:48, 9:260, 11:393–396, 12:58–59, 13:299, 14:36, 14:298–301, 15:22–23, 15:53, 15:72, 15:76, 15:120, 15:190, 16:60, 16:227, 16:315, 16:342, 17:44, 17:202, 18:15, 18:54, 18:157, 19:257–259; of rulers, 4:140, 5:35, 5:307, 5:391, 6:106, 7:433–435, 8:251, 9:48, 9:260, 11:399, 12:92, 13:299, 14:37, 14:303–304, 15:76, 16:60, 16:343, 18:159, 18:339, 18:341; of saints and angels, 1:33, 1:123, 2:162, 2:178, 2:318,

3:21, 3:355–357, 4:42–43, 4:59, 4:134–135, 4:154, 5:26–30, 5:137, 5:219, 5:302, 5:330–337, 7:391–395, 8:85–87, 8:149, 8:242, 8:245, 8:292, 9:42–45, 9:259, 11:189, 11:367–369, 12:72, 13:6, 13:104, 13:231, 13:297–311, 14:32–33, 14:285–290, 15:21, 15:74, 15:185–186, 16:56–57, 16:82, 16:180, 16:205, 16:328–332, 17:29, 17:79, 17:198, 17:263, 18:53–54, 18:153, 18:202, 19:234–236 (*see also* SI.XI e; and XI g); of superiors, 1:33, 1:44, 2:241, 4:46, 4:139, 5:35, 5:307, 5:391, 7:433–435, 8:218, 8:250, 9:48, 9:262, 11:393, 11:399, 13:5–6, 13:299, 14:36, 14:301–303, 15:191, 16:60, 16:343, 17:202–203, 18:55, 18:157–159, 19:261

Hope, 2:64, 2:150–151, 2:316, 3:32, 3:41, 15:32; act of (*see* SI.XV); supernatural (theological) (*see* SI.XI c)

Hospitality, 9:195, 12:64, 12:137–138, 12:252–254

Host, sacred, 1:70, 1:99, 1:131, 2:220, 3:102, 3:149, 5:93, 5:230–231, 6:134, 7:354, 8:142–143, 8:288, 16:264–267, 17:100, 18:204, 19:177–183; adoration of proper, 1:71, 1:99, 2:277, 2:291–292, 2:324, 3:116–117, 3:121–123, 4:11, 4:100, 5:95, 5:98, 5:162–163, 5:381–382, 5:387, 6:206, 6:219–220, 7:259, 7:266, 8:109, 8:284, 8:287, 9:94, 9:266, 12:288, 12:364, 13:85, 13:127, 13:260, 13:271, 13:341, 14:54, 14:382, 14:393, 15:94, 15:96–97, 15:166, 16:265–266, 17:66, 17:229, 18:171, 18:207, 19:176–178

Hours, liturgical. *See* Divine office

Humanity: of Jesus Christ (*see* SI.VIII b); redemption of, in Christ (*see* SI.VIII g); salvation of, in the Church (*see* SI.II a–b); unity of, in Adam (*see* SI.VII c–d)

Humiliation, 2:284, 5:16–17, 5:378, 5:389, 6:103, 7:286, 8:78, 10:174, 11:13, 11:81, 11:296, 13:112, 18:411–412

Humility, 1:29, 1:59, 2:81, 2:255, 2:330, 3:33, 3:37, 3:209, 3:266, 5:60–61, 5:65, 5:97, 5:238, 5:394, 6:46, 6:56–57, 6:144, 6:157–158, 6:167–168, 6:181, 7:80, 7:108, 8:228, 8:331, 9:245, 10:47, 11:17–18, 11:53–54, 11:296, 11:449–450, 12:26, 12:47–48, 12:283, 12:287, 13:112, 13:186, 13:229, 14:393, 14:433, 15:53, 15:98, 15:119, 15:176, 16:145, 16:242, 16:311, 17:11, 17:271, 17:275, 18:63, 18:179, 18:246, 18:270, 18:405, 19:150, 19:154–156, 19:229

Hunger, 1:10, 1:46, 1:132, 5:52, 5:347, 6:166, 7:165, 7:557, 8:78, 8:333, 10:108, 11:20, 11:132, 11:264, 11:410, 12:209, 12:391, 16:96, 16:121, 18:240–241, 19:314

Husband. *See* SI.XI k; and XII o

Hymn, 1:97, 4:216–225, 5:378, 6:99, 12:54, 12:307, 12:371, 13:48, 13:51–52, 13:219–220, 16:267, 16:358, 19:83, 19:176, 19:180

Hyperdulia, 1:33, 6:183–184, 8:77, 8:85–86, 8:245, 13:280–281, 13:284, 13:289, 14:33, 14:70,

14:288, 15:179–181, 16:105, 17:189–191, 18:153

Hypostatic union. *See* SI.VIII c–f

I

Icon(s). *See* SI.XI e

Iconoclasm, 2:176, 7:395–398, 9:46, 12:226–230, 14:288

Idol(s), 5:48–49, 5:212, 5:343–344, 19:127; definition of, 3:121, 3:301–302, 8:243, 9:259, 13:299, 16:273, 16:316, 17:196, 19:229; making of, 1:88, 2:173–174, 3:298, 4:43, 4:135, 5:27–28, 6:27, 7:487, 9:259, 10:272, 14:289, 16:273, 17:196; worship of, 1:32, 1:55, 2:172–174, 3:20, 3:295, 3:301–306, 4:43, 4:135, 5:219, 5:296–297, 5:333, 6:24, 6:84–86, 6:192, 6:222–223, 7:396, 8:243, 9:209, 9:272, 10:256, 10:297, 11:5, 12:140, 12:384–385, 13:299, 14:108, 14:283, 15:21, 16:116, 16:141, 16:176, 16:180, 16:272–273, 16:316, 17:42, 17:196, 18:94, 18:152

Ignorance, 1:10, 1:83, 1:133, 2:248, 5:280, 7:120, 7:129, 8:329, 9:5; culpable (vincible), 1:101, 3:323, 5:56, 5:191, 5:285, 5:311, 5:341, 6:93, 6:191, 6:199, 6:209–213, 6:220, 7:380, 8:104, 9:163–164, 9:166–167, 9:174, 11:93, 11:457, 14:253, 16:182, 16:198, 16:321–323, 17:42, 17:174, 17:194–195, 18:343; inculpable (invincible), 3:323, 5:184, 5:285, 5:333, 7:323, 7:441, 9:166, 9:174, 12:349, 14:253, 16:182–184, 17:21, 17:158, 18:144, 18:314, 18:323, 19:120

Illness, 4:72, 4:169, 4:209, 5:121–123, 5:256, 6:175, 6:195, 7:336–338, 8:172, 11:315–316, 12:337, 14:418, 16:121, 16:203, 16:248, 16:278–283, 17:63, 17:260, 18:37, 18:80, 18:220–221, 18:424, 19:205–208

Images, holy. *See* SI.XI e

Imagination, 4:14, 4:50–51, 4:103, 4:144, 5:359, 5:364–365, 5:368–369, 7:50, 7:544, 10:152, 11:408–410, 16:320, 19:43

Immaculate conception. *See* SI.VIII k

Immortality: of Adam (*see* SI.VII b); of reward and punishment (*see* SI.XIV a); of the soul (*see* SI.VI d)

Immunity: of the Church, 18:337; of the clergy, 8:163

Immutability, 5:193–194; of divine revelation (*see* SI.I b); of God (*see* SI.IV b)

Impassibility, 2:146, 2:220, 3:73, 3:103, 3:345, 5:199, 6:77, 6:142, 7:159, 8:71, 8:223, 11:75, 11:112, 11:117, 11:172, 14:260, 16:156–157, 18:150, 18:288–289

Impeccability, 5:211, 6:167, 6:183, 7:58, 8:83–84, 8:90–91, 8:101–102, 9:43, 9:144, 10:153, 11:103, 13:153, 14:199, 15:179

Impediments of marriage. *See* SI.XIII o

Impenitence, final, as a sin against the Holy Ghost. *See* SI.XV

Impetration. *See* SI.XI f

Imposition of hands, 7:360, 12:12; sacramental, 1:73, 1:77, 2:214,

2:231, 3:27, 3:66, 3:199, 3:336, 4:61, 4:157, 5:90, 5:227, 5:257, 5:264–265, 5:276, 6:136–137, 6:207, 7:337, 7:353, 8:140, 8:278, 9:85–88, 9:124, 11:244, 11:322, 12:16, 12:234, 13:221, 14:373, 14:420, 15:28, 16:215, 17:63, 17:92, 17:227–228, 18:223, 18:373–375

Imputability, 5:228–230, 5:282–288, 5:319–320, 5:368–369, 7:149, 8:63, 8:94–95, 9:156, 9:271, 11:150–151, 11:408–409, 11:446–447, 14:243

Incarnation. *See* SI.VIII a–f

Incense, 1:88–89, 2:305, 3:135–136, 3:275–276, 3:358, 5:377–378, 7:495, 10:137, 10:162, 10:215, 12:85, 12:134, 12:144, 12:230, 13:98–100, 14:447, 16:374, 18:335, 19:304

Incest, 1:47, 1:68, 2:192, 2:239, 4:52, 4:147, 4:200, 5:273, 5:310, 5:324, 6:203, 6:217, 7:313, 11:341, 16:66, 16:364, 17:52, 17:53, 17:216

Incomprehensibility: of divine mysteries (*see* SI.I b d); of God (*see* SI.IV b)

Incorporation: into Christ, 1:63, 7:218, 9:89–90, 18:390–391; into the Church, 1:17, 7:142, 9:103, 17:90–93

Incredulity. *See* Unbelief

Indifference, religious. *See* SI.I c

Indissolubility of marriage. *See* SI.XII o

Indulgences. *See* SI.XII l

Inequality: of men in society, 18:340–341; of true religion and falsehood, 5:213, 13:15, 13:328–329, 16:177–178, 16:182–184, 16:191–198, 17:155, 17:195

Inerrancy of scripture. *See* SI.I f

Infallibility: of the Church (*see* SI.II c–d); of the supreme pontiff (*see* SI.III f)

Infant(s), 2:212, 3:51–53, 3:68–69, 19:125–126; adoption of, 12:353–354; divine, Jesus, 12:342, 14:14, 14:110, 16:144–147, 16:301, 16:306, 16:344; massacre of by Herod, 2:210, 8:136, 9:157, 10:287, 11:15, 16:146, 16:344, 17:226, 18:95; prenatal murder of (*see* Abortion); sacramental Communion for, 3:85, 7:276–277, 8:131, 8:144–145, 11:265, 18:32

Infidelity, 5:82, 5:283, 7:530; of ancient Israel, 5:297, 19:25; in marriage (*see* SI.XII o); sin as, 1:34–35, 1:53, 2:116, 8:102, 8:104–105, 12:373, 14:336

Infidel(s): as outside the Church (*see* SI.II b); status and works of (*see* SI.VII d)

Ingratitude, 2:254, 4:69, 4:165, 5:106, 5:147, 5:254–255, 6:86–87, 6:107, 6:165, 7:585, 8:110, 10:101, 10:163, 11:447–448, 12:335, 12:366, 14:336, 14:340, 14:431, 15:102, 16:97, 16:220, 16:350, 18:96, 18:391, 19:61, 19:188–191

Inheritance, 1:48, 1:67, 1:128, 5:139, 5:279–280, 7:68, 7:71, 7:524, 8:62, 10:51, 16:205, 16:220,

16:293, 18:271, 18:292, 19:85, 19:285

Initiation: sacramental, of infants, 3:51–53, 11:265, 14:370, 17:222; sacraments of (*see* SI.XII c–h)

Injustice, 4:45, 4:49, 4:136–138, 4:142, 5:81, 6:90, 7:87, 7:305, 8:257, 10:67, 11:459, 15:78, 15:194, 16:187–188, 16:296, 16:322, 16:350, 18:280, 19:43, 19:191

Inspiration: of the Holy Ghost (*see* SI.I f); of scripture (*see* SI.XI p)

Institution of sacraments by Christ. *See* SI.XII a

Integrity: of confession (*see* SI.XII i); of the first man (*see* SI.VII b)

Intellect: divine (*see* SI.IV c); human (*see* SI.I c–e; and VII d)

Intention, 1:53, 14:50, 14:362–363, 19:208, 19:232–233; to deceive, 4:49, 4:69, 4:143, 4:166, 4:208, 5:321, 7:477, 7:481–482, 8:155, 11:284, 11:420, 14:318, 16:350; good not justifying evil means, 1:53–54, 4:49, 4:143, 5:44–45, 6:125, 11:366, 15:95; in moral acts, 5:282–286, 11:446–447, 16:130, 19:189; in sacraments (*see* SI.XII b)

Intercession: of angels and saints (*see* SI.XI e); of Christ, 5:374, 7:110, 7:510, 8:85, 11:56, 11:126, 11:464, 13:70, 13:252, 15:65, 19:75; of the Church, 5:217–218, 7:503–506, 12:125–128, 13:215; for the dead (*see* SI.XIV a); as a form of prayer (*see* SI.XI f); of Mary, 2:33, 3:289, 4:59, 4:88, 4:155, 5:146, 5:153, 5:166–167, 5:355, 5:371, 7:506, 8:86, 8:245, 9:35–37, 9:257, 11:214–215, 12:295–296, 12:347, 13:59, 13:153, 13:235–243, 14:288, 14:439, 15:20, 15:54, 15:85–86, 15:121, 15:179–181, 16:81–82, 16:329, 17:79, 17:190, 18:37, 18:63, 18:179, 18:184, 19:236

Interest, when usurious, 1:50, 1:54, 5:40–42, 5:287, 5:295, 5:315–316, 7:463, 8:257, 11:420, 14:314–315. *See also* Usury

Interdict, 3:168, 12:67, 16:225

Interior life. *See* Spiritual life

Interpretation: of the deposit of faith (*see* SI.I e; and I f); of holy scripture (*see* SI.I f); of laws, 5:307, 7:380, 8:14 (*see also* SI.II g)

Investiture, 10:145, 12:247–249, 14:125

Invocation, 1:122, 7:391, 15:185; of evil powers, 4:44, 4:135–136, 8:244, 10:156, 11:364–366, 14:284; of God, 4:137, 4:199, 5:381, 9:189, 9:259, 18:64, 18:180, 18:369; of the Holy Spirit, 2:216, 11:137, 18:375, 18:383; Trinitarian, 4:28, 4:118, 6:91, 11:97–99, 11:313, 13:259–260, 18:368, 18:369

Irreligion, 5:296, 10:31, 11:48, 11:363–364, 13:18, 14:134, 14:177, 14:280, 16:180, 18:153

Irregularity, 3:24, 5:309, 7:220, 11:325

Islamism, 1:35, 5:190, 5:297, 8:220, 11:138, 11:148, 12:217–220, 12:224–226, 12:259–261, 12:313–314, 13:250, 13:285–286, 13:289–290, 13:328, 14:122–124, 16:249–250

Israel, 1:7, 1:94, 7:387; chosen people of God, 10:61, 10:250, 12:151, 14:105, 16:162, 16:333–334, 18:91–95, 18:254, 18:433, 19:18; as the nascent Church before Christ, 10:337, 16:273, 16:313–314, 16:362

J

Jacobites, 18:280, 18:312, 18:370

Jansenism, 8:91, 8:104, 12:359–360, 12:367–368, 18:31–32

Jealousy, 19:43, 19:147; of God, 2:172, 7:400, 12:144, 15:53, 15:72; in marriage, 5:130, 6:61, 17:265; sinful (*see* SI.XV)

Jesus. *See* SI.VIII a–h

Joseph, 1:21, 1:98, 3:287–288, 7:67, 8:80, 8:251, 11:15, 14:15, 14:216, 19:187, 19:195; feast(s) of Saint, 3:262, 15:106–107, 15:124–125, 16:142, 18:167, 19:58–59, 19:235, 19:252; Jesus's submission to, 2:206, 4:221, 8:251, 10:258, 10:284, 11:17–18, 11:394, 11:440–441, 12:59, 14:15, 14:110, 14:299, 16:137, 16:147, 16:302, 18:95, 18:125, 19:257; old testament type of Christ, 3:80, 8:196, 10:160, 10:205, 10:225–231, 14:104, 14:209, 16:162–163

Joy, 1:24, 1:70, 1:114, 1:133, 2:243, 2:328, 5:72, 5:91, 5:210, 7:78, 7:496, 8:64–65, 9:207, 9:243, 9:275, 10:31, 10:139, 11:41–42, 15:33, 16:33, 16:221, 16:300, 16:375, 18:242, 18:246, 18:323, 19:201; as a fruit of the Holy Ghost (*see* SI.XV)

Jubilee, 3:174–175, 11:310, 19:204; indulgences and, 5:119, 5:253–254, 8:315, 11:307, 11:309–311, 14:416, 18:421, 19:204

Judgment, 1:21, 1:24, 1:118, 2:265, 2:329, 7:113–114; of conscience, 3:161, 5:186, 5:192, 6:111, 10:194, 16:183, 16:218, 16:244–245, 17:40, 17:41, 19:16, 19:226; as one of the four last things (*see* SI.XV); particular (*see* SI.XIV a); rash, 1:52, 2:194–196, 3:24, 4:36, 4:45, 4:49, 4:142, 5:43, 5:324–326, 6:112, 7:408–409, 7:413, 7:448, 8:258–259, 10:59, 11:430, 14:318, 14:320, 15:78, 16:63, 16:354, 17:47, 17:206, 18:164; universal (*see* SI.XIV b)

Jurisdiction, 8:28, 8:217, 18:160; of the Church (*see* SI.II e–f); of the supreme pontiff (*see* SI.III b–e)

Just, 1:45, 1:83, 2:181, 3:11, 8:17, 8:19, 19:22–23; Joseph as, 16:361, 19:24; those in state of grace (*see* SI.IX)

Justice, 1:10, 1:80, 1:132, 2:241, 3:33, 3:170, 11:418; as a cardinal virtue (*see* SI.XV); civil authorities and, 4:47, 4:140, 5:247–248, 5:308–309, 6:122, 7:440–441, 8:252, 9:160–161, 10:189, 11:401–402, 12:295, 12:305, 18:325, 19:263; of God (*see* SI.VII c–d; and IX); as holiness (*see* SI.IX); original (*see* SI.VII b); social (*see* SI.XI s)

Justification. *See* SI.IX

K

Keys: Peter given, 2:131–132, 3:203, 3:338, 3:370–371, 4:32,

4:122, 5:118, 5:211, 5:273–274, 7:146, 8:24, 8:209, 9:59, 11:35, 11:147, 14:111, 14:236, 17:23, 17:149, 18:302–305, 19:91; power of the, 2:132, 3:161, 3:170–171, 3:368–369, 4:32, 4:122, 6:169, 7:297, 9:22–23, 11:147, 11:164, 14:414, 15:32, 15:68, 17:72, 18:74, 18:209, 18:410

Killing, 1:45–47, 1:126, 1:128, 7:439–440, 8:136; the aggressor (*see* Defense); the criminal (*see* Execution); the innocent (*see* Murder); the preborn (*see* Abortion); the self (*see* Suicide); the suffering directly (*see* Euthanasia); unintentional not evil, 7:441, 11:401. *See also* SI.XI q

Kingdom of God, 1:21, 1:48, 5:72, 8:232, 11:200–201, 12:186, 19:46–48, 19:313; celibacy for, 2:205, 3:222–223, 7:366, 9:138, 9:214, 9:217, 19:280; the Church as, 3:320–321, 3:328–329, 4:32, 4:122, 10:27, 14:207, 16:77, 16:169, 16:219, 17:150; signs preceding fulfillment of, 11:130–132, 13:148; sins excluding from, 2:259, 3:161–162, 4:75, 4:173, 5:71, 5:104, 5:192, 5:283, 6:44, 6:116, 7:451, 7:460, 8:43, 8:57, 9:153, 9:272, 14:200, 14:262, 18:444; seeking first the, 6:177, 7:482, 7:534, 9:228–229, 10:37, 11:204, 11:442, 13:72–73, 18:83, 18:236, 19:10, 19:19

King, 1:30, 7:69, 9:14, 11:241, 11:252, 19:73–76; social reign of Christ as, 7:537–538, 12:94, 12:145, 12:250, 17:133–134, 17:148, 19:7, 19:44

Kiss, 1:100, 13:98, 13:103, 13:123, 13:132, 13:225; morality of, 1:47, 5:38, 5:247, 5:288, 5:311

Knowledge: of the faith, 2:147, 2:311, 4:40–41, 4:131–132, 5:126, 5:180–181, 5:184–185, 5:241, 6:4–5, 6:21, 6:199–200, 7:39–40, 7:42–43, 7:48–49, 8:12–33, 8:106, 8:183, 8:324–326, 9:12, 10:14–61, 11:99, 12:286–288, 14:164, 15:92, 16:48, 16:286, 17:63, 17:267, 18:31, 18:101, 18:231, 18:269, 18:408, 19:138; in general, 1:17, 1:59, 1:132, 3:32, 19:38 (*see also* SI.I a–e; IV a; and VIII f); as a gift of the Holy Ghost (*see* SI.XV); of good and evil, 2:247, 5:24, 5:54, 5:81, 5:282, 6:184–185, 7:65, 10:165, 10:170, 18:45, 18:91, 18:117, 19:38, 19:81; of the soul of Christ, 5:359, 8:82, 11:17, 17:251, 19:138

Kyrie eleison, 2:270, 2:285, 3:138, 3:146, 5:378, 13:101–102, 13:226, 14:87, 14:387, 16:267, 19:180, 19:184

L

Labor, 1:42, 1:91, 7:329, 7:462, 11:264–265, 19:41, 19:52; Jesus's manual, 11:16, 11:17–18, 16:147, 17:129; pains, punishment of Eve, 5:130, 6:184, 7:79, 10:167, 11:111, 11:213; remuneration of (*see* SI.XI s); rest from, 1:41–42, 2:44, 2:185, 3:22, 3:25, 3:197, 3:264, 3:266, 3:333–334, 4:46, 4:87, 4:139, 5:33, 5:305, 6:95–97, 7:420, 7:424, 8:249, 9:47–48, 9:260, 10:45, 10:107, 10:163–164, 11:381–388, 13:41–42, 13:204, 14:35, 14:42–43, 14:295–298,

14:324–328, 15:26, 15:89, 15:189–190, 15:198, 16:60, 16:154, 16:227, 16:339, 16:341, 17:44, 17:201, 18:15, 18:57, 18:166–167, 19:247

Laity, 2:131, 2:222–223, 5:185, 5:363, 7:202, 8:14, 8:218, 19:99, 19:219; rights of, 2:184, 8:132, 8:139, 8:157, 8:173, 18:349

Lamb, 1:100, 7:589, 13:133, 19:174, 19:314, 19:319; Abraham's sacrifice of, 10:218–219; type of Christ, 2:218, 3:89–91, 3:307, 5:383, 7:149, 7:281, 8:196, 9:98, 10:234, 11:52–53, 11:70, 11:254, 13:214, 13:220, 13:223, 14:105, 14:209, 16:85, 16:166, 18:286, 18:296–297, 18:419

Language, 7:114, 7:196, 7:456, 8:252, 12:194, 19:93, 19:146; liturgical (hieratic), 3:150–154, 5:161, 5:374–376, 13:13, 13:62–63, 14:388, 16:194, 16:366, 17:25, 17:243, 19:179

Last Supper, 7:110, 7:231, 19:168–170, 19:250–251; institution of the Eucharist during, 2:202, 2:218, 3:72, 3:83, 3:128, 3:336, 3:348–349, 4:11, 4:64, 4:100, 4:159, 5:228–229, 5:266, 7:282, 8:149–150, 8:284, 9:95, 11:54–55, 11:255, 12:366, 13:18, 13:143, 13:209, 14:378, 15:162, 16:41, 16:259, 17:64, 17:69, 18:70–71, 18:197, 18:377, 18:386, 19:166; institution of the priesthood during, 1:98, 2:231, 3:339, 4:64, 4:159, 8:317, 9:95, 9:101, 11:322, 14:53, 17:235, 19:167; Mass not a representation of (*see* SI.XII h)

Latria. See SI.XI e

Law: eternal, 3:265, 6:126, 11:445, 16:126–127, 16:364, 17:31; human, 4:47, 5:41, 5:306–307, 6:108, 6:222, 7:485, 9:157, 10:32, 10:79, 10:189–192, 11:445, 14:306, 15:172, 16:313, 17:268, 18:292, 18:411, 19:263, 19:264; natural, 2:190, 2:319, 5:185, 5:262, 5:311, 7:369, 7:417–418, 8:90, 8:105, 9:272, 10:204, 11:445, 15:138, 16:364, 18:144, 18:276, 18:341, 19:222–223; new (Christian), 1:41, 1:126, 2:184, 3:126, 4:27, 4:64–65, 4:117, 4:160, 4:194, 5:221, 5:373, 6:131–132, 6:197, 7:177, 8:16, 8:121, 8:248, 9:39, 9:264, 10:239, 10:334, 13:255, 14:383, 15:20, 15:91, 15:181–182, 15:200, 16:59, 16:273, 16:287, 16:341, 17:69, 17:238, 18:67, 18:71, 18:93, 18:186–187, 18:200, 18:361–363; old (Mosaic), 1:41, 1:126, 2:169, 3:126, 4:27, 4:65, 4:117, 4:160, 5:221, 5:302, 5:379, 6:84, 6:192, 7:385–387, 7:417, 7:451, 8:14, 8:121, 10:246, 10:239, 10:334, 12:15, 12:21, 13:255, 14:383, 15:20, 16:59, 16:190, 16:273, 16:286, 16:313, 16:341, 17:239, 18:93, 18:361, 19:14, 19:258; revealed, 6:215, 14:279, 16:129; sin as transgression of, 2:248–249, 2:329, 3:15, 4:33, 4:124, 4:196, 5:121, 5:247–248, 5:279, 5:282, 6:203, 9:142, 9:269, 10:170, 10:194, 11:80, 11:205, 11:445, 14:335, 15:16, 15:134, 15:151, 16:127, 16:129, 17:36

Laws. *See* SI.XI a; XI i; and XIII a

Laying on of hands, 3:177, 12:12; in baptism, 11:240, 13:221, 17:92, 19:131; in confirmation,

2:214–216, 3:27, 3:66, 3:69–70, 3:336, 4:61, 4:157, 5:89–90, 5:227, 5:264–265, 6:136–137, 8:140, 8:278, 9:85–88, 11:249–252, 14:373, 15:28, 16:30, 16:200, 16:215, 16:278, 17:63, 17:227–228, 18:195, 18:373–374; in holy orders, 1:73, 1:77, 2:231, 3:199, 3:201, 3:339, 5:257, 5:276, 6:207, 7:346, 7:352, 7:354, 8:162, 9:124, 11:322, 12:16, 12:234, 14:420, 16:278, 18:223, 19:210; symbolic of, 3:67, 3:142, 5:264, 18:375

Lector, 1:74, 2:234, 5:257, 6:140, 7:349, 8:162, 9:125, 10:44, 11:328, 14:422

Lent, 1:82, 1:90–92, 1:127, 2:299, 2:305, 3:251–252, 4:86–87, 5:47, 5:55, 5:342–346, 3:348, 5:386, 6:223, 8:264–265, 8:267, 9:185–187, 12:50, 12:247, 12:310, 13:137, 13:190–222, 14:42, 14:325, 14:329–330, 14:428, 15:26, 15:54, 15:80, 15:173, 15:200–201, 16:66, 16:248, 16:300, 16:362, 16:366, 17:90, 17:213, 18:59, 18:168–169, 18:412, 19:179, 19:250–255

Levite, 7:353–354, 10:62, 10:241, 16:362, 18:386–387

Lex orandi, lex credendi ("as we pray, so we believe"), 11:220–221, 11:333, 12:325, 13:8–12, 13:152, 13:317–322

Libertinism, 5:50, 5:192, 5:319, 5:329, 12:188, 12:373, 12:382, 13:18

Liberty. *See* Freedom

Lie(s), 1:53, 2:196, 3:24, 3:30, 3:162, 3:302, 3:324, 4:49, 4:69, 4:143, 4:166, 4:208, 5:44, 5:68, 5:321, 5:326, 6:124–126, 6:194, 6:202, 7:474–475, 7:477, 8:259, 9:50, 9:261, 11:103, 11:426–427, 14:40, 14:262, 14:318, 15:25, 15:31, 15:78, 15:160, 15:187, 15:195, 16:231, 16:241–242, 16:335, 17:47–48, 17:206–207, 18:214, 18:439, 19:290–291; devil as father of, 2:195, 3:378, 6:124, 6:185, 7:480, 10:215, 11:25, 11:426

Life: of Christ (*see* SI.VIII h); conjugal (*see* SI.XII o); consecrated (*see* Consecrated life); defense of (*see* Defense); eternal, reward of justice (*see* SI.XIV); of grace (*see* SI.VII a; and IX–X); moral (*see* SI.XI; and XIII); respect for human (*see* SI.XI q); temporal end of (*see* SI.XIV a); spiritual (*see* Spiritual life)

Lifting: of Jesus on the cross, 7:92, 11:67, 12:158, 13:212, 16:150; of mind and heart to God (*see* SI.XI f)

Light, 1:90, 1:93, 3:363, 7:217, 7:422, 19:54, 19:110; creation of, 10:82–83; of faith, 1:19, 2:214, 3:65, 3:135, 3:184, 5:8, 5:66, 5:357–358, 5:377, 7:32, 7:187, 8:207, 9:10–11, 9:249, 10:57, 13:274, 16:210, 17:6, 17:93, 18:182, 18:441, 19:149, 19:223; of glory, 3:184, 3:281–282, 3:283–284, 3:363, 5:385, 7:166, 8:47–48, 16:375, 18:114, 18:250, 18:455, 19:22, 19:244 (*see also* SI.XIV a); of grace, 2:306, 3:283–284, 3:363, 5:79, 5:154, 5:156, 5:385, 6:180, 7:217, 14:49, 15:41, 15:144; of

reason, 3:283–284, 3:363, 5:180, 5:290, 5:311, 6:174–175, 7:460, 8:6, 8:8, 8:165, 8:326, 11:141, 13:340, 14:100, 14:170, 18:103, 18:232–233, 18:253–254, 18:342; symbol of, 2:214, 3:65, 3:139, 3:184, 5:377, 5:385, 5:388, 13:24; of the world (*see* SI.VIII a–h)

Limbo: of the fathers, 1:21, 2:21, 2:125, 3:10, 3:198, 4:25, 4:115, 4:193, 5:18, 5:201, 5:204–205, 6:47–51, 7:87, 7:96–98, 8:202, 9:17, 10:258, 11:72, 11:115–116, 13:250–251, 13:319, 14:18, 14:222, 15:11, 15:63, 15:140, 16:19, 16:85–86, 16:142, 16:153–154, 17:139, 18:47, 18:127, 19:67–68, 19:73; of infants, 2:80, 5:198, 5:205–206, 8:43–44, 8:275, 11:116, 14:368, 16:153, 16:207–208, 17:171–172, 18:372. *See also* SI.XIV

Listening, 4:80, 5:5–6, 5:44, 6:123, 6:201, 8:218, 8:308, 16:232, 16:262, 16:279, 16:347, 17:30, 19:83, 19:253

Litanies, 3:40, 4:178–181, 4:222–225, 5:154–155, 7:350, 7:595, 11:216–217, 12:61, 12:291, 13:221–222, 13:248, 14:443, 15:41, 16:82–83, 16:85, 16:232, 16:329, 18:18

Liturgy: earthly, 10:238, 13:43–62, 13:94–140; in general (*see* SI.XI e; and XII); heavenly, 13:48, 13:75; locus of tradition, 5:374–377, 8:16, 13:8–12, 14:175, 17:240; music in, 13:13–14, 13:48, 13:63–65, 16:266, 19:101; seasons of, 8:267, 13:39, 16:264; source of theology, 8:16, 13:8–12, 18:178–179, 19:100

Living God, 3:121, 5:83, 7:135, 7:561, 9:224, 10:242, 10:293, 12:65, 12:110, 14:212, 17:126, 17:194, 18:262, 18:302–303, 19:29–33, 19:53, 19:127

Longanimity, as a fruit of the Holy Ghost. *See* SI.XV

Lord: in himself (God) (*see* SI.IV–V); Jesus is, 1:4, 1:20, 2:62, 2:121, 3:5, 3:7, 4:29, 4:119, 4:195, 5:10, 5:26, 5:158, 6:4, 7:72, 7:537–538, 8:195, 9:14, 9:250, 10:224, 11:106–107, 12:173, 13:122, 13:251, 14:13, 14:204–205, 15:137, 16:85, 17:17, 17:99, 18:46, 18:120, 18:130, 18:280, 18:286–287, 18:386, 19:47, 19:74, 19:157

Love: act of (*see* SI.XV); for the Church (*see* SI.XI m); of enemies, 2:167–168, 3:36, 3:42, 4:52, 4:58, 4:146, 4:154, 4:199–200, 5:35, 5:141, 5:293–294, 7:445, 7:574, 8:119–120, 8:253, 8:328, 11:353–354, 12:243, 12:297, 13:202, 13:215–217, 14:29, 14:271–273, 15:37, 15:42, 15:144, 15:176, 16:173–174, 17:192, 17:274; for the fatherland (*see* SI.XI m; and XI o); for God (*see* SI.XI d); of God for creatures (*see* SI.VI; and VIII g); God is, 6:63, 7:51, 10:46–47, 10:54, 11:347, 11:362, 14:9, 14:185, 19:31; in marriage (*see* SI.XI k; and XII o); new commandment of, 3:36, 4:52, 4:144–146, 4:199–200, 6:194, 9:39, 9:51–52, 12:149–150, 13:211, 17:270,

19:147; for others (*see* SI.XI d); as a theological virtue (*see* SI.XI d; and XV)

Lust, as a capital sin. *See* SI.XI r; and XV

Lutheranism, 3:96–97, 3:220, 3:228, 3:373, 3:377–378, 3:379–381, 5:214, 5:216, 5:229, 5:271, 8:67, 8:179, 11:184, 12:316–320, 12:323–326, 14:126–128, 14:132–133, 16:155, 16:196, 18:406, 18:420–421, 19:122

Luxury. *See* SI.XI s; and XV

M

Macedonianism, 11:100, 12:185–186, 13:111–112, 14:230

Magic, 2:44, 2:173, 3:308, 3:363, 4:83, 5:30, 5:296, 6:28, 6:192, 6:201, 6:221, 9:42, 10:157, 11:98, 11:364, 12:11, 12:14–15, 12:26, 12:154, 14:262, 14:284, 16:164, 16:276, 16:319, 19:229

Magisterium: extraordinary (*see* SI.II d; and III f); ordinary (*see* SI.II c–d)

Magnetism, 8:57, 10:156, 11:365

Magnificat, 3:261, 13:58–59, 16:301, 17:188, 17:190

Mahometan(s). *See* Islamism

Major orders. *See* SI.XII n

Man, 1:17, 10:48, 18:114; end of (*see* SI.VI d; VI f; VII a; and XIV); fallen (*see* SI.VII d); origin of (*see* SI.VI d); in paradise (*see* SI.VII b)

Manichaeanism, 3:218, 3:248, 5:47, 5:342, 6:29–30, 6:38–39, 6:64, 9:185, 12:190, 13:30, 14:391, 17:235, 18:316

Manna, 2:218, 3:84, 7:269, 7:564, 9:104, 10:235–236, 11:34, 11:255, 11:262, 12:53, 13:85, 13:111, 14:106, 14:209, 16:151–152, 16:167, 16:314, 17:230, 19:18, 19:176

Marcionism, 3:218, 3:248, 5:277, 5:343, 13:30

Mark(s): of the Beast, 8:224; of the Church (*see* SI.II a). *See also* Sacramental Character

Marriage. *See* SI.XI k; and XII o

Martyrs, 1:23, 1:53, 3:197, 3:359, 5:87, 5:225, 5:275, 5:309, 7:158, 7:282, 8:135–137, 10:40, 12:70–72, 16:180, 16:198, 16:212, 19:54, 19:179; feasts of, 3:135, 3:262, 7:423, 9:45–46, 13:38, 15:106, 16:146; veneration of, 1:34, 1:46, 2:276, 3:142, 3:279, 3:292–297, 5:331, 7:282, 7:423, 11:120, 12:71–72, 12:84, 12:209, 13:22–23, 13:70, 13:98, 13:320, 14:289–290, 14:449, 16:83, 16:116, 16:179, 17:199, 18:154, 18:329–330

Mary, Blessed Virgin. *See* SI.VIII i–k

Masons. *See* Freemasonry

Mass. *See* SI.XII f–h

Masturbation, 1:47, 1:58, 2:192, 5:38, 5:288, 5:310–313, 6:194, 6:217–218, 7:450–451, 9:171, 15:77, 15:193

Materialism, 10:154, 14:339

Matrimony. *See* SI.XI k; and XII o

Matter, sacramental. *See* SI.XII a

Mediator. *See* SI.VIII g

Mediatrix. *See* SI.VIII k

Meditation, 1:49, 1:99, 1:134, 7:161, 7:317, 18:73, 18:178, 18:206, 19:153, 19:219; as a form of prayer (*see* SI.XI f)

Meekness, 1:10, 1:27, 1:132, 1:133, 2:246, 2:328, 3:33, 3:37, 3:270, 5:38, 5:76–77, 5:91, 6:111, 7:94, 8:333, 9:49, 9:275, 10:234, 10:266, 10:282, 11:460, 12:47–48, 12:192, 12:202, 12:299, 14:347–348, 16:220, 17:271, 17:275, 18:240–241, 18:246, 19:149, 19:219

Melchisedech, 2:233, 3:125, 7:69, 7:283, 7:344, 9:96, 19:46; type of Christ, 8:196, 9:98, 10:205, 10:213, 10:216, 11:106, 14:209, 14:384, 17:238, 19:169–170

Members of the Church. *See* SI.II b

Memorial, 3:21, 7:256, 7:421, 10:203, 12:46–47, 14:386, 15:21, 15:29, 16:58, 16:334, 17:242, 18:71

Mendicants, 3:228, 3:230–231, 12:282–288, 14:124–125

Mercy, 1:28, 1:83, 1:126, 1:132–133, 3:286, 7:189, 7:193, 7:398, 19:199–207; divine, 1:17, 1:34, 1:60, 2:262, 3:272, 5:31, 5:68, 5:133, 5:272, 5:291–292, 6:99, 7:91, 8:43, 8:102, 8:193–194, 9:164–165, 10:153, 14:386, 15:184, 16:112, 18:313, 18:410–412, 19:30, 19:199; works of, necessary, 1:2, 1:9–10, 1:126, 1:133, 2:66, 2:73, 2:244–245, 2:326–327, 3:32–33, 3:247, 3:349, 4:46, 4:83–84, 4:138–139, 5:74–75, 5:351–354, 6:195, 7:118, 9:193–200, 9:273–275, 11:353–357, 14:273–274, 15:33, 15:161, 16:38, 16:248–250, 17:88, 19:276–278 (*see also* SI.XIII d; and XV)

Merit(s): of Christ (*see* SI.VIII g); of good works (*see* SI.XIII b); of the saints (*see* SI.II b; XII l; and XIV a); shared in the Church (*see* SI.II b; and XII l)

Messiah. *See* SI.VIII g–h

Mildness, as a fruit of the Holy Ghost. *See* SI.XV

Minister(s), 7:36, 7:42, 18:394; of the sacraments (*see* SI.XII b; *and individual sacraments*); support of the Church's, 2:50, 2:203, 2:320, 3:25, 4:52, 4:55, 4:147, 4:150, 4:200, 5:55, 5:295, 5:349–350, 5:391, 6:106, 6:220–221, 7:434, 8:266–267, 8:319, 9:243, 14:45, 14:324, 14:334, 16:66, 16:228–229, 16:362–364, 17:202, 17:215, 18:15, 18:61, 18:173

Ministry, 7:518, 18:44, 18:113; of the Church (*see* SI.II; and XII n); public, of Jesus (*see* SI.VIII f)

Miracle(s), 1:23, 1:36, 2:180, 3:5, 3:293–294, 3:301, 3:308, 3:364–365, 5:186, 5:338, 7:88, 7:177, 11:78–79, 16:89, 16:195–196, 16:198, 18:105, 19:69, 19:173; of Jesus as signs, 2:144, 3:86–87, 3:96, 3:233, 5:195, 6:24, 7:97, 8:196, 11:79, 13:148–149, 14:211, 16:86, 16:155, 16:333, 17:15, 18:95, 18:121, 18:381, 19:47, 19:71; worked by the first disciples, 3:295, 4:83, 5:211, 7:144, 11:75–76, 11:79, 12:7–12, 16:168, 17:24

Mission(s), 19:83–85, 19:107–108; canonical (*see* SI.II); of the Holy Ghost (*see* SI.V d); of the laity, 7:343; of the Son (*see* SI.VIII g–h)

Missionary, 11:274, 12:170, 12:206–207, 12:223, 12:333–335, 12:369–372, 16:78, 16:180, 16:189, 16:212, 16:257, 19:115; mandate of the Church, 7:222–223, 8:23, 10:38, 10:194, 11:148, 12:6, 12:170, 13:249, 14:114, 14:235, 16:251, 16:322, 18:158, 18:337, 18:352, 18:438, 19:107–108

Model(s), 6:146–147, 19:130; Christ as, 3:37, 3:252, 4:24, 4:43, 4:114, 4:135, 4:192, 5:17, 5:89, 5:371, 6:45–47, 6:50–51, 7:104, 7:448, 9:20, 9:51, 9:221, 11:27, 11:112–113, 11:380–381, 11:437–445, 12:10, 13:249, 13:295, 14:48, 14:272, 14:354, 14:425, 15:37, 15:92, 15:139, 15:186, 16:252, 17:275, 19:150; Mary as, 3:273, 5:147, 6:181–182, 11:111, 13:155–158, 13:181–183, 13:236, 13:277–279, 13:287–289, 14:443, 15:181; saints as, 3:237, 3:273, 3:293, 4:43, 4:135, 5:29, 5:219, 6:106, 6:181, 7:225, 9:43, 11:15, 11:239, 12:72, 12:296–298, 12:307, 13:40–41, 13:104, 13:145–146, 13:303–305, 14:119–120, 14:286, 14:290, 14:370, 15:74, 15:151, 15:186, 16:29, 16:58, 16:212–214, 16:334, 16:358, 17:62, 17:277, 19:130, 19:234

Modernism, 8:337–339, 18:254

Modesty, 1:133, 2:244, 2:328, 3:32, 3:38, 3:41, 4:48, 4:50, 4:141, 4:143–144, 5:38, 5:91, 5:152, 5:311–312, 5:329, 6:117, 7:314, 7:450, 7:456, 8:292, 9:49, 9:208, 9:261, 10:225, 10:233, 11:190, 11:263, 11:406–407, 11:411, 12:48, 12:50–51, 12:58, 12:106, 12:145, 12:192, 13:288, 14:130, 14:354, 14:427, 15:33, 15:38, 15:41, 15:88, 15:96, 15:110, 15:193, 16:33, 16:61, 16:221, 16:347, 17:270, 18:242, 19:281–284; as a fruit of the Holy Ghost (*see* SI.XV)

Molinism (Quietism). *See* SI.XIII d

Monarchy, 12:216, 12:251, 12:288; Church constituted as (*see* SI.II a)

Monasteries, 3:224, 12:202–205, 12:238–240, 14:121, 16:251, 18:335, 18:416, 19:177, 19:284

Money, 1:49–50, 1:54, 7:462–465, 7:476, 19:285–287; love of, root of evil, 2:255, 5:62, 6:127, 9:150, 14:338–339, 19:285; as payment (*see* SI.XI s). *See also* Simony; and Usury

Monks, 3:226–227, 3:228–229, 9:137, 12:202–205, 12:261–263, 14:119, 16:251, 16:284, 18:335, 19:219, 19:240

Monogamy. *See* SI.XII o

Monophysitism, 12:197, 18:287

Monotheletism, 5:217, 8:82, 12:220–221, 18:267, 18:287, 18:291

Montanism, 6:64, 10:278

Moral law. *See* Law

Morality, 7:132; fonts of, 5:282–286, 11:446–447, 16:130, 19:189;

of passions, 5:84, 5:117, 5:357–358, 6:111–114

Mortification, 2:257, 3:245–258, 3:267, 4:54, 4:148, 5:47, 5:50, 5:115, 5:238, 6:99, 6:129–130, 7:457, 8:190, 8:264, 8:311, 9:113, 9:123, 10:234, 10:271, 11:308, 11:450, 11:460, 12:48–50, 12:60, 12:185, 12:310–312, 12:368, 13:158–162, 13:187–200, 14:313, 14:362, 15:201, 15:203, 16:65, 16:251, 16:332, 16:360, 17:49–50, 17:213–214, 17:274–276, 18:163

Moses, Law of, 1:41, 1:86, 2:169, 2:319, 3:379, 4:76, 5:188, 5:388, 6:84, 7:385–387, 7:417, 7:451, 8:107, 9:40, 9:96, 10:60, 10:188, 10:246, 10:326, 12:15, 12:21, 13:255, 14:105, 14:363, 15:182, 16:301, 17:239, 18:93, 18:151, 18:433

Motives of credibility. *See* SI.I d

Murder: as grave sin (*see* SI.XI q); origin of, 2:260, 6:112, 16:354, 18:91, 19:38; unjust hatred tantamount to (*see* SI.XI q); willful, as a sin that cries vengeance (*see* SI.XV)

Muslim(s). *See* Islamism

Mutilation. *See* SI.XI q

Mystagogy, 11:237–238

Mysteries: of faith (*see* SI.I b d); of the life of Christ (*see* SI.VIII h); of the rosary (*see* Rosary; and SI.XV)

Mystical body of Christ, the Church. *See* SI.II a

Mystical life. *See* Spiritual life

Mythology / myth, 10:54, 12:57–58, 12:166, 14:138

N

Name, 1:8, 1:39–41, 1:52, 1:114, 1:126, 3:18, 3:69, 6:88–93, 13:285–286; baptismal, 1:60–61, 3:59, 5:227, 7:225, 8:276, 11:239, 12:61, 12:233, 13:28, 14:370, 15:151, 16:29, 16:209, 16:212–214, 17:62, 19:130–131; of Jesus, 1:64, 2:120–121, 3:21, 4:18, 4:57, 4:108, 4:152, 4:191, 4:201, 5:15, 5:27, 5:29, 5:135–136, 5:331, 5:337, 6:152, 6:223, 7:96, 7:514, 8:195, 8:227, 8:246, 9:14, 10:202, 11:12, 11:101–102, 11:105, 12:302, 13:124, 13:171–173, 13:275, 14:13, 14:203, 15:156, 16:85, 16:305, 17:80, 18:63, 18:179, 18:352, 19:74, 19:238–239

Nation(s), 1:84, 1:91, 7:66, 7:117, 8:19, 8:23, 8:210, 9:203, 10:19, 10:64, 10:215–216, 12:7, 12:12, 13:222, 14:303, 18:64, 18:91, 18:158, 18:181, 18:337, 18:352, 19:305, 19:309

Nativity, 7:71, 7:78–79, 12:72; of Christ (*see* SI.VIII h); feast of Christ's, 2:295, 3:262, 3:266–267, 4:24, 4:86, 4:113, 4:192, 5:167, 5:369, 5:388, 12:187–188, 12:201–202, 12:230, 13:36–37, 13:143, 13:163–169, 14:326, 14:329–330, 15:26, 15:81, 15:106–108, 15:123–126, 15:200, 17:135, 18:167, 19:249; feast of John the Baptist's, 13:284; feast of Mary's, 2:300, 3:272, 12:265, 13:283–284, 15:124–125

Naturalism, 12:372–373

Nature, 1:73, 1:81, 1:99, 19:56, 19:82; Christ possessing two (*see* SI.VIII c); divine (*see* SI.IV, V); human (*see* SI.VI d–f; and VII); origin and end of created (*see* SI.VI, XIV)

Necessity, 2:207–208, 7:35; of baptism, 1:60, 2:210–211, 2:248, 3:51–52, 3:57–58, 3:316–317, 4:61, 4:73, 4:156, 4:171, 4:203, 4:210, 5:87, 5:190, 5:225, 6:71, 6:135, 7:206, 8:135, 8:276, 9:265, 11:228, 14:51, 14:367–368, 15:150, 16:7, 16:28, 16:97, 16:207–208, 16:211, 17:61–62, 17:171–172, 17:218, 17:223, 18:69, 18:190, 18:194, 18:371, 19:134–135; of the Church for salvation (*see* SI.II a); of faith, 1:19, 1:24, 2:114, 2:133, 2:313, 3:5, 3:318, 3:322, 3:373, 5:8, 5:188, 6:4–5, 6:21, 6:199–200, 7:45, 7:65, 8:105–111, 9:25–26, 9:239–240, 10:27, 10:175, 11:79, 11:89–90, 14:165–167, 15:6, 15:128, 15:153, 15:184, 17:13, 17:30–31, 17:98, 17:119–122, 18:35, 18:82, 18:100, 18:106, 18:231–232, 18:438, 18:441; of grace (*see* SI.X c); of observing laws (*see* SI.XI e; and XIII a); of prayer, 3:16–17, 3:38, 3:150, 5:134, 5:147, 5:157, 7:493, 8:227, 9:273, 11:187, 11:194, 11:449, 14:431, 15:76, 15:136, 15:160, 15:176, 16:52, 17:78–79, 17:183, 18:63, 18:178–179, 19:152; of the sacraments for salvation (*see* SI.XII b; *and individual sacraments*)

Neighbor, 1:9–10, 1:51–54, 2:167, 3:23–24, 7:489, 7:504, 8:252–255, 10:202, 10:336; love of, 1:9, 1:54, 1:124–125, 1:127, 2:44, 2:167–169, 2:319, 3:32, 3:42, 4:10, 4:40, 4:42, 4:51, 4:131, 4:133, 4:145–146, 4:199, 5:25, 5:34–35, 5:65, 5:73–74, 5:292–295, 6:84, 6:194–195, 6:200, 7:427–430, 8:119–120, 8:328, 9:50–52, 9:262–263, 10:14, 10:31–32, 10:190, 10:217, 11:28–29, 11:38, 11:351–357, 12:56–66, 13:211, 13:262, 14:29, 14:270, 15:33, 15:42, 16:53, 16:221, 16:315, 17:192, 17:270, 18:56, 18:83–84, 18:165, 18:235–237, 18:322, 18:445, 19:147–149, 19:286, 19:323

Nestorianism, 2:165, 5:216, 5:369, 6:39–40, 8:221, 11:110, 12:197, 13:231, 13:277, 14:216, 18:291–292

Newspapers, 10:197, 14:314, 15:193, 16:62, 16:339–340, 16:347

New testament, 1:55, 1:60, 1:86, 3:342, 7:252–253, 8:12, 19:166–167, 19:170; books of (*see* SI.I f); time of, 4:76, 10:63–64, 12:5–78, 14:101, 16:84, 16:173, 16:195, 16:206; unity of the old and, 3:90, 3:329, 4:78, 9:67, 10:65–66, 10:204, 16:205, 18:120, 18:257

Nicene Creed, 2:272–273, 3:55, 3:139, 3:319, 5:193, 5:214–215, 5:380, 6:29–30, 6:34, 6:38, 6:53, 6:62–64, 6:71, 7:53, 7:134, 8:173–174, 11:100, 12:173, 13:111–112, 14:213, 14:242, 17:156

Noah, 1:44, 10:210–214, 13:25, 13:38, 14:103, 17:238; ark of, type of the Church, 6:67, 7:132, 7:140, 8:211, 9:22, 9:248, 10:213,

11:149–150, 12:46, 13:220, 17:158, 18:315

Notes: of the Church (*see* SI.II a); theological (*see* SI.I c; and I e)

Nourishment: Eucharist as, 1:31, 1:70, 1:131, 2:31, 2:158–159, 2:221, 3:97, 4:64, 4:160, 5:55, 5:222, 5:228–229, 5:231, 6:166, 6:206–207, 7:183, 7:249, 7:275, 8:145, 8:234, 8:285, 9:75, 10:31, 10:201, 11:260–262, 11:263–266, 12:53, 13:58, 13:134, 14:56, 14:389, 15:28, 16:268, 16:374, 17:59, 18:204, 18:251–252, 18:361, 19:111; material, 2:158, 5:35, 5:47–48, 5:174, 5:343–344, 5:347, 6:102–103, 6:163–166, 6:219–220, 8:233–234, 8:256, 9:30, 9:255, 10:148, 10:167, 14:305, 15:19, 15:55, 15:84, 15:121, 15:178, 18:26, 18:58, 18:162, 18:391, 19:253

Novatianism, 6:139, 6:168, 7:310–311

Number, 3:37, 3:158, 11:139, 13:44, 13:56; in the Blessed Trinity (*see* SI.V a; and IV e); of orders (*see* SI.XII n); of the sacraments (*see* SI.XII a)

Nuns, 2:205, 3:220, 3:224–225, 3:230–233, 8:156, 9:136, 12:125, 13:241, 13:286–287, 16:251, 16:285

Nuptials. *See* SI.XII o

O

Oath, 1:78, 3:21, 7:406–413, 8:246–247, 9:47, 10:341, 11:373–374, 15:74–75, 15:187, 19:241–242; conditions for licit, 1:39, 2:181, 4:45, 4:137–138, 4:199, 5:298–299, 6:89–91, 7:408, 8:247, 11:374–375, 14:292, 16:58–59, 16:335–336, 17:200, 19:242; false as perjury, 1:40, 2:181, 3:21, 4:45, 4:138, 4:199, 5:298–300, 6:90, 7:412, 11:375–376, 14:292–293, 15:75, 15:187, 16:59, 16:335, 17:43, 17:200, 19:241, 19:242; against Modernism, 8:337–339, 18:254

Obedience, 1:29, 1:59, 1:82, 2:206, 3:34, 3:222–223, 3:249, 7:162, 7:180, 9:36, 9:48, 9:260, 10:47, 11:14–15, 11:358, 11:380, 11:394, 12:59, 12:298–299, 13:199, 13:288, 13:331; Adam's refusal of (*see* SI.VII c); to civil authorities (*see* SI.II g; XI i; and XI o–q); as an evangelical counsel (*see* Evangelical counsels; SI.XIII e; and XV); sin in general as refusal of (*see* SI.XIII c)

Obligation. *See* Duty

Obsession, demonic, 3:200, 5:257, 8:58, 12:319, 14:196

Obstinacy in sin, as a sin against the Holy Ghost (*see* SI.XV)

Occasion of sin, 1:66, 1:104, 1:109, 2:161, 2:225, 3:29, 3:157, 3:159–160, 3:168, 3:241–242, 4:90, 4:149, 5:107, 5:111, 5:120, 5:236, 5:238, 5:294–295, 6:54, 6:129–130, 7:455–457, 7:541–542, 7:576, 8:236, 8:250, 8:255, 8:304, 9:49, 11:410–411, 11:446–447, 12:66–69, 14:77, 14:84–85, 14:305, 14:313, 14:405–406, 15:30, 15:43, 15:136, 15:158, 15:196, 16:36, 16:121, 16:237–238, 16:367,

17:74, 17:249, 18:76, 18:86, 18:103, 18:247, 19:186–187

Offertory, 2:273–274, 2:288, 3:139, 3:147, 5:374, 5:380, 13:113–121, 14:55, 14:88, 14:387, 14:389, 16:265, 16:267, 18:70–71, 18:127, 18:197, 18:201, 18:296, 18:393, 19:181–182

Oil(s), 7:68–69, 7:476, 19:132, 19:163; sacramental (*see* SI.XII a; XII c; and XII m); symbol of, 2:215, 3:71, 5:90, 5:265, 6:136, 8:278–279, 9:75, 9:120, 11:244–245, 14:375, 16:200, 16:215, 16:278, 17:228, 18:373, 18:423, 19:44

Old age. *See* Elderly

Old testament, 1:55, 7:152–153, 7:399; books of (*see* SI.I f); prophecies of Christ (*see* SI.VIII h); time of, 3:264, 4:76, 5:343, 8:196, 10:61–63, 14:100–101, 16:77, 18:96, 19:65; unity of the new and, 3:90, 3:329, 4:78, 5:350, 5:379, 10:65–66, 10:204, 14:97, 14:136, 16:205, 18:105, 18:120–121

Omission, 3:30, 3:51, 3:164–165, 3:238, 3:255, 7:380, 19:198, 19:296; sins of, 1:108, 2:248, 2:323, 3:41, 4:33, 4:53, 4:68, 4:90, 4:124, 4:147, 4:165, 4:196, 4:207, 5:57–58, 5:280, 5:285, 5:351–352, 6:202, 6:210–211, 6:215, 7:146, 8:297, 9:161, 11:177–178, 11:205, 11:406, 14:45, 14:335, 15:41, 15:100, 15:134, 16:14, 16:125, 16:127, 17:36, 17:44, 17:143, 18:85, 18:87, 18:153, 18:242, 18:452, 19:198

Omnipotence. *See* SI.IV c

Onanism. *See* Masturbation

One: Church (*see* SI.II a); God (*see* SI.IV b; and V a)

Oppression of the poor, as a sin that cries vengeance. *See* SI.XV

Order, 1:56, 1:86, 11:351–352; of creation (*see* SI.VI); religious (*see* Consecrated life); social or public (*see* SI.II g–i; XI o–q; and XI s)

Orders, holy. *See* SI.XII n

Ordination. *See* SI.II f; and XII n

Original sin. *See* SI.VII c

Orthodox, schismatics, 5:216, 8:21, 12:312–313, 14:122, 14:380, 19:122

"Our Father." *See* SI.XV

Ownership. *See* Property

P

Paganism, 3:255, 3:302–306, 3:366, 5:137, 5:190, 5:208, 5:297, 7:355, 7:463, 8:8, 10:75–76, 10:156, 10:344, 12:152, 12:314–315, 12:382–385, 13:155, 13:175, 13:276, 14:118, 16:273, 16:303, 16:316, 17:125, 18:312, 18:431

Pain, 1:21, 1:118, 1:128, 3:40, 6:31, 7:83, 7:118, 19:262; absent in heaven (*see* SI.XIV a); in childbirth, 1:31, 5:130, 6:184, 7:78–79, 8:81, 10:167, 10:336, 11:111, 11:213, 12:105, 13:164

Pantheism, 10:154

Parable(s): of the Good Samaritan, 9:199, 19:145; of the Importunate Friend, 19:156; of the Lost Sheep, 11:41–42, 19:52; of the Mustard Seed, 12:36, 17:150;

of the Net, 7:132, 17:150; of the Pharisee and the Publican, 6:144, 9:190, 19:156; of the Prodigal Son, 7:497, 11:42–43, 12:34, 19:198, 19:228; of the Rich Man and Lazarus, 9:224, 14:184, 17:161, 19:300; of the Sower, 3:80, 5:266, 13:108, 17:150; of the Talents, 5:390, 19:269; of the Tares and the Wheat, 7:132, 12:126, 14:184; of the Ten Virgins, 3:65, 7:132; of the Two Gates, 9:119, 9:155; of the Unforgiving Servant, 11:37, 19:30; of the Unjust Judge, 19:156; of the Unjust Steward, 16:79; used by Christ to teach, 3:75–81, 5:266–267, 11:41, 19:49, 19:311; of the Wedding Feast, 19:9

Paraclete. *See* SI.I f; II c; V d; and XII e

Paradise, 1:70, 1:92, 3:198, 7:519, 7:581, 19:39–41, 19:271; eternal (*see* SI.VII a; and XIV a); terrestrial (*see* SI.VII b)

Parents, 1:33, 1:44–45, 1:80, 7:377; duties of children toward (*see* SI.XI k); first (Adam and Eve) (*see* SI.VI d; and VII b–d); Jesus subject to his, 2:206, 4:94, 4:221, 8:251, 9:215, 10:258, 10:284, 11:17–18, 11:394, 11:440–441, 12:59, 14:15, 14:110, 14:299, 16:137, 16:147, 16:302, 18:95, 18:125, 19:258; rights and duties of (*see* SI.XI k; and XI p)

Parish, 4:149–150, 5:53–54, 5:340, 8:218, 8:262, 8:266, 8:288, 16:180, 16:191, 16:288, 18:35, 18:170, 19:148, 19:212

Parousia. *See* SI.XIV b

Partaking, as a way of being accessory to sin. *See* SI.XV

Pascha, 5:302, 11:52–53, 11:254, 13:223–224, 18:343, 18:416, 19:251–252

Paschal banquet, 7:241, 7:281, 11:52–53, 18:172, 19:70, 19:74, 19:251

Passion of Christ. *See* SI.VIII h

Passion(s), 3:36–37, 7:550, 11:452, 13:64, 13:96; mastery of, 4:54, 4:88, 4:148, 4:165, 4:207, 4:221, 5:50–52, 5:117, 5:231, 5:328, 7:162, 8:285, 10:171, 11:431, 11:457, 12:160, 12:218, 13:324–325, 15:201, 16:65, 16:134–135, 16:360, 17:274, 19:273; in moral action (*see* SI.VII d; and VIII f); nature and function of, 5:84, 5:357–358, 6:111–112, 13:96, 16:88

Passover (Pasch), 3:264, 7:247; Jewish, 5:295, 5:302, 5:387, 10:234, 11:52–53, 11:254, 13:214, 13:223, 16:161, 16:166–167, 18:93, 18:387. *See also* Easter

Pater Noster. See SI.XV

Patience, 1:10, 1:83, 1:133, 2:84, 2:243, 2:260, 2:326, 2:328, 2:330, 3:32, 3:270, 5:66, 5:74, 5:142, 5:359, 6:31, 6:45–46, 6:103, 6:147, 6:176–177, 7:94, 7:445, 7:597, 8:170, 8:260, 8:331, 9:149, 9:207, 9:243, 10:177, 10:201, 11:459, 12:92, 12:95–96, 12:103, 14:217, 15:33, 15:88, 15:104, 16:33, 16:220–221, 17:270, 17:275, 18:83, 18:97, 18:234, 18:242, 18:341, 19:27–30; as a fruit of the Holy Ghost (*see* SI.XV)

Patriarchs, 12:182–183, 19:44; ecclesiastical, 3:94, 3:208–209, 5:270, 16:288, 18:27; of the old testament, 1:97, 1:100, 3:283, 6:40, 6:48, 7:67, 7:386, 8:211, 10:73, 14:100–101, 16:117, 16:162, 16:206, 18:47, 18:127, 18:330, 18:432, 19:13, 19:67, 19:79

Payment for labor. *See* SI.XI s

Peace, 1:25, 1:100, 1:132, 1:133, 2:243, 2:328, 3:32, 3:72, 7:169, 9:207, 9:243, 9:275, 11:295, 15:33, 16:33, 16:61, 16:207, 16:221, 16:345, 18:240–242, 18:341; as a fruit of the Holy Ghost (*see* SI.XV)

Pelagianism, 6:136, 11:184, 12:190

Penance, 1:34, 1:92, 7:287, 9:177, 19:250–253; forms of, 3:248, 4:54, 4:70, 4:148, 4:167, 4:208, 5:48, 5:115–117, 5:238, 5:248–249, 5:252–254, 5:395, 6:129–130, 6:205, 8:295, 9:113–119, 16:38, 16:245–247, 16:251, 16:258, 16:332, 18:169, 18:403, 19:193, 19:196; meritorious for the dead, 4:37–38, 4:127–128, 4:197–198, 5:274, 6:51, 8:312, 11:159–160, 14:367, 15:148, 15:203, 16:247, 19:204, 19:299; sacrament of (*see* SI.XII i); virtue of (*see* SI.IX b)

Pentateuch, 10:61, 10:63, 14:171, 19:106

Pentecost, 1:64, 1:71, 2:199, 2:297, 3:12, 3:58, 3:262, 3:271–272, 4:27, 4:86, 4:117, 5:302, 5:387, 6:136, 7:194, 7:238, 8:206, 10:35–36, 10:240, 10:337–338, 11:19, 12:6–7, 13:253–259, 14:114, 14:325, 16:20, 16:160–161, 17:281, 18:48, 18:96–97, 18:132, 18:374, 19:78–88, 19:95–97, 19:252

Perfection, 1:131, 3:222, 7:259, 19:149–150; charity as bond of, 2:168, 6:101, 9:39, 9:72, 11:28–29, 19:149; of creatures, 1:107, 4:61, 4:156, 4:203, 6:101, 7:53, 8:7, 8:54, 10:150, 11:86–87, 13:332–333, 14:47, 15:12, 15:183, 16:54, 16:317–319, 17:56, 18:264; of Mary, 2:33, 3:284–285, 4:112, 6:167, 6:180–184, 8:18, 8:85–86, 8:238, 8:245, 9:36–37, 9:257, 11:212–214, 13:152–158, 13:284, 14:33, 14:70, 14:288, 15:179–180, 19:125

Perjury, 1:40–41, 1:55, 2:181, 3:165, 3:173, 4:45, 4:138, 4:199, 5:62, 5:283, 5:300, 6:90, 6:194, 7:412–413, 7:474, 9:150, 11:375, 14:293, 15:75, 15:187, 16:335, 17:43, 17:200, 19:241–242

Persecution, 7:575, 7:597, 19:25, 19:306; of Catholics, 2:246, 3:224, 5:78, 5:90, 5:187, 5:191, 6:69–70, 6:173–174, 7:155, 8:10, 8:135, 8:213, 8:333, 10:202, 10:291, 11:444–445, 12:156, 13:272, 13:338, 14:116, 15:34, 16:150, 16:179, 16:221, 16:300, 17:258, 18:97, 18:441; of Christ, 11:444–445, 18:95

Perseverance, 1:107, 8:165–166, 11:459, 14:311, 14:344; in faith, 2:298, 3:84, 7:104–105, 8:326, 9:72, 9:175, 11:183, 12:359, 13:25, 14:377, 17:58, 18:323, 19:305–306; final, 2:145, 2:151, 5:209, 5:362, 8:91, 8:229, 11:183, 14:431–432, 15:144, 16:22, 16:175, 18:74, 18:206–207,

19:155; in prayer, 2:151, 3:84, 4:57, 4:152, 4:201, 5:136, 6:130, 6:145, 7:170, 7:514, 8:206, 8:228, 11:187, 11:191–192, 12:189, 12:244, 13:244, 13:319, 14:114, 14:433–434, 14:441, 15:176, 16:52, 16:308, 16:311, 17:13, 18:63, 18:179, 19:154–155

Person(s): angelic (*see* SI.VI c; and VII a); of the Blessed Trinity (*see* SI.V); of the Blessed Virgin Mary (*see* SI.VIII i–k); of Christ (*see* SI.VIII a–h); human (*see* Man; SI.VI d–e; and VII a–d)

Pertinacity, 2:254, 5:60, 5:68, 5:190, 7:128, 7:446, 8:104, 9:149, 11:138, 11:149, 11:449, 12:34, 12:139, 18:324, 18:466

Perversion: as loss of supernatural faith, 10:215, 10:280; sexual, 2:264, 12:40, 12:324–325

Pessary. *See* SI.XI r

Peter (Apostle), 1:86, 3:203, 3:370–372, 5:211, 12:7–10, 12:13–15, 12:26–27, 14:111, 14:114–115, 16:167–169, 19:91–99; Church founded upon (*see* SI.III a); confession of, 2:131, 7:135–136, 10:34–35, 11:146, 14:210, 18:303, 19:53; successors of (*see* SI.III a)

Petition, 11:160, 18:202, 19:97, 19:151–154; as a form of prayer (*see* SI.XI f)

Pharisee, 3:294, 5:50, 5:336, 7:433–434, 7:477, 9:129, 9:166, 10:329, 11:6, 12:151, 14:109, 14:111, 14:318, 16:303, 18:95–96, 19:156, 19:195

Philosophy, 12:89, 12:155, 12:365–366, 12:377, 12:382, 13:325–330, 18:328, 18:439–440; relationship to faith (*see* SI.I s; and II h)

Physician, 7:316, 7:492, 16:253–254; Christ as divine, 9:175, 10:33, 10:38, 10:165, 11:13, 11:438, 11:453, 18:409

Piety, 2:184, 10:30, 16:46, 16:275, 16:340, 18:239, 19:81–82; filial, 7:437, 9:197, 11:393–396, 12:58–59, 13:242, 13:299, 13:327, 18:159, 18:239; as a gift of the Holy Ghost (*see* SI.XV)

Pilgrimage, 1:89, 2:179–180, 3:296, 5:337, 6:205, 6:224, 7:242, 7:534, 8:226, 10:225, 11:310–311, 12:28, 12:280, 13:295–297, 14:449, 16:250, 19:243, 19:257

Places, sacred, 2:179, 5:296, 5:337, 7:526, 9:47, 10:43, 11:364, 12:72, 12:260, 13:295–297, 14:284, 14:435, 16:151, 16:202, 18:210, 19:110

Pleasure, 1:52, 1:57, 1:111, 7:387, 7:486, 11:453, 16:115, 16:312, 16:316; moderated by temperance, 5:64, 5:76, 6:196, 7:455, 7:457, 9:184, 9:201, 11:21, 11:460, 12:48–50, 14:347, 19:254 (*see also* SI.XV); sexual (*see* SI.XI r)

Pneumatomachians. *See* Macedonianism

Political authority. *See* SI.XI g

Pollution, 5:38, 5:288, 5:310–313, 6:194, 6:217–218. *See also* SI.XI r

Polyandry. *See* SI.XII o

Polygamy: in the new law (*see* SI.XII o); in the old law, 6:116, 7:370, 8:164, 11:338

Polytheism, 2:174, 4:13, 4:17, 4:102, 4:105, 4:190, 6:26–28, 6:84–88, 10:75, 11:104, 11:371, 12:19, 12:37–38, 17:125

Pontiff, Roman. *See* SI.III a–i

Pope. *See* SI.III a–i

Pornography, 5:329, 7:456–457, 8:255, 14:82, 14:290, 14:309, 14:311, 15:193, 17:205

Possession, demonic, 1:107, 3:200, 5:257, 7:349, 7:494, 7:539–540, 10:266, 11:25, 11:37, 11:51, 12:17–18

Poverty, 1:44–45, 1:48, 19:286; of Christ, 2:122, 4:24, 4:114, 4:192, 6:46–47, 7:80, 8:260, 9:214–215, 9:221, 11:13, 11:81, 11:380, 11:442, 12:51, 12:160, 13:171, 14:16, 14:322, 16:18, 16:145, 17:16; as an evangelical counsel (*see* Evangelical counsels; SI.XIII e; and XV); of spirit, 2:246, 2:328, 3:33, 5:77, 6:59, 8:260, 8:332, 11:28, 12:51–52, 13:302, 14:322, 15:34, 16:219–220, 17:88, 17:271

Power(s), 1:28, 1:73–74, 1:117, 13:339–340, 19:196–197; of the Church (*see* SI.II c–d); of death, 9:17, 11:454, 17:247, 19:68; of evil, 1:61, 1:88, 4:20, 4:109, 5:148, 5:164, 5:205, 7:389, 7:552, 8:37–38, 8:57, 8:190, 10:155–156, 14:371–372, 16:210, 16:299, 18:387, 19:306; of the keys, 2:132, 3:170, 3:368, 4:32, 4:122, 6:169, 7:297, 9:23, 11:147, 11:164, 14:414, 15:32, 15:68, 17:72, 18:74, 18:209, 18:410; as one of the nine choirs of angels (*see* SI.XV); of prayer, 4:81, 5:137–138, 5:165, 7:493–495, 7:497–498, 8:227, 9:189–191, 10:218, 10:240, 11:165, 11:192–193, 12:119–120, 12:189, 13:45, 13:92, 13:248, 14:432, 15:82, 15:87, 15:110, 15:176–177, 17:81, 17:183, 18:63, 18:147, 18:178–179, 19:155; occult, 8:57–58, 10:155–156, 11:364–366; of the state (*see* SI.XI g)

Power of God, 1:25, 1:70, 1:116, 2:261, 3:99, 3:101–102, 7:99, 7:148, 10:85, 19:68–69; made perfect in weakness, 11:39, 12:217; as unlimited (*see* SI.IV c)

Praise(s), 1:29, 1:83, 1:121–122, 3:34, 7:284, 7:405, 9:159, 13:52, 16:180, 16:329, 19:88; creation renders to God, 4:58, 4:89, 4:153, 10:122, 13:52, 14:431, 16:115; as a form of prayer (*see* SI.XI f); psalms as, 13:49, 16:358, 19:142, 19:159; as a way of being accessory to sin (*see* SI.XV)

Prayer. *See* SI.XI f

Preaching, 1:98, 1:102, 1:116, 2:287–288, 3:12, 3:155, 3:200, 3:222, 3:230, 3:380, 4:77–78, 5:34, 5:149, 5:277, 5:305, 5:379, 6:209, 7:117, 8:70, 8:125–126, 10:38, 11:18–19, 12:10, 12:285–286, 13:110–111, 14:99, 16:147, 16:197, 18:95, 18:123, 18:400–401, 19:48–49, 19:90, 19:92

Preamble of faith. *See* SI.I d

Precepts of the Church. *See* SI.XI m

Predestination. *See* SI.X g–i

Pre-existence of souls. *See* SI.VI d

Prefigurement(s), 2:218, 3:91–92, 3:349–350, 4:65, 4:160, 5:349,

8:196, 10:62, 10:176, 10:187, 10:203, 18:361, 18:387, 19:169

Preparation for receiving the sacraments. *See* SI.XII a–b; *and individual sacraments*

Presbyterate. *See* Priest/priesthood

Presence, Eucharistic. *See* SI.XII f

Presentation: of Jesus in the Temple, 1:134, 2:296, 3:262, 3:268, 3:290, 4:84, 5:369, 5:388, 11:14–15, 13:183–186, 14:15, 14:80, 14:442, 16:301–302, 17:87, 18:18, 19:249; of Mary in the Temple, 2:300, 3:272–273, 13:286–287

Presumption, 1:37–38, 1:61, 2:89, 2:151–152, 2:330, 3:33, 4:35, 4:41–42, 4:133, 5:31, 5:67–68, 5:133, 5:292, 6:50, 6:85, 7:49, 7:150, 8:113–114, 8:436, 9:27, 9:164–165, 9:264, 9:271, 10:164, 11:181, 11:449, 12:110, 14:281, 14:342, 15:34, 15:184, 16:56, 16:326–327, 17:41, 17:195, 18:234–235, 18:244, 19:141–142; as a sin against the Holy Ghost (*see* SI.XV)

Pride, 1:48, 2:81, 10:153, 10:314, 18:45, 18:112, 18:245, 18:270–271, 19:43; as a capital sin (*see* SI.XV)

Priest/priesthood, 1:68–73, 1:96–101, 2:233, 3:29, 3:127, 3:346, 10:41, 10:282, 11:241, 11:252–253, 18:80, 18:223; of Christ (*see* SI.VIII g; and XII h); of the old covenant, 5:277, 7:353–354, 9:63, 10:61, 10:216, 10:244, 10:301, 13:99, 13:125, 14:420, 16:273, 16:362, 17:238, 18:386, 19:44, 19:169; sacrament of (*see* SI.XII n)

Primacy: of Christ, 11:12, 11:63, 11:105, 11:443; of God, 11:361–363; of the Roman Church, 2:139, 4:31–32, 4:122, 8:175, 9:59, 11:146–147, 12:234, 13:224, 16:191, 18:306–307, 19:98; of the supreme pontiff (*see* SI.III)

Private property. *See* Property

Privilege(s), 7:81, 7:103, 16:245, 16:286–287, 19:42, 19:58; of the Blessed Virgin Mary (*see* SI.VIII k)

Procession: as an act of worship, 1:89, 2:296–299, 2:303, 3:123, 3:268, 3:272, 8:226, 10:262, 10:269, 11:49, 13:85, 13:89–93, 13:206–207, 13:225–226, 13:243–244, 13:248, 13:268, 14:449, 16:284, 19:73, 19:75, 19:110; of the Holy Ghost (*see* SI.V d)

Procreation of children, as primary end of marriage, 1:47, 2:236, 3:233, 6:141, 9:133, 12:57–58

Profanation, 2:185, 3:22, 4:45–46, 4:72, 4:137, 4:139, 4:170, 4:210, 5:34, 5:296, 7:413–414, 8:244, 8:306, 10:329–331, 11:22, 11:385, 12:154, 12:260, 12:285, 12:384–385, 13:18, 14:33, 14:284, 15:22, 15:90, 15:105, 17:266

Profession, 1:85, 1:98, 3:331, 3:333, 7:49; of the evangelical counsels (*see* Evangelical counsels; SI.XIII e; and XV); of faith, formulaic (*see* Creed); of faith publicly required at times, 1:114, 2:111, 3:46, 3:60, 3:71, 4:40–41, 4:62,

4:131–132, 4:158, 4:204, 5:187, 5:227, 5:380, 7:189, 7:405, 8:173, 8:219, 9:124, 11:99, 11:177–178, 12:70–72, 14:178, 14:298, 14:449, 15:91–92, 15:152–153, 15:183–184, 16:55, 16:210, 16:325–326, 17:42, 18:103, 18:233, 18:327, 19:110, 19:132

Progress, 18:440, 18:442, 19:201; dogmatic an error, 8:337

Promise(s), 1:52, 1:61, 1:128, 3:84, 3:170, 11:340, 19:44–45, 19:141; baptismal (*see* SI.XII c); of God (*see* Covenant); made to God (vow), 2:182, 3:62, 3:219–221, 4:44–45, 4:136–138, 5:32, 5:88, 5:277–278, 5:295, 5:299, 6:87, 6:92–93, 6:224, 7:412, 8:247–248, 10:331, 11:378–381, 14:294, 15:75, 15:188, 16:58–59, 16:247, 16:251, 16:290, 16:336–337, 17:200, 19:243; marital (*see* SI.XII o)

Property, 2:193, 2:197, 6:202, 9:216, 9:261, 10:143, 10:343, 16:196, 19:285–288; of marriage, 3:235, 6:115, 7:366, 8:164–165, 10:32, 11:419, 16:293, 16:295, 18:226, 18:349; renouncing, 2:112, 3:222, 5:56, 11:380, 12:139, 14:351, 16:132, 16:180, 19:220, 19:286; right of man to (*see* SI.XI s); spiritual, communion of (*see* SI.II b; and XII l)

Prophecy, 1:96, 4:78, 7:68, 8:88, 10:277, 10:285, 13:106, 16:177, 17:14, 18:92, 18:105, 18:255, 18:441, 19:45–46, 19:67

Prophet(s), 1:91, 1:93, 3:283, 5:219, 5:336, 6:63–64, 7:68, 7:144, 8:80, 8:211, 10:20–25, 10:177, 10:187–188, 10:277–278, 11:106, 11:241, 11:253, 12:75–76, 13:106, 14:100–101, 14:107–109, 16:145, 16:168, 16:177, 16:196, 16:333, 17:9, 17:117, 18:94–95, 18:121, 18:256–257, 18:298, 18:354, 19:21, 19:44

Propitiator, 5:206, 5:234, 9:174. *See also* SI.VIII g

Prostitution, 12:152, 14:312

Protestantism, 1:93, 1:101, 2:136, 3:153–154, 3:299, 3:319, 3:328–329, 3:374–381, 5:192, 5:212–216, 5:259–260, 5:298, 5:331–335, 5:376–377, 7:37–38, 8:21, 8:103–104, 8:109, 8:221, 10:64, 11:158, 11:222, 12:316–326, 13:328–329, 14:126–136, 16:191, 16:195–198, 16:216, 16:291, 16:331, 17:147, 17:224, 19:122

Providence. *See* SI.VI g

Provocation, as a way of being accessory to sin. *See* SI.XV

Prudence, 10:47, 19:290; as a cardinal virtue (*see* SI.XV)

Psalms, 1:74, 7:86, 12:191, 19:142; in the liturgy, 2:268–269, 3:136–137, 3:140, 3:185–186, 3:258–261, 5:384–385, 13:48–49, 13:100–101, 13:136, 16:358; in scripture, 1:93, 10:62, 10:279, 10:342, 14:171, 18:257, 18:382, 19:106

Public heretics, 4:41, 4:79, 4:132, 7:128, 7:133, 8:17, 8:221, 11:138, 11:222, 11:407, 12:172–174, 12:185–186, 12:190, 12:194, 12:197, 12:256–257, 12:294, 12:304–305, 12:316–326, 12:359–360, 13:111–112, 13:127, 13:231, 14:250, 16:184, 16:196, 16:323, 17:42, 17:158, 17:194–195, 18:51,

18:142–143, 18:233–234, 18:322, 19:122

Pulpit, 10:33, 10:44, 10:60–61, 11:328, 13:21

Punishment, 1:54, 1:81, 1:118, 1:128, 3:30, 3:173, 3:354–355, 11:138, 18:218–219; death as (*see* SI.VII d; and XIV a); ecclesiastical (*see* SI.II b; II e; and XII k); eternal (*see* SI.XIV a); fear of sufficient, for penance (*see* SI.XII k)

Purgatory. *See* SI.XIV a

Purification of the Blessed Virgin Mary (feast), 2:296, 3:262, 3:268, 5:369, 5:388, 12:275, 13:180–181, 14:448, 16:300, 19:249

Purity, 6:183–184, 6:212, 7:81, 7:377–378; 7:455–457, 11:412, 12:50–51, 19:282–283; of heart required to see God, 1:10, 1:132, 2:246, 2:328, 3:33, 5:77, 5:378, 6:175, 8:333, 9:211, 9:275, 11:28, 13:302, 14:353, 15:34, 17:88, 17:271, 18:241; of intention, 1:109, 3:116, 3:234, 4:72, 4:170, 4:210, 5:299–300, 5:312, 5:315, 7:554, 10:234, 11:29, 11:50, 11:191, 11:338–339, 14:50, 14:362–363, 15:173, 17:204, 19:232–233

Purpose of amendment. *See* SI.IX b; and XII i

Q

Quicumque (Athanasian Creed), 1:24, 3:261, 6:4–5, 6:199, 7:59–60, 8:50, 11:100, 13:54

Quietism (Molinism). *See* SI.XIII d

R

Race, injustice based on, 19:146

Rationalism, 10:50, 10:154, 12:315, 12:320, 13:155

Reading of scripture. *See* SI.I f

Reason, 1:72, 1:125, 3:25, 3:68, 3:120, 7:549–550, 8:33; age of, 16:7, 16:28–29, 16:97, 16:206, 16:361, 19:293–294; and faith (*see* SI.I d–e; and XI b); and morality, 5:180, 5:290, 5:363, 5:368, 10:31, 16:206, 16:208, 16:346, 17:40; and the passions, 1:45, 4:23, 5:329, 6:111–113, 16:133, 18:283–284; sin as contrary to, 1:57, 5:288, 5:311, 7:487, 9:185, 10:278, 15:135

Rebaptism, 1:61, 1:87, 2:212, 3:51, 3:317, 4:73, 4:171, 4:210, 5:88, 5:224, 6:135, 6:213–214, 7:219, 8:126–127, 8:174, 8:272, 9:81–82, 9:268, 11:219, 11:232, 14:370, 16:27–28, 16:203–205, 16:211, 18:365, 18:372, 19:134

Rebellion, 4:21, 4:80, 4:110, 6:161, 7:367, 8:193, 10:141, 10:195, 12:76, 12:250, 12:304–305, 14:303, 17:167

Reception of heretics, 9:22, 14:370, 17:90–93

Reconciliation. *See* SI.XII i

Redeemer. *See* SI.VIII g

Redemption. *See* SI.VIII a–h

Reflection, 5:106, 5:171, 7:77, 7:81–82, 10:61; in human acts, 5:282, 5:328–329, 6:41, 8:90–91, 8:298, 10:171, 11:446, 15:134, 17:250, 18:77, 18:213

Regeneration: baptism, sacrament of (*see* SI.XII c–d); by justification (*see* SI.IX a)

Regulars. *See* SI.XIII e

Reincarnation, 13:326

Relation(s), 19:259–260; between Church and state, sciences, culture (*see* SI.XI e)

Relics. *See* SI.XI e

Religion(s), 1:44, 1:102–103, 3:20, 7:371, 7:455, 14:164, 19:146; acts of, 1:80, 1:95, 3:221, 4:64, 4:160, 4:205, 5:166, 5:191, 5:295, 5:354, 7:416–427, 9:94, 12:279, 16:45, 16:272–273, 18:152, 19:139; Catholic the one true, 2:133, 3:35, 3:322, 4:29–30, 4:41, 4:119–120, 4:132–133, 4:195, 5:186, 8:10, 8:20, 8:209, 9:9, 10:43, 10:50, 10:186, 11:96, 12:91, 12:101, 12:177, 12:235, 13:15, 13:324, 14:5–6, 14:166–169, 16:90, 16:126, 16:178, 16:190–199, 17:83, 17:155, 18:136, 18:314, 18:331, 19:7, 19:101; virtue of (*see* SI.XI e)

Religious life. *See* Consecrated life

Remission of sin. *See* SI.IX

Renunciation of riches, 5:56, 9:214–216, 11:380, 12:51–52, 12:163, 14:351, 19:286

Reparation, 11:429; Christ makes perfect (*see* SI.VIII g; and XII l); of human nature (*see* SI.VIII a–h); of scandal (*see* SI.XI d); for sin through good works (*see* SI.XII l)

Reprobation. *See* SI.X g–i

Reservation, mental, 11:426

Resisting the known truth, sin against the Holy Ghost. *See* SI.XV

Resolution, 3:252, 18:73, 18:76, 18:206, 18:211; in the sacrament of penance (*see* SI.XII i)

Responsibility. *See* Duty

Rest, 3:10, 7:130, 8:73, 13:59–61, 13:144, 13:204, 19:123, 19:160; enjoined by God, 1:41, 2:182, 3:22, 3:25, 3:197, 3:264, 3:266, 3:333–334, 4:46, 4:139, 6:93–101, 7:423–425, 8:249, 9:47–48, 9:260, 10:163–164, 11:381–388, 13:41–42, 14:35, 14:42–43, 14:295–298, 14:324–328, 15:26, 15:89, 15:189–190, 15:198, 16:339, 17:44, 17:201, 18:156, 18:300, 19:247

Restitution, 1:50–51, 2:193, 3:23, 3:24, 3:168, 4:142–143, 5:42–43, 5:112, 5:117, 5:120, 5:316–318, 5:326–327, 6:121, 6:205, 6:221, 7:461, 7:465, 8:157, 11:406, 11:421–422, 14:315, 15:24, 15:25, 15:78, 15:194, 16:228, 16:246, 16:352, 17:47, 17:206, 18:161, 18:163, 19:288

Resurrection: of Christ (*see* SI.VIII h); of the dead (*see* SI.XIV b); feast of (Easter), 1:93–94, 2:297, 3:252, 3:262, 3:270–271, 4:55, 4:146, 4:149, 4:200, 5:18, 5:384–387, 6:214, 9:66, 13:223–227, 14:44, 14:329, 14:332–334, 16:155, 16:248, 17:51, 18:59–60, 18:156, 18:170, 18:343–344, 19:251

Retribution, divine (eternal). *See* SI.XIV

Revelation. *See* SI.I

Reward: eternal (*see* SI.XIV c); of good works (merit) (*see* SI.XIV c)

Riches, 2:255–256, 3:37, 5:62, 5:142, 5:236, 5:287, 5:327–328, 6:46–47, 6:126–128, 6:165–166, 7:490, 8:332, 9:214–216, 10:99, 10:157, 10:198, 11:452, 12:38–39, 12:51–52, 14:193, 14:339, 16:197, 17:275, 18:52, 18:147, 18:396, 18:441, 19:31

Right(s): of the baptized, 5:149, 5:376, 8:132, 8:139, 8:157, 8:173, 16:245, 19:135–136 (*see also* SI.XI l); of children, 5:35–36, 5:57–58, 5:307, 11:111, 14:305; of citizens, 5:307, 5:318, 16:192, 18:55, 18:157, 18:349, 19:256, 19:263; of civil authorities, 5:307, 18:229, 19:263–265; of clergy, 5:54, 5:349–350; of ecclesiastical superiors, 2:232, 5:211, 5:307, 14:37, 15:146, 16:188, 18:227; of parents, 5:35–36, 5:58, 5:211, 5:261, 5:307, 10:189, 14:36, 18:226

Rite(s), 7:180–181, 7:203, 10:24, 10:336; of the Church (*see* SI.XI e); different rites in the universal Church, 9:79, 9:240, 13:7–8, 17:70, 18:170, 18:208, 18:307, 19:121, 19:175; of the sacraments (*see individual sacraments*). *See also* Liturgy; and Tradition

Roman pontiff. *See* SI.III

Roman Rite, 2:139, 13:8, 19:121, 19:179–180

Rome, city of, 1:23, 1:88, 2:301, 3:13, 3:210–211, 3:370–372, 4:31–32, 4:122, 7:135, 7:258, 8:180–181, 11:146–147, 12:37–70, 17:151, 18:49, 18:134, 18:261, 18:318, 19:98–99, 19:203

Rosary, 1:34, 2:102, 2:331–333, 3:289–290, 4:84–85, 5:166–168, 5:369–370, 8:239, 8:293, 11:390, 12:286, 12:371, 13:242–243, 13:290, 14:80, 14:442, 15:86–87, 16:300–304, 17:87, 17:281, 18:18, 18:185, 19:237, 19:240, 19:326. *See also* SI.XV

S

Sabbath, 1:55, 7:416, 19:244–245; rest and holiness of, 1:8, 1:41, 2:174, 2:182–185, 3:21–22, 3:25, 3:264, 3:266, 3:333–334, 4:45–46, 4:53, 4:138–139, 4:147, 5:33–34, 5:301–306, 6:93–101, 6:193, 6:201, 7:416–427, 8:249, 9:47, 9:260, 10:163–164, 10:236, 11:381–392, 13:41–42, 13:144, 14:35, 14:42–43, 14:295–298, 14:324–328, 15:26, 15:89, 15:189–190, 15:198, 16:60, 16:341, 17:44, 17:201, 18:54, 18:155–156, 19:247; Sunday as fulfillment of, 1:41–42, 2:183–185, 3:22, 3:262–265, 4:76, 5:33, 5:301–302, 6:94, 6:100–101, 7:417, 7:422–423, 8:248, 8:263, 11:383–384, 12:324, 13:41–42, 14:35, 14:295–296, 15:22, 15:76, 15:189, 16:59, 16:340–341, 17:43, 17:201, 18:156, 19:244–249

Sabellianism, 5:193, 6:34, 6:35

Sacrament(s). *See* SI.XII a–o

Sacramental character, 2:209, 6:134, 17:220, 18:68, 18:189, 18:365 (*see also* SI.XII a): of baptism (*see* SI.XII c); of confirmation (*see* SI.XII e); of holy orders (*see* SI.XII n)

Sacramentals. *See* SI.XII p

Sacred Heart, 12:366, 13:270–276, 16:277, 16:320, 17:82, 18:377, 19:52, 19:175

Sacred scripture. *See* SI.I f

Sacrifice(s), 1:33, 1:95, 1:118, 10:154–155, 10:299, 11:106, 11:363, 12:87–88, 13:12, 13:65–66, 19:149, 19:171; in antiquity, 3:126, 5:49, 5:158, 6:98–99, 7:280, 8:146–147, 8:290, 9:96, 9:266, 10:68–69, 10:239, 11:54, 11:122, 13:66–69, 13:263–264, 14:107, 14:383, 16:140–141, 16:146, 16:161, 16:272–273, 16:317, 17:238, 17:239, 18:91, 18:280, 18:387, 19:65–66, 19:169; of the Mass (*see* SI.XII h)

Sacrilege, 1:47, 1:49, 2:192, 2:193, 2:212, 2:227, 3:67, 3:150, 3:162, 3:317, 3:378, 4:62, 4:69, 4:72, 4:157, 4:166, 4:170, 4:203, 4:208, 4:210, 5:222, 5:224, 5:231, 5:240–242, 5:245, 5:248, 5:296, 5:310, 5:314, 5:330, 6:115, 6:195, 6:203, 7:320, 7:460, 8:244, 8:266, 8:271, 9:47, 9:76, 10:329–331, 11:364, 12:86, 12:384–385, 13:271–272, 14:284, 14:365, 15:90, 15:99, 15:105, 15:149, 15:160, 16:27, 16:44, 16:202, 16:232, 16:234, 16:242, 16:269, 17:197, 17:266, 18:68, 18:72, 18:153, 18:447, 19:173, 19:199, 19:240

Sadness, 4:68–69, 4:165–166, 4:207–208, 5:64, 5:68, 5:288–289, 6:145, 7:288, 7:338, 9:152, 9:154, 10:14, 11:46, 11:50, 14:263, 18:75–77, 18:212–213, 18:409

Saint(s): canonization of, 12:328, 12:364, 13:124, 13:305–311, 16:89; communion of (*see* SI.II b; and XII l); example of, 3:5, 4:43, 4:135, 5:37, 5:219, 6:106, 6:181, 7:225, 10:332–333, 11:15, 11:239, 12:72, 12:170, 12:332, 13:40–41, 13:104, 13:145–146, 13:303–305, 14:119–120, 14:286, 14:290, 14:370, 14:449, 15:74, 15:151, 15:186, 16:180, 16:322–323, 17:62, 17:277, 19:253; intercession of, 1:24, 1:122–123, 2:33, 2:142–143, 2:317, 3:18, 3:274–291, 3:355–364, 4:43, 4:128, 4:134, 4:198, 5:143, 5:217–220, 6:150–151, 7:394, 7:507, 8:86, 8:245, 8:292, 9:43–45, 9:259, 10:218, 11:189, 12:72, 13:6, 13:302, 14:25, 14:33, 14:255, 14:286–288, 15:67, 15:74, 15:185–186, 16:57, 16:89, 16:329–330, 17:79, 17:186, 18:329, 18:358, 19:123; veneration of (*see* SI.XII i; and XIII b)

Salvation, 1:26, 1:98, 3:17, 3:233, 3:322, 7:29, 7:284, 10:75, 10:335; Church and (*see* SI.II a–b); distribution of grace of (*see* SI.X g); Mary cooperating in (*see* SI.VIII i–k); redemption meriting (*see* SI.VIII g); sacraments necessary for (*see* SI.XII b; XII d; and XII i–k)

Sanctification. *See* SI.IX–X; and XII

Sanction, divine. *See* SI.XIV a

Sanctuary, 3:137, 3:152, 3:298, 3:366, 7:79, 7:190, 10:43, 10:268, 12:57, 12:151, 13:22, 14:107, 19:251

Sanhedrin, 12:8, 12:32–33, 18:96

Satan. *See* Demon

Satisfaction. *See* SI.VIII g; XII l; and XIV

Savior. *See* SI.VIII g

Scandal. *See* SI.XI d

Schism. *See* SI.II b; and XI d

School(s), 19:107, 19:117; and the Church (*see* SI.II g; and XI p); parents may utilize, 11:397, 17:52, 17:195, 19:262

Scholastics, 2:216, 7:173, 7:547, 8:12, 8:32–33, 12:317–318, 18:385–386

Science, 1:10, 1:42, 7:358, 7:503, 10:51, 10:53; and faith (*see* SI.I d–e); (knowledge) as a gift of the Holy Ghost (*see* SI.XV)

Scripture, sacred. *See* SI.I f

Seal of the confessional. *See* SI.XII k; and Sacramental character

Second coming of Christ. *See* SI.XIV b

Secrecy, 3:281–282, 11:426, 11:430; in confession, 2:226, 3:163–164, 6:204–205, 7:316, 8:307, 12:301–302, 14:408, 16:253, 17:255, 18:217, 18:410–412; professional, 5:322–223, 5:391, 16:221, 16:354

Sects, 1:17–18, 1:67, 2:133, 3:153, 3:319, 3:328–329, 4:78, 5:186, 6:66, 7:138, 8:10, 8:209, 9:209, 9:249, 10:27, 10:53, 10:75, 12:89, 12:155, 12:219, 12:235, 14:168, 14:245, 16:183, 17:22, 17:203, 19:267, 19:309

See, Roman. *See* SI.III i

Sedition, 3:379, 7:594, 9:157, 12:187, 14:303, 18:159–160, 18:339, 18:436

Self-denial. *See* Asceticism

Self-mastery, 11:252, 11:431, 11:457, 12:160, 17:274, 19:283

Selfishness, 10:193, 10:199, 11:127–128, 11:372, 11:459, 12:40, 14:277–278, 16:127, 16:296, 19:216

Seminaries, 7:607, 12:402, 16:82, 19:212–213

Semipelagianism, 18:279, 18:295, 18:354

Sense(s), 1:48, 1:103, 7:140, 7:257, 19:132; bodily, 1:56–58, 1:72, 3:99–101, 3:178, 5:122–123, 5:267–268, 6:139, 6:195, 8:131, 8:160, 8:316, 9:74, 9:245, 10:88, 11:453, 12:153, 12:218, 12:317, 13:325, 13:335–337, 14:313, 16:42, 16:47, 16:262, 16:279, 16:347, 16:371, 17:65, 18:163, 18:382; of the faith, 4:79, 7:266, 16:95, 16:168, 16:308; interior religious (Modernist), 8:337–338, 18:362; moral, 5:180, 14:281, 16:37, 16:52, 16:240, 16:242, 16:315; of scripture, 3:75–81, 3:316, 4:78–79, 5:189, 6:55, 7:573, 8:13–15, 14:101–102, 14:172–173, 16:335, 17:91

Separation: of Church and state an error, 18:145–146, 18:327 (*see also* SI.II g); of spouses (*see* SI.XII o)

Sermon on the Mount, 7:533, 9:275, 18:240

Servant(s), 1:17, 1:81, 3:125, 3:277, 7:41, 7:73, 7:425, 11:399, 19:29, 19:138; employment of, 2:189–190, 4:47, 4:140, 5:318, 10:341–342, 13:331, 16:357, 18:159–160, 18:341

Sheol, 19:67

Shepherd(s), 9:219–220, 11:11–12, 14:14; bishop as, 4:32, 4:122, 11:463, 12:30, 12:336, 19:98, 19:116; Christ as Good, 4:30, 4:120, 4:179, 5:333, 7:130, 10:34, 10:288, 11:23–24, 11:41–42, 12:46, 17:156; pastor as, 5:53, 6:210, 11:324–325, 16:288; pope as, 4:32, 4:122, 11:147, 11:463, 17:151, 17:152, 18:139, 18:319, 19:98, 19:116

Sick, 1:37, 1:58, 7:118, 7:182; anointing of (*see* SI.XII m); caring for, 1:9, 1:83, 1:133, 2:70, 2:207, 2:327, 4:83, 5:122, 5:306, 5:353–354, 6:195, 6:206, 8:136, 11:273–274, 12:276–279, 13:138, 13:327, 14:327, 16:177, 16:249–250, 16:252, 16:339, 19:107, 19:276

Sign(s), 1:85, 1:94, 1:114, 7:105, 10:133–134, 10:284–286, 10:302, 11:130–132, 13:148, 19:112; of the cross (*see* Cross); liturgical, 2:288–290, 2:292–293, 3:133–136, 5:377–388, 8:121, 11:220–221, 11:333, 13:6–9, 13:49, 13:94–140, 14:367, 14:445, 19:112; sacramental (*see individual sacraments*)

Silence, 2:253, 2:331, 3:34, 7:273, 7:317, 9:159, 10:67, 10:136, 11:376, 19:22, 19:213; obsequious, 5:285, 18:321; as a way of being accessory to sin (*see* SI.XV)

Simony, 1:49, 5:283, 5:287, 5:391, 6:195, 6:203, 9:50, 11:364, 12:11, 12:247–248, 14:285, 16:276, 18:153

Simplicity, 7:429, 7:575, 11:43, 12:48, 19:109; divine (*see* SI.IV b)

Simulation of sacraments, 4:44, 4:136, 8:130, 12:117, 17:263–264, 19:111–112

Sin(s): forgiveness of (*see* SI.VII c; IX; XII c; and XII i–k); inclination to (*see* Concupiscence); kinds (*see* SI.XIII c; and SI.XV); leading others to (*see* SI.XI d; and SI.XV); occasion of (*see* occasion of sin); reward of (*see* SI.VII c–d; XIII c; and XIV)

Slander. *See* Calumny

Slavery: institutional, 5:346, 12:148, 13:327, 16:136, 16:141, 16:303; of Israel in Egypt, 10:160, 10:232–233, 11:236, 14:105, 16:161, 16:164, 18:92; of sin, 3:62, 3:114, 5:150, 5:172, 6:43–44, 6:87–88, 7:157, 7:389, 8:194, 8:330, 9:146, 10:146, 10:245, 11:24, 11:461, 15:137, 16:136, 16:222, 16:358, 17:37, 18:109, 18:123, 18:400

Sloth, 7:423, 19:43; as a capital sin (*see* SI.XV); spiritual, 1:76, 5:289, 9:154, 14:341, 15:136

Society, 1:77, 7:131, 7:140, 7:179, 19:108; Christ the king of, 7:537–538, 10:262, 12:94, 12:145, 12:250, 17:133–134, 17:148; Church as a perfect and divine (*see* SI.II a); civil and domestic (*see* SI.II a); legitimate defense of (*see* SI.XI q)

Societies, clandestine, 8:24, 16:336–337, 17:203, 19:267

Sodomy, 1:47, 1:81, 2:264, 2:331, 3:34, 4:36, 5:69, 5:310–311, 6:217–218, 7:450–451, 8:331–332, 9:169–171, 10:343, 11:452,

14:342–343, 15:35, 17:272, 18:245; as a sin that cries vengeance (*see* SI.XV)

Son of God. *See* SI.V c; and VIII a–h

Song(s), 1:47, 6:99, 6:129, 6:224, 7:456; of angels at Christmas, 2:271, 3:138, 7:78, 11:12, 13:165, 14:387; liturgical, 1:98, 6:199, 7:241, 12:54, 12:291, 12:371, 13:48, 13:51–52, 13:63–65, 16:285, 19:180; of Mary (*see* Magnificat)

Soul, 1:9, 1:34, 1:118, 1:124, 3:4–5, 7:125, 10:139; care of (*see* SI.II b); of Christ (*see* SI.VIII b; and VIII f); of the Church (*see* SI.V d); indelibly marked (*see* Sacramental character); rational, in man (*see* SI.VI d)

Species, Eucharistic. *See* SI.XII f

Spirit(s), 1:82, 1:93, 1:132, 7:349, 7:353; angels as pure (*see* SI.VI c); God as pure (*see* SI.IV b); man as body and (*see* SI.VI d); poverty of (*see* Poverty)

Spirit, Holy: fruits of (*see* SI.XV); in general (*see* SI.V d); gifts of (*see* SI.XV); sins against (*see* SI.XV)

Spiritism, 8:244, 10:156, 11:365, 14:284, 15:21, 15:183, 16:54, 16:319–321, 17:42, 17:197, 18:152

Spiritual exercises, 3:38–42, 3:252, 4:46, 5:173, 5:361, 12:52–54, 12:61, 12:332, 15:38–44, 15:88–89, 15:109–110, 17:276–280, 19:276

Spiritual life, 1:25, 7:105, 7:122, 9:143, 11:438–440, 16:15, 16:129, 16:201, 17:59, 18:44, 18:113, 18:349; Eucharist and, 2:221, 5:265, 6:72, 7:607, 8:144–146, 8:285–289, 9:103, 10:30, 12:61–62, 15:104, 15:166–168, 16:201, 17:67, 17:102; progress in, 3:277, 5:358, 5:361, 6:71–72, 6:129–130, 6:132, 8:94–120, 8:323–328, 10:29, 12:52–56, 15:148–149, 17:222; as progress in divine charity, 2:169, 5:169, 10:33; scripture and, 4:80, 5:356, 6:99–100, 12:54, 13:43–62

Sports, 7:420, 10:340, 14:354

Spouses. *See* SI.XI k; and XII o

Stars, consulting of, 4:44, 4:135, 6:26–28, 6:84–85, 10:105–106, 12:373, 13:339. *See also* Astrology

State(s): duties of (*see* SI.XI k–n); of grace (*see* SI.X f; XIII b; and XIV a); graces of, 5:258, 8:316, 8:319, 11:322, 11:330, 11:334–335, 12:270, 14:49; laws of (*see* SI.XI o); of life, free choice of, 1:80, 1:106, 2:238, 3:224, 5:259, 8:318, 8:321, 10:143, 11:381, 11:398, 12:363, 14:305, 16:126–127, 16:296, 18:160, 18:273, 18:353, 19:328; of original justice and holiness (*see* SI.VII b); power of (*see* SI.II g; and XI o–q); relationship to Church (*see* SI.II g; and XI o–q)

Sterilization, 1:46

Subdiaconate. *See* SI.XII n

Suffering, 7:91, 7:94, 19:300–301; of Christ redemptive (*see* SI.VIII g; IX b; XII h; and XII l); offered in reparation with Christ, 1:64, 1:89, 2:246, 3:37, 3:40, 5:66,

8:236, 10:79, 12:125–129, 14:434, 15:88, 18:466, 19:26, 19:208

Suicide, 1:45, 5:310, 6:108–109, 6:110, 7:442, 7:473, 8:252–253, 11:403–405, 12:74, 13:326, 14:308, 15:192, 16:133, 16:328, 16:346, 16:365, 17:45, 18:55, 18:161, 19:268

Sunday, 1:79, 1:92, 13:41–43; as the first day of the week, 7:419, 7:423, 11:383, 13:142, 14:295, 15:189, 16:59, 16:340; as fulfillment of the sabbath, 1:41–42, 2:183–185, 3:22, 3:262–265, 4:76, 5:33, 5:301–302, 6:94, 6:100–101, 7:417, 7:422–423, 8:248, 8:263, 11:383–384, 12:324, 13:41–42, 14:35, 14:295–296, 15:22, 15:76, 15:189, 16:59, 16:340–341, 17:43, 17:201, 18:156, 19:244–249; obligation to rest on, 1:42, 2:174, 2:185, 2:320, 3:22, 3:25, 3:264, 3:266, 3:333–334, 4:46, 4:139, 5:33, 5:284, 5:305, 5:391, 6:95–97, 7:423–425, 8:249, 9:47–48, 9:260, 10:197, 11:381–388, 13:41–42, 14:35, 14:42–43, 14:295–298, 14:324–328, 15:26, 15:89, 15:189–190, 15:198, 16:60, 16:227, 16:339, 16:341, 17:44, 17:201, 18:15, 18:57, 18:167, 19:247–248; obligation to worship on, 1:42, 1:55, 2:47, 2:174, 2:182–185, 2:198–199, 2:320, 3:149, 3:262, 4:45, 4:53, 4:138, 4:147, 5:33, 5:147, 5:160, 5:286, 5:305, 5:391, 6:96, 6:193, 6:201, 7:421–423, 8:262, 9:263, 10:43, 11:388–392, 12:61, 13:41–43, 14:35, 14:42–43, 14:295–298, 14:324–328, 15:22, 15:79, 15:189, 15:198, 16:216, 16:227–228, 16:308, 16:339, 17:44, 17:201, 17:210, 18:15, 18:57, 19:245, 19:266

Supernatural: acts (*see* SI.VII a; and X a–e); beatitude (*see* SI.VII a; and XIV a); order (*see* SI.VII a); virtues (*see* SI.XI a–d)

Superstition, 1:55, 2:172, 3:264, 3:280–281, 3:295, 3:307, 3:324, 3:360, 4:44, 4:81–82, 4:135–136, 5:163–164, 5:296–297, 5:333, 5:336, 5:338, 6:193, 6:201, 7:404, 8:243, 9:42, 9:185, 9:259, 9:262, 10:75, 10:331–332, 11:364–366, 12:42, 12:219, 13:10, 14:283–284, 14:289, 14:331, 15:183, 17:42, 17:197, 18:152, 18:419, 19:114, 19:229

Supplication. *See* SI.XI f

Supreme Pontiff. *See* SI.III a–i

Syllabus of Pius IX, 18:433

Symbol. *See* Creed

Synod. *See* Council

Systems, moral, 4:76, 12:218, 12:324–325

T

Tabernacle, 1:92, 1:95, 3:122, 3:152, 3:284, 3:333, 5:302, 7:170, 9:78, 9:228–229, 10:240–243, 10:337–338, 12:364, 12:369, 13:16–17, 13:83, 16:151–152, 16:179, 16:262, 16:265–266, 16:274, 17:134, 18:204, 19:176–177, 19:313

Table, 7:272, 7:428, 8:241, 16:179, 19:166; meal prayers at, 1:6–7, 2:336, 4:8, 4:97, 4:185–186, 5:156, 11:98, 11:188, 12:54, 12:121, 14:77, 14:354, 15:55, 15:88, 15:121, 16:96, 17:86, 17:107–108,

17:278, 19:157, 19:160, 19:322 (*see also* SI.XV)

Talents, 7:171, 16:170, 16:292; parable of, 19:269–270

Tax collector, 10:194; parable of, 5:390, 19:51

Teacher(s), 3:93, 3:324, 6:116, 7:36, 7:143, 8:216–217, 10:38, 11:17, 11:27–30, 11:399, 12:110, 12:340–341, 12:366–367, 18:171, 19:74–76; bishops as authorized (*see* SI.II c–d; and XII n)

Temperance, 2:330, 3:33, 7:455, 12:48–50; as a cardinal virtue (*see* SI.XV)

Temple, 1:48, 1:90, 1:95, 1:122, 7:407, 13:259; body of Christ as the true, 7:100, 13:317, 14:206, 14:222; body of the Christian as, 1:122, 2:192, 3:60, 3:70, 3:292–293, 4:43, 4:135, 5:337, 7:123, 7:443, 7:453, 8:245, 9:151, 10:137, 11:240, 11:369, 11:408, 11:411, 12:57, 13:84, 13:260, 13:322, 14:289–290, 19:85–86, 19:134–135, 19:303; of Jerusalem, 2:154, 2:296, 3:152, 3:268, 3:272, 3:290, 5:28, 5:369, 5:382, 5:384–385, 7:195, 7:353, 10:20–21, 10:272, 11:7, 11:22, 11:69, 12:151, 12:179–180, 13:286–287, 14:107–108, 14:211–212, 16:151, 16:161, 16:301–302, 18:94, 19:20–21; Jewish destroyed, 8:9, 10:295, 12:75–78, 14:107, 14:116, 14:207, 16:338, 18:94, 18:97, 19:25; Church as, 2:153–154, 3:61, 3:150, 3:244, 6:67–68, 11:22, 13:16–18, 13:316–317, 16:152, 19:90–92, 19:119

Temptation, 1:28–29, 1:53, 1:70, 3:18, 3:40, 3:118, 5:141–142, 5:146, 5:367–368, 6:171–174, 7:578, 7:583, 11:363, 14:438; avoiding, 1:49, 1:56–58, 1:108–109, 2:160–161, 3:38, 3:240, 4:58, 4:91, 4:154, 5:81, 5:150, 5:157, 5:186–187, 5:313, 5:329–330, 6:22, 6:54, 6:111–114, 6:129–130, 6:171–175, 7:455–457, 7:541–542, 7:576, 8:90, 8:190, 8:229–230, 9:31, 9:256, 10:58, 11:20, 11:207–208, 11:408–412, 11:446–447, 12:66–69, 13:159–161, 14:68, 14:311, 15:88, 15:136, 16:47, 16:52, 16:79–80, 16:123–125, 16:135, 16:217, 16:254, 16:347, 17:103, 17:130, 18:44, 18:76, 18:86, 18:247, 19:140, 19:158, 19:185–188 (*see also* occasion of sin); of Jesus in the desert, 11:19–21, 19:185

Ten Commandments. *See* SI.XI e–t

Testament, old and new. *See* SI.I f

Thanksgiving, 1:98, 1:100, 7:405; Eucharist as, 2:218, 3:28, 3:72, 3:351, 4:63, 4:158, 5:159, 5:234, 5:383, 7:241, 8:148, 9:89, 9:95, 10:122, 11:255, 14:378, 15:29, 17:68, 18:70, 18:183, 19:168–169, 19:174–175; as a form of prayer (*see* SI.XI f)

Theft. *See* SI.XI s

Theology, 7:29, 8:12, 16:138; method of, 10:14, 18:26–27; teachers of, 10:14. *See also* SI.I c; and I e

Thought(s), 1:49, 1:108–110, 1:128, 2:129, 3:11, 6:26, 7:491, 8:232, 8:237, 10:33, 16:50, 16:307, 16:309, 18:21, 18:42, 18:108,

19:20–21, 19:27–28, 19:155–159; impure, sinful when entertained, 1:48, 1:53, 1:67, 1:08–109, 2:197, 3:24, 4:50–51, 4:143–144, 5:39, 5:142, 5:246, 5:312, 5:328–330, 5:368, 5:391, 6:129, 6:203, 7:487–488, 8:254, 9:49, 11:408–410, 11:446–447, 12:153, 14:41, 14:311, 15:25, 15:78, 15:193, 15:196, 16:63, 16:127, 16:132, 16:221, 16:227, 16:355, 17:46, 17:207, 18:76, 18:165, 19:282

Throne(s): of the civil sovereign, 5:30, 12:158; of God, 3:132, 3:276, 3:364, 4:20, 4:110, 5:121, 6:55–56, 7:392, 7:410, 8:227, 9:217, 10:238, 13:119, 15:83, 16:12, 16:92, 16:115, 16:359, 17:163, 17:186, 18:271, 18:298, 19:73, 19:228, 19:311–314; as one of the nine choirs of angels (*see* SI.XV)

Time, 3:14, 13:36, 13:140–141; beginning of (*see* SI.VI); end of (*see* SI.XIV); liturgical, 2:51, 3:116, 3:175, 3:255–257, 8:267, 13:36–37, 13:43–62, 13:140–340, 16:160–161, 16:264, 19:244–254

Tithe, 1:45, 1:127, 2:50, 2:320, 3:25, 3:252, 4:52, 4:55, 4:147, 4:150, 4:200, 5:55, 5:295, 5:349–350, 5:391, 6:106, 6:220–221, 7:463, 7:558, 8:266–267, 9:243, 11:6, 12:9, 14:334, 15:26, 15:54, 15:81, 15:202, 16:363, 17:32, 17:51–52, 17:202, 17:215–216, 18:15, 18:61, 18:173, 19:266

Tomb, 3:188, 3:258, 3:364, 4:25, 4:115, 4:193, 7:95, 7:109, 8:81, 10:280, 10:302, 11:71, 12:44–47, 13:22–25, 13:34–35, 13:70, 13:83, 13:210, 13:320, 16:154, 16:179, 17:140, 18:298, 19:68, 19:71

Tonsure, 1:75, 3:199, 5:257, 5:377, 6:140, 6:223, 7:347, 11:325–326, 12:366, 13:15, 16:284–285, 19:212

Tradition, 1:18, 1:23, 1:59, 3:332, 7:42, 7:96, 8:15–17, 17:10, 19:104–106; ecclesiastical (*see* SI.I f); of instruments in holy orders (*see* SI.XII n); liturgy as locus of, 8:16, 13:8–12, 14:175, 17:240; and scripture equally the Word of God, 3:330, 4:76, 4:79, 5:183, 5:189–190, 7:42–43, 10:15, 10:63–64, 10:67, 10:161, 14:6, 14:170, 14:174, 16:333, 17:28, 18:105–106, 18:256–258, 19:103–106. *See also* SI.I f

Transcendence, divine. *See* SI.IV; and VI a–b

Transfiguration, 2:298, 5:337, 7:160, 11:36, 13:199, 16:156, 19:53

Transgression, 3:14, 6:220, 7:298, 10:47; sin as, 4:33, 4:124, 4:196, 5:25, 5:288, 5:303, 5:307, 5:365, 8:329–330, 9:142, 10:170, 10:194, 11:80, 11:205, 11:445, 14:45, 15:16, 15:134, 15:151, 16:14, 16:127–128, 17:36, 17:48, 18:280, 18:404, 19:188

Transubstantiation. *See* SI.XII f

Treasury of the Church. *See* SI.XII l

Tree, 1:82, 1:93, 3:197, 3:379, 11:143, 12:223, 13:202, 18:41, 18:103, 18:126, 18:288, 18:296; of good and evil, 4:20, 4:109, 6:184–185, 7:65, 10:16, 10:148–149, 10:165, 13:55, 14:102,

16:119–120, 17:130, 18:45, 18:91, 18:117, 19:38, 19:40–41, 19:45

Trent, Profession of, 3:316–318, 3:373, 8:173–175, 14:97, 14:421

Trial(s): of Adam and Eve (*see* SI.VII c); of the angels (*see* SI.VI c); of the Church, 12:169, 12:172–174, 12:234–235, 12:314–315, 12:365–366, 19:305–306; opportunity for merit, 2:161, 2:197, 4:23, 4:112, 5:142, 6:145, 6:176, 7:583, 8:110, 10:37, 11:409, 12:112, 12:169, 13:272, 14:438, 16:344, 17:130, 17:132, 17:161, 19:185

Trinity, Blessed. *See* SI.V

Trust, 1:26–27, 1:33–34, 3:32, 3:100, 6:158, 7:91, 8:14, 9:26, 12:395, 16:22, 16:52, 16:172, 16:308, 16:310–311, 17:13, 17:180, 18:64, 18:83, 18:180, 18:234–235, 18:352, 18:404, 19:187, 19:305–307

Truth, 1:23, 3:13, 3:126, 3:302, 7:70; faith as assent to, 3:5, 3:62–63, 3:92–94, 3:111, 3:322, 3:323, 4:39, 4:129–130, 5:183, 5:195, 6:25, 8:31, 8:108, 9:71, 10:28, 11:90, 15:73, 15:118, 16:6, 16:21, 16:94, 16:172, 16:195, 16:209, 16:322, 18:82, 18:106–108, 18:232, 18:255, 18:459, 19:83, 19:87; God the source of all, 2:137, 3:5, 3:41, 3:147, 3:195–196, 3:293, 3:324–326, 3:364, 6:24, 6:124, 7:45, 8:103, 9:11, 10:186, 10:187, 11:87, 14:5, 14:318, 15:6, 15:41, 15:51, 16:182, 16:190, 16:199, 16:260, 17:121, 19:14; inerrantly taught in scripture (*see* SI.I f); Jesus as, 1:94, 3:74, 3:324–325, 9:19, 9:191, 10:84, 11:87, 13:328, 14:211, 18:264, 18:308, 18:367; makes one free, 3:159, 11:90; neglect or rejection of revealed, 2:262, 2:330, 3:34, 3:322–3:323, 4:35, 5:68, 8:87, 8:104, 8:221, 9:57–58, 9:166–167, 10:195, 11:90, 14:137, 15:34, 15:183, 16:182–183, 16:191, 16:242, 16:323, 17:158, 18:140, 18:144, 18:233, 18:244, 18:272–273; oath-taking and, 2:181, 5:299, 6:89, 7:408, 8:246–247, 9:260, 11:374–375, 14:293, 15:74–75, 15:187, 16:58, 16:335, 17:43, 17:200, 19:241; offenses against, 1:51–53, 2:90, 2:116, 3:322–3:323, 5:44, 5:321, 6:124–126, 6:194, 6:202, 7:412–415, 7:472–477, 11:425–431, 13:328–330, 15:183, 15:195, 16:62, 16:198, 16:228, 16:353, 18:377, 19:289; resisting the known, sin against the Holy Ghost (*see* SI.XV)

Typology, 3:52, 3:89–92, 3:126, 3:338, 4:65, 4:160, 5:297, 5:331, 5:349, 7:85, 7:149, 7:281, 7:449, 8:196, 9:98, 10:20, 10:301, 11:12, 11:254–255, 13:125, 13:128, 13:214, 13:220, 13:223, 14:104, 14:209, 14:384, 17:239

Tyrannicide, 12:78, 12:116

U

Unbelief, 2:126, 2:180, 3:86–88, 3:322, 3:239, 7:339, 7:511, 8:58, 8:104–105, 8:107–109, 8:216, 8:325, 10:50, 10:71, 10:214, 10:303, 11:35, 11:47–48, 11:73, 11:93, 12:162–169, 13:21, 14:166, 16:110, 16:113, 18:351, 18:444, 19:137, 19:139

Unction, extreme. *See* SI.XII m

Understanding, 1:40, 1:117, 3:4, 7:85, 8:14, 8:50, 19:20, 19:39; and faith, 2:113, 3:150–154, 3:330, 4:16, 4:105, 5:91, 5:189, 6:42, 7:50–53, 8:107–109, 8:326, 10:57–58, 11:457, 14:165–166, 16:14, 16:101, 16:123, 17:127, 18:104, 18:252–253, 18:438, 19:87–88, 19:226; as a gift of the Holy Ghost (*see* SI.XV)

Union, 1:106, 7:125, 19:155; of body and soul in man (*see* SI.VI d); with Christ by grace and the sacraments (*see* SI.XII c; and XII g); hypostatic (*see* SI.VIII c–f); marital (*see* SI.XI r; and XII o)

Unity, 1:25, 1:103, 7:45, 7:53, 19:121; of body and soul in man (*see* SI.VI d); of the divine nature (*see* SI.IV b; and V a); of mankind in Adam (*see* SI.VI d); mark of the Church (*see* SI.II a); of spouses (*see* SI.XI k; and XII o)

Universe, 5:198, 7:62, 8:38, 8:187, 8:188, 12:5, 14:244, 16:77, 16:100, 18:262–263, 18:268, 19:32–35, 19:222

Universities, 12:301, 12:336

Unleavened bread, 3:104–105, 5:228, 7:246–247, 8:142–143, 10:234, 10:268, 11:54, 11:256, 18:373, 18:384, 18:389, 19:178

Usury, 1:50, 1:54, 2:193–194, 2:256, 5:40–42, 5:287, 5:295, 5:315, 5:391, 6:120, 6:194, 6:202, 6:221–222, 7:463, 8:256–257, 9:50, 9:203, 9:261, 11:420, 12:154, 14:314, 14:339, 15:194, 18:296

V

Value, 7:149, 19:189–190, 19:232–233; of good works (*see* SI.XII i; and XIII b); of the sacraments (*see* SI.XII a)

Veneration, 7:421, 16:224; of angels and saints, 1:33, 1:36, 2:178, 2:301, 3:21, 3:355–357, 4:42–43, 4:134–135, 5:26, 5:31, 5:218–220, 5:302, 5:335–336, 6:179–180, 7:391–395, 7:507, 8:86–87, 8:245, 9:42–46, 9:259, 11:189, 11:367–369, 12:72, 13:6, 13:104, 13:297–311, 14:32–33, 14:285–290, 15:21, 15:74, 15:185–186, 16:105, 16:331, 17:29, 17:79, 17:198, 17:263, 18:53, 18:153, 18:329, 19:157, 19:234–236 (*see also* SI.XI e; and XI g); of images, 1:33, 1:36, 2:175, 3:301, 4:43, 4:82, 4:134–135, 5:27–30, 5:385, 5:330–337, 7:395, 7:397–398, 8:245, 9:46–47, 9:56, 9:259, 11:370–371, 12:46, 12:230, 13:6–7, 13:294–295, 14:288, 15:21, 15:74, 15:186, 16:331, 17:79–80, 17:91, 17:198–199, 18:53, 18:154, 18:329, 19:234; of Mary, 1:33, 2:164, 2:300, 3:284–291, 4:59, 4:154, 5:166–168, 5:302, 5:370, 6:94, 6:180–186, 7:78–79, 7:506, 8:86–87, 8:245, 9:33–37, 9:257, 11:210–216, 12:272–273, 13:280–281, 13:284, 13:289, 14:288, 15:20, 15:54, 15:85–86, 15:121, 15:179–181, 16:105, 18:53, 18:153, 19:236–237 (*see also* SI.VIII k; XI e; and XI g); of relics, 1:33, 1:36, 2:178, 3:292–296, 3:364, 4:43, 4:135, 5:30, 5:296, 5:336, 7:393–395, 8:87, 9:45, 11:369–370, 12:72, 12:84, 12:209,

13:98, 13:292–294, 13:320, 14:290, 15:21, 15:74, 15:186, 16:57, 16:330–331, 17:79–80, 17:91, 17:198–199, 18:53, 18:329, 19:234; of scripture, 7:42–43, 7:405, 12:71, 12:129, 12:194, 13:105–106, 13:108–111, 18:10, 18:257, 19:105

Venial sin. *See* SI.XII i; and XIII c

Vernacular, 8:14–15, 11:198, 12:194, 14:173; and liturgical language, 3:150–154, 5:161, 5:374–377, 8:150, 13:62–63, 14:388, 16:194

Vespers, 2:155, 3:255, 4:46, 4:138, 5:305, 5:383–384, 12:61, 12:265, 12:296, 13:56–59, 15:89, 16:285, 16:301, 16:339, 16:359, 19:245

Vessels, sacred, 1:96, 3:299, 6:96, 7:279, 9:97, 10:291, 11:364, 12:112, 12:187, 12:191, 12:230, 13:84–85, 14:444, 15:99, 16:202, 16:264–265, 17:197, 18:335, 19:110, 19:178, 19:240

Viaticum, 1:71, 3:115, 5:96, 5:232, 5:341–342, 7:242, 8:172–173, 8:287, 11:256, 12:193, 12:203, 12:241, 12:287–288, 12:396–397, 13:282, 14:378, 15:95, 15:96, 15:167–168, 16:270–271, 16:282, 17:237, 18:31, 18:204, 19:209–210

Vicar of Christ. *See* SI.III a–i

Vice(s), 1:2, 1:54, 1:107, 3:31, 7:90, 7:458, 8:330–331, 15:32, 18:243, 19:188–189, 19:253; capital (sins) (*see* SI.XV); correction of, 1:82, 5:23–24, 5:47, 5:65, 5:130, 6:130, 6:164–166, 6:210, 8:303, 9:159–160, 9:161, 9:197, 9:274, 11:354–355, 11:397, 11:400–401, 12:62, 12:195, 14:407, 15:37, 15:191, 16:171, 16:254, 16:282, 17:248–249, 18:441

Victim: Christ as priest and, 2:222–223, 3:127, 4:11, 4:65, 4:101, 4:160, 5:373, 7:283–284, 8:147–148, 8:290, 9:98, 10:239, 11:389, 11:443, 13:69–70, 13:94, 14:54–55, 14:383, 15:168–169, 16:45, 16:274, 17:70, 17:241, 18:71, 18:201, 18:297, 18:393, 19:66, 19:170–171; in Holy Mass, 2:278, 3:124, 4:65, 4:160, 5:373, 5:381, 7:280, 7:284, 8:147, 8:290, 9:98, 10:38, 10:239, 11:389, 13:69–70, 13:94, 14:54–55, 14:385, 16:45, 16:274, 17:241, 18:72, 18:203, 18:385, 19:170–171

Victory: of Christ over sin and death, 1:93, 1:110, 6:56, 7:159, 7:588, 9:17, 10:258, 13:223, 13:251–252, 14:223, 14:448, 17:138, 18:285, 19:24–25, 19:251; over temptation, 2:161–162, 5:141, 5:367, 6:129–130, 6:174–175, 7:589, 8:90, 8:141, 8:160–161, 8:190, 8:235–236, 8:306–307, 10:177, 11:20, 11:409, 11:411–412, 12:124, 12:185, 12:202, 16:79, 16:88, 19:274, 19:283, 19:314

Vigilance, 3:38, 5:76, 5:329, 7:205, 7:517, 10:156, 11:398, 12:246, 13:46, 13:150, 13:162, 15:38, 15:136, 15:192, 17:276, 19:185–186

Vine: Christ as the true, 3:78, 14:362, 17:181, 19:85; fruit of the, 1:70, 3:98–99, 7:248, 10:97, 13:196, 18:389

Violence, 1:49, 1:72, 3:22–23, 5:310, 5:314, 5:356, 5:393, 6:119, 6:194, 6:201, 7:457, 7:509, 8:57, 8:92, 8:256, 9:49, 9:150, 9:261, 11:405, 12:69, 12:361, 15:136, 18:159, 18:326, 18:339–340

Virginity, 6:141, 7:217, 7:366, 10:201, 19:280; of the Blessed Virgin Mary perpetual (*see* SI.VIII k); in the consecrated life, 2:204–205, 7:366, 7:452, 9:136, 9:213, 11:380, 11:444, 12:17, 12:347, 13:240, 14:351, 18:174, 18:227

Virgin Mary, Blessed. *See* SI.VIII i–k

Virtue(s): advancing in, 1:104–107, 5:67–68, 5:77, 5:174, 6:171–172, 6:207, 8:126, 8:185, 8:229, 8:236, 12:192, 12:221, 12:301, 13:187–189, 13:331, 14:350, 14:374, 15:37, 15:148–149, 16:78, 16:135, 16:171, 16:213, 16:334, 16:358, 18:241; cardinal (*see* SI.XV); in general (*see* SI.XI a); as one of the nine choirs of angels (*see* SI.XV)

Vision of God (beatific). *See* SI.VII a; and XIV a

Vocation, 2:233–235, 3:200–201, 3:223–224, 3:267, 5:78, 5:124–128, 7:341–343, 7:357–359, 7:553, 8:162–163, 8:318, 9:272–273, 10:58, 10:107, 11:325, 11:338, 11:381, 11:398, 12:223, 12:270, 12:362, 14:422–423, 14:430, 15:171, 16:126–127, 16:286, 17:56–57, 18:174, 18:224, 19:211, 19:271

Voice, 1:7, 1:124, 7:495, 12:189; of conscience (*see* SI.II g); of God in scripture (*see* SI.I f)

Vow(s). *See* SI.XI g

Vulgate. *See* SI.I f

W

Wage(s), 19:288, 19:298; defrauding laborers of, as a sin that cries vengeance (*see* SI.XV); as remuneration for labor (*see* SI.XI s); of sin is death, 6:59, 8:62, 8:329, 10:170, 11:446, 15:16, 15:69, 15:133–134, 15:148, 17:35, 17:37, 17:174

War(s), 1:72, 19:37, 19:275; legitimacy of just, 2:45, 2:190, 5:308–309, 6:108, 7:441, 8:252, 10:247, 11:401–402, 12:259–261, 16:250, 19:43, 19:268; sign of second coming, 2:128, 19:305

Water, 1:87–88, 3:104, 3:307–309, 7:325, 19:304; baptismal (*see* SI.XII c); mixed with wine in Eucharist (*see* SI.XII f); from the side of Christ, 2:221, 2:288, 3:105, 5:228, 5:380, 5:382, 10:206, 11:70, 11:256, 13:88–89, 13:201, 14:113, 18:389, 19:325

Way(s), 1:67, 7:492; of being accessory to another's sin (*see* SI.XV); of the cross, 13:295–297, 14:221, 16:297, 17:82, 19:149–150; to the Father, Jesus the only, 3:35, 10:334, 13:93, 13:251–253, 15:35; parable of the two (gates), 9:119, 9:155

Weakness, 1:28, 7:433, 7:501, 19:60–61; God's power made perfect in, 2:525, 8:112, 10:162, 10:204, 11:39, 12:217; Holy Spirit helps in our, 7:587, 8:88–89, 11:137, 11:142, 18:65, 18:183

Wedding, 7:273; at Cana, 2:235, 3:233, 3:267, 11:335, 13:176, 16:260, 18:381, 19:170; of the Lamb, mystical, 9:228–229, 13:222, 19:9–10. *See also* SI.XII o

Widow(s), 1:76, 1:81, 2:164, 2:205, 2:264, 2:331, 3:190–191, 3:213, 3:217, 3:340, 5:69, 5:277–278, 7:425, 7:514, 9:171–172, 9:218, 9:271, 10:329, 11:14, 11:32, 12:51, 12:191, 12:300, 13:23, 13:184, 13:240, 14:342, 18:457, 19:276

Wife. *See* SI.XI k; and XII o

Will: of angels (*see* SI.VI c; and VII a); of Christ (*see* SI.VIII c); of God (*see* SI.IV b; V a; and V e); of man (*see* SI.VI d; VII b; and VII d)

Wine, 1:60, 1:70, 3:247, 7:248, 7:255; Eucharistic (*see* SI.XII f)

Wisdom, 1:10, 1:25, 1:44, 1:62, 1:132, 7:50, 18:110, 18:267, 19:35, 19:75; as a gift of the Holy Ghost (*see* SI.XV)

Witness, 1:40, 1:86, 1:98, 16:93, 19:233; bearing false, 1:9, 1:51–53, 2:45, 2:194–196, 2:320, 3:23, 4:49–50, 4:142–143, 5:246, 6:121–122, 6:194, 6:202, 7:471–474, 8:247, 8:258, 9:50, 9:261, 10:70, 11:425–426, 12:10, 14:40, 14:317, 15:24, 15:53, 15:78, 15:194, 16:62, 16:149, 16:228, 16:316, 17:47, 17:206, 18:15, 18:56, 18:164, 18:447, 19:289, 19:241; in marriage (*see* SI.XII o); martyrdom as, 8:136, 11:79, 11:150, 12:70, 19:71

Woman, 3:243, 7:365, 11:111–112; blessing (nuptial) of the, 3:237, 16:48, 16:288–289, 19:213; caught in adultery, 2:192, 6:116, 7:303; consecrated (*see* Nuns); Eve the first (*see* SI.VI d; and VII b–d); ineligible to receive holy orders (*see* SI.XII n); Mary the perfect (*see* SI.VII c; and VIII k). *See also* SI.XI k

Word of God, 1:28, 1:90, 6:36, 6:99–100, 7:42, 10:84; incarnate (*see* SI.V c; and VIII a–f); scripture as inspired (*see* SI.I f); in the Trinity (*see* SI.V b; and VIII a–e)

Words, 1:18, 1:34, 1:100, 1:121, 2:129, 3:75, 6:35–36, 8:110, 11:67–69, 13:216–217, 19:212, 19:214; authoritative in exorcism, 7:223, 7:349, 11:25, 11:37, 13:86–88, 19:131; in sacramental form (*see individual sacraments*)

Work. *See* Labor

Works, 1:107, 1:117, 3:16, 7:71, 7:117, 19:275; of Christ reveal his divinity, 3:86–87, 3:96, 3:233, 4:26, 4:116, 11:79, 11:90–91, 11:106, 13:148–149, 14:189; of the flesh, 1:47–49, 1:53–54, 3:322, 5:63, 5:287–288, 6:22, 6:128–130, 6:172, 6:204, 7:549, 9:209, 9:272, 11:142–143, 12:314–315, 12:319–320, 12:323–325, 12:385–386, 14:438, 15:25, 15:37–38, 15:78, 17:275; good and bad (*see* SI.XIII a); of mercy (*see* SI.XV); of penance, 1:66, 1:68, 3:165, 3:172, 4:70, 4:167, 4:207–208, 5:53, 6:176, 6:205, 7:325, 7:329, 8:154, 8:311, 9:185–187, 9:273–274, 11:308, 11:450, 11:460, 12:187–188, 13:158–162, 13:187–200, 15:104, 15:160, 15:163, 16:38,

16:245–247, 16:251, 16:258, 16:332, 19:193, 19:196

World, 1:20, 1:31, 3:37, 6:173, 7:36, 7:73, 15:38; Christ the Savior of (*see* SI.VIII g); Church sent into the entire, 2:116, 2:135–136, 2:301, 2:314, 3:327, 4:32, 4:77, 4:123, 5:381, 6:68, 10:38, 10:194, 11:148, 12:6, 12:170, 13:249, 14:116, 19:107–108; creation of (*see* SI.VI a); ending of (*see* SI.XIV b)

Worship, 1:32–33, 1:42, 1:126, 3:5, 8:85–87, 8:242, 9:73–74, 19:228–229; of angels and saints (*see* Veneration); of the Eucharist, 1:71, 1:99, 2:277, 2:291–292, 2:324, 3:116–117, 3:121–123, 4:11, 4:100, 5:95, 5:98, 5:162–163, 5:381–382, 5:387, 6:206, 6:219–220, 7:259, 7:266, 8:109, 8:284, 8:287, 9:94, 9:266, 12:288, 12:364, 13:85, 13:127, 13:260, 13:271, 13:341, 14:54, 14:382, 14:393, 15:94, 15:96–97, 15:166, 16:265–266, 17:66, 17:229, 18:171, 18:207, 19:176–178; of images (*see* Veneration); of Mary (*see* Veneration); public, official (*see* SI.XI e; and XII); of relics (*see* Veneration); true retained in the 8:6, 10:336, 11:149, 11:366–367, Church alone, 2:172–173, 5:212, 12:271, 13:10, 13:104, 13:133, 14:98, 16:9, 16:25, 16:193, 16:198, 17:21, 17:157, 18:93, 18:146, 19:109–110

Wrath, 1:11, 1:17, 1:109, 7:79, 7:193, 19:92; as a capital sin (*see* SI.XV)

Y

Youth, 1:46, 1:101, 7:457, 7:607, 10:128, 11:442, 19:117; parents' duty to educate (*see* SI.XI p)

Z

Zeal, religious, 1:63, 2:242, 2:261, 2:330, 5:67, 6:161, 7:42, 8:126, 9:116–117, 10:180, 11:22, 11:193–194, 12:328, 12:333–334, 13:263, 14:130–131, 14:217, 14:280, 18:94–95, 18:260, 19:50

Zwinglianism, 1:22, 8:21, 11:255, 12:320–321

ABOUT THIS SERIES

Tradivox was first conceived as an international research endeavor to recover lost and otherwise little-known Catholic catechetical texts. As the research progressed over several years, the vision began to grow, along with the number of project contributors and a general desire to share these works with a broader audience.

Legally incorporated in 2019, Tradivox has begun the work of carefully remastering and republishing dozens of these catechisms which were once in common and official use in the Church around the world. That effort is embodied in this *Tradivox Catholic Catechism Index*, a multi-volume series restoring artifacts of traditional faith and praxis for a contemporary readership. More about this series and the work of Tradivox can be learned at www.Tradivox.com.

SOPHIA INSTITUTE

Sophia Institute is a nonprofit institution that seeks to nurture the spiritual, moral, and cultural life of souls and to spread the Gospel of Christ in conformity with the authentic teachings of the Roman Catholic Church.

Sophia Institute Press fulfills this mission by offering translations, reprints, and new publications that afford readers a rich source of the enduring wisdom of mankind.

Sophia Institute also operates the popular online resource CatholicExchange.com. *Catholic Exchange* provides world news from a Catholic perspective as well as daily devotionals and articles that will help readers to grow in holiness and live a life consistent with the teachings of the Church.

In 2013, Sophia Institute launched Sophia Institute for Teachers to renew and rebuild Catholic culture through service to Catholic education. With the goal of nurturing the spiritual, moral, and cultural life of souls, and an abiding respect for the role and work of teachers, we strive to provide materials and programs that are at once enlightening to the mind and ennobling to the heart; faithful and complete, as well as useful and practical.

Sophia Institute gratefully recognizes the Solidarity Association for preserving and encouraging the growth of our apostolate over the course of many years. Without their generous and timely support, this book would not be in your hands.

www.SophiaInstitute.com
www.CatholicExchange.com
www.SophiaTeachers.org